Mediating Madness

D1375810

Martiai
el: 019

Mediating Madness

Mental Distress and Cultural Representation

Simon Cross

palgrave
macmillan

First published 2010 by
PALGRAVE MACMILLAN

Palgrave Macmillan in the UK is an imprint of Macmillan Publishers Limited, registered in England, company number 785998, of Houndmills, Basingstoke, Hampshire RG21 6XS.

Palgrave Macmillan in the US is a division of St Martin's Press LLC, 175 Fifth Avenue, New York, NY 10010.

Palgrave Macmillan is the global academic imprint of the above companies and has companies and representatives throughout the world.

Palgrave® and Macmillan® are registered trademarks in the United States, the United Kingdom, Europe and other countries.

ISBN 978-0-230-00531-0   hardback

This book is printed on paper suitable for recycling and made from fully managed and sustained forest sources. Logging, pulping and manufacturing processes are expected to conform to the environmental regulations of the country of origin.

A catalogue record for this book is available from the British Library.

Library of Congress Cataloging-in-Publication Data

Cross, Simon, 1964-
    Mediating madness : mental distress and cultural representation / Simon Cross.
        p. cm.
    Summary: "Mediating Madness examines how mediations of madness emerge, disappear and interleave, only to re-emerge at unexpected moments. Drawing on social and cultural histories of madness, history of art, and popular journalism, the book offers a unique interdisciplinary understanding of historical and contemporary media representations of madness"–Provided by publisher.
    Includes bibliographical references and index.
    ISBN 978-0-230-00531-0 (hardback)
    1. Mental illness in mass media. I. Title.
    P96.M45C76 2010
    362.2–dc22

                                                                    2009047526

10   9   8   7   6   5   4   3   2   1
19   18   17   16   15   14   13   12   11   10

For Lizzy and Gabriel, with love

Contents

List of Figures

The author and publisher wish to thank the Wellcome Library, London, for permission to use Figures 2.1, 2.3, 2.4, 2.6; Rod Dickinson for Figure 2.2; Royal Society of Medicine for Figure 2.5 and Mirrorpix for permission to use Figures 4.1 to 4.3.

Acknowledgements

Producing scholarly work is often described as a solitary enterprise. In my experience, however, it is both solitary *and* collective.
Consequently thanks are always due to other people and rightly
so. In the long gestation period that has finally seen the arrival of
Mediating Madness, I have amassed numerous debts to many people
all of whom have encouraged my work, believed in its importance
and stood by me when the going was tougher than they, or I, could
ever imagine. To each of you, my heartfelt thanks. It is not my inten-
tion however, to be evasive about whom I would like to single out for
special thanks since without a number of you actively looking out for
me, this book would probably never have been completed.

The origin of this book began life in a *very* different form as a Ph.D.
thesis in the Department of Social Sciences, Loughborough University.
My first debt of thanks is therefore to my former supervisor, Graham
Murdock. Graham's remarkable insights, sound advice and intellectual
generosity have guided my thinking on madness and media as well as
many other topics. Graham has also co-written Chapter 6 of this book
and it gives me great pleasure to see ideas hatched over Belgian beer and
accompanying fries come to fruition in this way. Thanks Graham!

I also owe an enormous debt to other scholars in Loughborough's
Social Sciences department. In particular, David Deacon and Michael
Pickering have encouraged me through difficult writing periods. Their
confidence-boosting insights, advice and friendship have been inspi-
rational and I shall always be grateful for their willingness to read
drafts, make suggestions and generally help me bring this project to
a conclusion. The intellectual contours of this book would also have
been poorer had it not been for important conversations at just the
right moments with Dominic Wring, John Corner, Ralph Negrine,
Tim O'Sullivan, Richard Keeble, Barbara Cairns, Ann Gray, David
Sleight, James Stanyer, Sarah Codman, Roger Dickinson and Luke
Goode. However, none of the above has any responsibility for errors
of fact or judgment that may remain.

I have also benefited from the support of my colleagues in the
Communication, Culture and Media team at Nottingham Trent

University. Moving (back!) to NTU midway through the writing period of this book was daunting but my new colleagues were welcoming and were interested in what I was doing. Joost van Loon also came up with financial help just when I needed it, so grateful thanks. My thanks to Sage for permission to publish a revised version of an article that originally appeared in *Television and New Media*, and which appears here as Chapter 5. Thanks are also due to the patience and enthusiasm of my editor at Palgrave Macmillan, Christabel Scaife. Thanks to *The Guardian* newspaper for permission to reproduce material cited in Chapter 4, which is copyright Myra Hindley/Guardian News & Media 1995.

Significant others outside of my academic life have shown resilience in maintaining (or perhaps feigning) enthusiasm for my preoccupation with mediations of madness. For the countless good laughs over the years, I would especially like to thank Debra Elliot, Claire and Neil Cross (no relation), David and Sarah Weller-Sheffield, Jane and Russell Harrison-Paul, Cal and Tim Mountfort-Lisle. Special thanks to the great Richard Thompson. My mum and dad, Barbara and Philip Cross, will be delighted to see this book on their shelf and my love to them for supplies of proper Lancashire Parkin (none of that Yorkshire rubbish) and 'those biscuits'.

Finally, my biggest thanks go to two very special people. The love, influence and support of Lizzy Gilliland are etched into every page of this book. Her willingness to sooth my anxieties about where the next idea is heading is the single most important contribution to finishing this book. Both in my work and away from it, she has kept me going through the good times and a few not so good times. I will always be amazed and grateful to what Lizzy adds to my life. She is also mummy to the most adorable boy in the world. The arrival of our son Gabriel James Gilliland Cross during the latter stages of writing this book has been the final inspiration to completing this project. Gabriel's arrival in the world has provided immense joy and more laughs, nappies and sleepless nights than one could possibly imagine. He also managed to chew over a couple of important pages. This book is dedicated to Lizzy and Gabriel: the loves of my life in a world of relative madness and sanity.

Introduction

Recognising madness

The cause of madness, as the old saw has it, is the mystery of mysteries. Yet despite its causes existing beyond everyday understanding, we all can recognise the appearance of madness. A true, but apocryphal-sounding tale is instructive here. Some years ago, a canteen worker in a psychiatric hospital was overheard advising a nervous and distracted-seeming arrival at the staff dining room as to the whereabouts of the patients' own dining area. About to be ushered away, the visitor frostily announced that he was in fact a newly appointed psychiatrist and that he preferred to dine with his colleagues. The mutual embarrassment of the canteen worker and psychiatrist was painfully obvious to all who witnessed the scene, including myself.

At that time I was a trainee psychiatric nurse working in a busy mental health unit. The inherent comedy in this encounter – cases of mistaken identity in a psychiatric hospital assume multiple comic proportions especially when a psychiatrist is on the receiving end of the joke – was long enjoyed by nursing and canteen staff, though possibly not medical staff. What has stayed with me about this incident has been a nagging interest in the canteen worker's (mis)recognition that there was something in the psychiatrist's odd appearance that warranted her 'diagnosis' and intervention.

This anecdote could be viewed as a classic example of what can happen to the appearance of sanity in the cuckoo's nest: that which is normal assumes the appearance of the abnormal such that even those who interact only minimally with psychiatric patients, such as hospital canteen workers, misrecognise what is normal. There is a sting in this tale, however. Within months of the incident I have just recounted the same psychiatrist *was* admitted as a patient into another psychiatric hospital (such confidential details are hard to secure). What had previously been nothing more than a hilarious case of mistaken identity now took on new comic dimensions around the canteen worker's ability to see what senior psychiatrists on the interview panel evidently could not! How can we understand this incident?

Though the events took place in a psychiatric hospital, I think that the explanation is to be found not in the professional world of psychiatry but in the public sphere of mediated images, representations and meanings about madness. Indeed, the puzzles that are posed by what we variously call madness, lunacy, insanity, psychosis and mental illness, covers a multitude of sin, and it is in the enigmatic and sometimes disturbing appearance of the 'mad' that we call upon notions of madness as ways of telling what is 'different' or just plain wrong about some people (Phillips, 2001).

While 'madness' is a grass roots construction it has been a real presence in the popular mind long before psychiatry made it its object of professional expertise. For example, in the eighteenth century, public exhibitions of madness by beggars and vagrants were recognisable to all who cared to look: 'Madness advertised itself in a proliferation of symptoms, in gait, in physiognomy, in weird demeanour and habits. It was synonymous with behaving crazy, looking crazy, talking crazy. Villagers, churchwardens and doctors alike – all could spot "antic dispositions"' (Porter, 1997, p.35). Porter's point is that no specialist knowledge was needed to recognise madness back then and as my hospital anecdote above suggests, it remains the case.

How do we all come to recognise the signs of madness? Whether we are seventeenth-century villagers or twenty-first century town or city dwellers, we have learnt to do so through mediated images and representations of madness. It is important to note that I am not suggesting here that 'signs' of madness are based on some or other 'genuine' psychiatric symptomology, since, as we shall see, my argument is that the meaning of madness is mediated in and through cultural forms that construct its appearance such that we know that this is what madness 'looks like'. Nor do I want to imply that it is the *same* basic message about 'madness' that we recognise, as though an eighteenth-century ballad about a mad beggar serves for instant recognition by a twenty-first century listener. While there are continuities over time in mediated images of madness there are also important changes to consider.

My approach to mediations of madness in this book considers historical and contemporary media ranging across single paintings, songs and photographs depicting insanity to the more familiar mass reproductions of madness in the tabloid press, television and via the Internet. Though society today defines itself as rational, the image of the irrational is never far away. As Sander Gilman (1982) notes in *Seeing the Insane*, his important visual history of cultural images and stereotypes of madness: 'Today the appearance of the madman has supposedly receded in importance in art as well as medicine .... Yet underlying our understanding of the mentally ill is the continued presence in society of older images of the insane, images that overtly or covertly color our concept and serve to categorize them upon first glance' (p.iii).

Gilman's cultural-historical work has proven an important marker in identifying the continuing importance of a culture of madness within 'sane' society. By this I mean that cultural images and representations of madness have by and large emerged out from everyday perceptions, rather than taking our terms *ex cathedra* from psychiatrists and other 'certified experts' (pun intended) on what madness really means. Thus, at no point in this book do I argue that mediated images or depictions of madness fall short of more 'accurate' depictions of mental illness preferred by anti-stigma campaigners. This is a false argument, because as Stephen Harper (2005, p.463) has rightly insisted, madness 'problematizes the pathologising implications of phrases such as "mental illness"'. By side-stepping the reductionist tendencies of clinical psychiatric language, I hope to be able to explore the versatility of madness and 'mad folk' (real and imagined) as a recurring cultural presence.

Mediating Madness has been written as a contribution to media studies concern with stereotypical images and representations of madness. However, it also goes beyond media studies' typically restricted concern with the present, to explore how stereotypes of madness appear on the historical landscape, only to disappear and then re-emerge later in some very surprising ways. Approaching the culture of madness in this way, I have plundered the work of scholars across diverse fields including social and cultural history of psychiatry, journalism studies, literary and women's studies, as well as contemporary media and cultural studies. By doing so, I see madness as a protean figure in the popular imagination, one whose masks have shifted to reflect, and also to influence, his contemporary sociocultural climes (Lavis, 2005). The interplay of popular ideas about madness and culture is where I begin my discussion about the mediations of madness in historical and contemporary media.

Thus, in Chapter 1, I begin by considering why the lay concept of 'madness' remains as a persistent and paradoxically *meaningful* category in the popular imagination. To understand why we need to directly engage with popular views of madness such as reported in the popular press. Thus, rather than blaming, say, the tabloid press for stigmatising psychiatric patients as 'mad' rather than psychiatrically ill, which is the standard view, my own approach takes account of the social and psychiatric policy context in relation to which distrustful images of madness appear. My strategy is to consider how contemporary media images of madness silence or censure the lived experience of mental distress. This is why I also make the case in this chapter for retaining the terminology of madness as an important counterpoint to a culturally limiting psychiatric discourse of 'mental illness'. By doing so, I am able to apply notions of 'madness' and 'insanity' in historical and cultural media contexts.

With historical media culture in mind, Chapter 2 examines change and continuity in visual images of madness beginning with the early modern English stereotype of 'Tom o'Bedlam' before moving on to consider clinical photographs and painted images of female insanity in the late-nineteenth century. Such images may appear to be the proper concern of historians not least because contemporary media stereotypes of madness seem to demand more urgent critical attention. I differ from this view, however, and argue that how we see and read historical images of madness is crucial to our understanding of the nature of continuity and change in stereotypes of madness. Thus, I offer in this chapter an analytic strategy for reading historical images of madness that enables us to see that while forms and figures of madness change there are threads of continuity. Indeed, my argument is that we can only really understand continuity in the visual image of madness in relation to change.

Journalists are often identified by historians of psychiatry as having made significant campaigning interventions on psychiatric policy gone awry. However, these accounts have seldom been analysed for how they represent the recipients of psychiatric policy-in-practice. Chapter 3 examines selected British and US reporting on psychiatric patients in three historically important sites of specialised care: the asylum, the psychiatric hospital and 'the community'. I illustrate the interrelationship between reporting on a policy trajectory that has seen psychiatric patients relocate from the asylum into the community, and concomitant images of human (sometimes *in*human) suffering. I show that in documenting the abuse of patients in their historical-psychiatric context, journalists trade on stereotypical images of madness.

Chapter 4 is focused on historical and contemporary press reporting on 'psy expertise' and the 'dangerous mind'. There is no shortage of tabloid reporting on this particular topic because ideas about the grotesqueness of madness and criminality have been the bread and butter of popular journalism since the beginning of the penny dreadful periodicals in the 1830s. However, my approach to reporting on psychiatry and criminals in this chapter bypasses concern about the tabloid press's sensationalist overemphasis on mad murderers since this tends to obscure the role played by the popular press negotiating the fluid boundaries of sickness, madness and badness. Instead, I take the fluidity of these boundaries as my starting point to probe the complex interplay between popular journalism, psychiatry, and criminals who are also patients.

Chapter 5 explores the continuities between traditional iconographies of madness and images of mental illness mobilised by contemporary television programme makers. In particular, it shows how contrasting forms of British TV documentary visualise 'dangerous' mental patients abroad in the community. In constructing the argument, particular attention is focused on the role of documentary television in making visible the lives of schizophrenics vis-à-vis changing notions of mental health care in the community. By doing so, the chapter adopts an approach to public representations of madness, which takes account of documentary television as a cultural form with social responsibility. The chapter concludes by emphasising television's cultural importance as *visual* medium capable of promoting or undermining the symbolic presence of mad folk within the community.

Using the example of voice hearing, one of the most widely accepted symptoms of mental disorder, in Chapter 6 Graham Murdock and

I examine how the experience of voice hearing has been mediated in actuality TV formats. The discussion also examines other recent and contradictory developments in the mediation of public talk about mental disorder. Firstly, we discuss how access to a public voice for the psychiatrically ill has been squeezed by reality television formats while making space for celebrity accounts of the experience of mental distress. Secondly, we discuss the migration of voice hearers to web forums where they can share their experiences and promote counter explanations and images of their situation. In the context of recent arguments for an enlarged public sphere in the digital age rooted in the integration of public broadcasting with the Internet, the chapter also asks what implications such a development has for the cultural rights of those with a psychiatric history.

My overall aim in this book is to illustrate how contemporary images and representations of madness are a consequence of the cultural legacy of ways of seeing 'the mad' under changing social and psychiatric conditions. Thus, as my plan of the book suggests, I have purposefully opted to explore historical and contemporary images of madness as discrete 'case studies' that I hope illustrate how and why images of madness and mad folk appear and disappear, only to re-emerge later in surprising ways. I make no claim to have written a comprehensive account of mediated images and representations past and present. What I do claim however is that we need to marry growing interest in the presentism of stereotypes of madness with a historically informed cultural analysis that together illuminates what it is that we find so fascinating about the human condition that we recognise as madness.

1
Madness and the Popular Imagination

Madness in the public sphere

My aim in this chapter is to illustrate how images and representations of the 'mad, bad and dangerous' are not simply the outcome of poor journalism, which is the standard view, but rather the cultural legacy of ways of seeing 'the mad' under new social and psychiatric conditions. The mythology of violence that underpins popular assumptions about the psychiatrically ill suggests that we must confront the cultural legacy of misrecognition in the public sphere. The social consequences of misrecognition, the philosopher Nancy Fraser (2000, p.113) has warned, are that people are 'denied the status of a full partner in social interaction, as a consequence of institutionalized patterns of cultural value that constitute one as comparatively unworthy of respect or esteem'. This is not just a philosophical point.

On New Year's Eve 1992, visitors to the lion enclosure in London Zoo saw a young man climb over the safety barrier. Despite urgent appeals to him to return to the safety of the viewing area he walked towards the lions, knelt and was then mauled. The man, Ben Silcock, survived the ordeal, though surgery to repair the damage reportedly took eight hours (Jones, 1993). The incident, captured on film by an amateur camcorder enthusiast, was aired by TV news organisations in Britain and across the world. Its newsworthiness was added to when it transpired that Silcock had recently asked for, but had been refused, medical help. He had apparently recognised that his psychotic symptoms were worsening but like the character Yossarian in Joseph Heller's *Catch 22*, doctors interpreted Silcock's request as evidence that he did *not* need treatment.

The footage of Silcock's mauling was deeply disturbing and, in Britain, sparked debate about the wisdom of deinstitutionalisation policies. But in the aftermath of recriminations and explanations it was never made clear why Silcock entered the lion's den, aside from popular explanations that he was simply 'mad', as in the *Daily Mirror* headline: 'My Mad Son' (2 January 1993, p.12). The *Daily Mirror* report was undoubtedly ventriloquising Silcock's father because in a television interview given some months after the event, Bryan Silcock, a journalist, spoke movingly of how his son often visited the zoo because he felt a particular communion with the caged lions, and that he had brought chickens to feed the lions when he was mauled. He made the point that his son had previously told him that being a community psychiatric patient was akin to being an unwelcome guest at a party, and he suggested that his son felt that he had more in common with animals than with people.

The symbolism of Silcock's mauling continues to carry two differing meanings. Firstly, it remains a *cause celebre* for those who maintain that care in the community policy is not working. Secondly, it also suggests the difficulty that the psychiatrically ill encounter in forging a sense of belonging in the community.

Writing on the pernicious social effects of psychiatric stigma, Sayce (1995, 1998, 2000) has suggested that public fear of mentally ill people, reported to be on the rise in the 1990s, was because of saturation media coverage of a small number of cases of homicide. While I am sympathetic to the socially progressive aims of anti-stigma campaigners like Sayce, my own approach to mediated images of the mentally distressed in this book aims to avoid this variant on the 'media effects' thesis. I want to argue instead for a revised approach to understanding the mediation of images and representations of madness, one that understands that their revivification in, say, tabloid reporting is part and parcel of a deformation of group identity, in which individual characters such as Ben Silcock are the epitome of *human matter out of place* (to borrow Mary Douglas's well-known anthropological term).

By this, I mean that the inane are so inextricably associated with belonging 'elsewhere' that we struggle to imagine that they might belong among us (I shall consider the implications of the words 'we', 'they', 'us' later in this chapter). For instance, following the closure of Britain's network of Victorian-built asylums in the 1980s and 1990s, the mentally distressed have reappeared as familiar figures on our streets and in other public spaces. At the same time however, their cultural image as 'mad, bad and dangerous to know' has reinforced their psychiatric otherness. As the feminist philosopher Anne Phillips (1999, p.81) puts it in the context of her argument about how we devalue human worth: 'it is proximity to those different from ourselves that resurrects long-buried ideas about social superiority and social inferiority, and that it is easy to conceive of others as your equals when you are not exposed to the details of their lives'. Recognising mentally ill people's humanity all too easily collapses in the face of recalcitrant experience (Barham, 1992; Barham and Hayward, 1991).

A brief example illustrates this point. In 1989, the then newly formed pressure group SANE (Schizophrenia: A National Emergency), launched by the *Sunday Times* journalist Marjorie Wallace, mounted a 'Stop the Madness' campaign predicated on public concern about the 'problem' of medicating psychiatric patients in the community. Its campaign also blamed psychiatrists who, SANE argued, did not use their power to compulsory treat as often as they should (Barham, 1992). SANE's campaign included a poster that appeared on public transport across the south of England showing the face of a young man alongside a caption that read:

HE THINKS HE'S JESUS
YOU THINK HE'S A KILLER
THEY THINK HE'S FINE

However, as critics within the psychiatric service user community noted:

If they [the public] half closed their eyes, what key words stood out? Killer. Voices. Lies. Nothing. Jesus. Madness. Their conclusion might well be that not only did 'those people' inhabit some completely different world but also that 'those people' pose a particularly awful menace, the true dimensions of which can only be alluded to in public.

(quoted in Crossley, 2006, p.195)

What the antics of SANE also illustrate is how the category of madness provides a template for mythologising about dangerous mental patients in the community. But why the modern scientific notion of 'schizophrenia' has not swept away the lay category of 'madness' is the begged question here.

The persistence of madness as a category of popular knowledge steers us towards the ways in which our culture draws from a reservoir of themes, premises and messages about being out of one's mind. Throughout history the image of madness has shifted to reflect changing social and psychiatric contexts (Sass, 1994; Porter, 2002). The mutable figure of madness has influenced my own approach to the mediation of images of madness in this book. Thus, I show how historical images have shaped, firstly, the popular image of Bedlam and later, photographic representations of female insanity in the nineteenth-century asylum (Chapter 2). More recent images of the mad as victims of psychiatric and social policies (Chapter 3), the criminally insane (Chapter 4), schizophrenics abroad in the community (Chapter 5) and voice hearers (Chapter 6) also reflect the resilience of 'madness' as an important category in popular thought.

The Italian Marxist Antonio Gramsci argued that the popular thought of the masses, what he calls 'common sense', could be understood in cultural–historical terms as the accretion of sediments of knowledge laid down in the social stratum over centuries (Gramsci, 1971). I want to borrow this trickle-down theory of knowledge to suggest that in the ebb and flow of our scientific and intellectual histories of madness, as each philosophical current of explanation comes and goes, it leaves behind a trace element in relation to popular ways of thinking about madness, where the latter has been historically effective in its own terms. It is worth noting here that across the centuries of human history, 'madness' has for the most part been interpreted and also managed by individuals and communities who find themselves confronted with mental symptoms that are, not incidentally, social infractions (Scull, 2006).

In a practical sense, then, madness is a category of lay knowledge grounded in the practical business of managing offensive anti-social behaviour. Moreover, the lay categories of the 'madman', the 'loony', the 'crazy', 'the nutter' and so on, have practical importance for how we not only recognise but also how we deal with it. For instance, in 1981, Peter Sutcliffe, known as the Yorkshire Ripper, was on trial for the murder of 13 women and the attempted murder of seven others.

During the proceedings the trial judge asked one psychiatrist who had diagnosed Sutcliffe as a schizophrenic to explain the condition. He replied: 'In layman's terms it is madness, but what I wish to say is that because people might be clinically mad, they are not necessarily out of contact with reality' (quoted in Bilton, 2003, p.517). I shall return to the Sutcliffe case later in Chapter 5. Here I simply want to underscore how madness remains a category of popular knowledge that we cannot easily dispense with.

Gramsci's insights into the historical resilience of lay knowledge suggest why popular categories of madness are easily revived, for example in our contemporary tabloid press. Thus the tabloid inventory of terms such as 'schizo', 'crazy', 'nutter', 'loony' and so forth, which are daily deployed in politically charged coverage of apparent dangers posed by community psychiatric patients, mobilises elements, premises and assumptions drawn from historically elaborated discourses on madness as dangerousness embedded in the popular imagination. Drawing on this inventory of madness is one way of imaging and imagining those who would once have been institutionalised out of sight, out of mind. In this sense, the standard anti-psychiatric stigma view that tabloid terminology for psychiatric patients is derogatory and should therefore be challenged misses how such terminology is expressive of a popular consciousness that contradicts what science tells us about 'mental illness'.

The symbolic image of madness re-emerged in the fading years of the twentieth century, precisely at the moment when many Western nations became familiar with the presence of mentally distressed vagrants forced to shift for themselves in the wake of asylum closures. In Great Britain for instance, semi-institutional places have sprung up to redirect the social disturbance wrought by ex-psychiatric patients. For instance, in Great Britain, mapping of social networks through which ex-psychiatric patients are now required to move through (Parr, 2000) has revealed new urban geographies whereby schizophrenics, for example, are steered from zones of public interaction to 'drop-in' centres, church halls and homeless shelters, that is, places where 'we' are not overtly bothered by 'them'. Thus, while madness remains a fixed cultural reference point within the political economy of local urban mythology, social relations with the mentally ill are negotiated via a *spatial* relationship in which mad lives exist at some remove from the not so mad.

Caroline Knowles (2000) has pointed out how public exhibitions of madness in the post-asylum era are now part of the grammar of urban space in the Canadian city of Montreal. In her interviews with homeless schizophrenics we see how they encounter misconceptions about their condition – that they have a split personality, are violent, dangerous and so on – which are worked into both their own self-understandings and their relations with others: 'Schizophrenics' conceptions of madness form a part of the public regimes for disposal of private terror. It forms a part of the ways in which they walk the streets of the city' (Knowles, 2000, p.101). I draw on Knowles' work here because I suggest that a sociologically informed understanding of the politics of mental distress and homelessness, both of which rarely feature in commentaries on media misrepresentations of madness, should be more appreciated as key indicators for what appears to be 'wrong' in the appearance of people for whom taking a bath or keeping clean clothes are no simple choices.

Knowles has termed post-asylum geographies in Montreal as 'Bedlam on the streets', which underlines how popular imagery of the chaos of mad lives from past times appear in contemporary accounts of mental distress (see Chapter 2). Thus, Knowles' account of what Bedlam on the streets *looks like* – she uses photographs to illustrate individual mad lives in transit around Montreal – reflects shared cultural knowledge; in this case, the popular image of Bedlam as a place of pandemonium and craziness. It therefore makes sense (out of non-sense, as it were) that the mad bring with them their 'natural' condition (crazy appearance, hazardous behaviour and so on) when they are relocated to the community. But as Knowles cautions: 'Appearance and behaviour combined with a renewed public visibility feeds popular perceptions of dangerousness, but this should not in itself be interpreted as dangerousness. What *looks* dangerous is not so necessarily' (Knowles, ibid., pp.142–3, emphasis in the original).

Whereas in the asylum, the mad were secluded literally and symbolically 'off the map', outside the community of 'normal' folk, they now occupy a liminal zone (Glass, 1989) in which they are neither fully immersed in the world of psychiatry, nor incorporated in the world of citizens. Deinstitutionalisation has ushered in a new (and for some disturbing) scenario in which former mental patients 'may be more of a mystery today, living among us, than they were when hidden away in the asylum. We do not know them, because they are neither outside society in the world of exclusion, nor are they full citizens – individuals who are like the rest of us' (Lewis et al., quoted in Barham and Hayward, 1991, p.143). In the next section, we shall see how the apparently violent nature of these people has resulted in the popular press relying on stock images and representations of psychiatric patients as socially disturbing figures.

Disturbing figures and the fear of madness

Before we look at images of madness in this book, what are we able to glean through dispassionate analysis of mental disorder and violence? To answer the question I shall bring popular press reporting on dangerous psychiatric patients together with real-world indicators of mental disorder and homicide. My focus here on the popular press is for three reasons. Firstly, representations of madness that I use later in the book mainly derive from popular journalism, past and present. Secondly, journalists use official (and quasi-official) figures on mental disorder and violence to fuel the idea that psychiatric patients pose a risk to the public. Thirdly, I want to consider accusations that media reporting exacerbates social fear of madness.

I noted earlier Caroline Knowles' interviews with homeless schizophrenics in the Canadian city of Montreal. She reveals how, cut off from the support network they once had in the hospital, they are now forced to wander through the liminal spaces of the city where they daily encounter popular misconceptions of their condition; that they have a split personality, are violent and dangerous, and so on. As a sociologist, Knowles is aware how popular assumptions about madness and danger fit neatly with social anxieties about the unpredictable character of violence in urban environments:

> Madness underwrites and gives meaning and content to the randomness and senselessness of urban violence: and this is its place in the overall political economy of urban mythology. The mad have re-entered the demonology of modern urban life – lurking beneath the surface, indistinguishable from the rest of the population, an insidious threat that gives new form to the long-standing social anxiety that surrounds the *anomie* of urban existence.
>
> (Knowles, ibid., p.137)

In the main cultural arena that daily constructs the symbols of urban terror, the tabloid press, the mad have taken their place in the pantheon of other modern folk devils including predatory paedophiles, child killers and serial killers. This is not to say that the tabloids are *frightening* their readers, since this view misunderstands not only the pleasures of reading tabloid journalism but also genuine public interest in the risks posed to the public by community-care policies. Here, the notion of community 'at risk' is not one cooked up by tabloid journalists, though they are implicated in its ideological construction in their reporting on psychiatric risks (Castel, 1991).

Thus, the sociologist Nikolas Rose (2005) has noted how psychiatric governance is now dominated by 'risk-thinking', which until recently was the concern of only a small number of forensic psychiatrists but has since the 1990s been replaced by a requirement that psychiatrists assume that *every* patient carries the potential for risk to self or others. In his other work on psychiatric governance and risk calculation, Rose (2002) has also noted how the equation of madness with risk is not new but that psychiatric patients are now centre stage in a public debate transfixed by newspaper headlines about predatory madmen discharged from hospitals and poised to kill members of the public because they lack self-control. Rose also points out how the tenor of public debate about psychiatric policy has mutated from seeing patients as victims of institutionalised asylum-based policies to seeing the public as victims of new community-based mental health policies. Rose pithily sums up change in the tenor of the debate as 'from care in the community to scare in the community' (Rose, 2002, p.182).

From the outset, public debate about community care was influenced by media construction of schizophrenia as the epitome of risky madness. In December 1992, just a few months before the policy became formally implemented, Jonathan Zito, a recently married musician, was stabbed to death on the London Underground. The newsworthiness of Zito's murder was heightened when it was revealed that his killer, Christopher Clunis, was a violent schizophrenic recently released from hospital.

The personal tragedy of Zito's murder became a public emblematic of the perils of mental health care in the community. For instance, a report in the *Daily Mail* ('Killers in the Community', 25 February 1994, p.7), listed 17 schizophrenics who had killed family members in the year or so following Zito's murder. Thus, Zito's random murder of a stranger provided a template explaining other murders by schizophrenics regardless of individual circumstances. The *Mail* report underscored that (i) Zito's murder is part of a pattern of offending by violent schizophrenics, which is (ii) predicable given (iii) the circumstances in which schizophrenics *per se* are inadequately supervised/medicated in the community. Why schizophrenics are presumed to require supervision/medication is the begged question here.

The answer, according to a study by Leudar and Thomas (2000) of British national newspaper coverage of 14 named individuals who had killed, coheres around the interlinking topics of 'voices and violence'. They highlight the case of Anthony Smith, a paranoid schizophrenic who shortly after being discharged from hospital murdered his mother and brother. What is unusual and welcome about their study of the Smith case is that it is concerned with broadsheet reporting, which is traditionally seen as more serious, less trivialising journalism than what is written in the tabloid press.

Broadsheet reporting on Anthony Smith's violent schizophrenic condition highlights the 'common sense' view that he should not have been discharged unless he was heavily supervised and medicated for 'hearing voices', which he apparently was not. But as they point out, press reporting of his case is best seen 'not as objective representations of events, but as accounts aligned in a controversy concerning the place in the community for people with a mental illness' (Leudar and Thomas, 2000, p.155). I have already noted how 'the community' is not a place where those diagnosed with schizophrenia can easily feel at home (cf. Rogers, Pilgrim and Lacey, 1993).

In their analysis of reporting on the Smith case, Leudar and Thomas point out how Smith is discursively transformed by journalists into an 'aggressor' rather than a family member so as to distance him from the normality of family relations, which he has shattered by his murderous actions. They also note that 'the journalist does the binding of violence to schizophrenia and the categorisation of Smith as a schizophrenic in the narrator voice' (Leudar and Thomas, ibid., p.156). What they mean by this is that the category 'schizophrenia' is deployed in newspaper reporting to dissolve the binding of social membership: 'This is just to say that in a technical way that an insane person is in some respects outside the moral order' (ibid.). There is a temptation here to wrongly conceive of schizophrenic violence as meaningless.

By contrast, newspaper reporting of Smith's murderous attacks render his violence *meaningful* but only in relation to his 'voices', as he becomes through them an irrational agent (a violent and dangerous paranoid schizophrenic) ultimately absolved from the responsibility by the courts because of his 'hearing voices'. Later in Chapter 6, Graham Murdock and I will offer a counterpoint to conventional news media reporting of voice hearers. For now, I want to stress how journalists reporting on schizophrenics need not emphasise the core symptoms of the condition such as 'hearing voices' to impart a sense of fear and loathing. A case in point concerns how the findings of a British study on schizophrenics who had come before the courts was used by one tabloid as a stick to beat the community-care policy.

In 1998, the Royal College of Psychiatrists' *Bulletin* journal published a study (see Perry et al., 1998) that reported that 23 schizophrenic patients were found to have carried weapons during psychotic episodes. The research was reported *the next day* in the *Sunday Express* with the headline, 'Armed and dangerous' (*Sunday Express*, 22 February, 1998, p.1). The story extrapolated that 1250 mentally ill patients in the community carried weapons and posed 'a serious threat to public safety'. The paper also quoted a Zito Trust figure (a charity set up in memory of Jonathan Zito to campaign on the politics of mental health) that claimed, '5000 schizophrenic patients in the community are a danger to themselves or others' (p.1). The *Bulletin* study became a classic tabloid tale of 'armed and dangerous' schizophrenics in the community and underlines why the tabloids more than any other media are accused of whipping up public anxiety that the mentally ill are more dangerous than the sane.

Mental illness and violence has been a consistently skewed theme of British tabloid and broadsheet reporting on mental illness and community care (see for instance Philo, Henderson and McLauglin, 1993; Philo, 1996; Read and Baker, 1996; Busfield, 2002; Hallam, 2002; Foster, 2006). In their widely cited research on mental illness themes appearing in the British tabloids following the launch of community care in 1993, Philo, McLaughlin and Henderson (1996), found that the commission of a violent attack was the most common news item involving a mental illness, which led to their conclusion that 'This is a media world populated by "psychopaths", "maniacs" and "frenzied knife men"' (p.50). Nor is this a uniquely British media phenomenon.

A similar skewed emphasis on mental illness and violence is found in tabloid newspapers in other English-speaking countries including the US (e.g. Wahl, 2004), Canada (e.g. Olstead, 2002), New Zealand (e.g. Wilson et al., 1999) and Australia (see a special edition on news reporting of mental illness in the *Australian Journalism Review*, 2005). All these countries are ex-colonies of Britain and while there are significant national differences between their respective media and mental health systems, these countries have implemented broadly similar deinstitutionalisation and community-care policies to the UK. This cross-national policy similarity helps explain not only similarities in media images of community psychiatric patients as violent or dangerous but also that there is a universal legacy of cultural misrecognition. Of especial concern in this international literature is that tabloid stories daily construct schizophrenics as modern day folk devils, synonymous with violence or danger.

The drip-by-drip association of mental illness with violence prevalent in media reporting has been criticised for its prejudicial portrayal of the risks psychiatric patients pose to the public. The writer Sara Maitland is typical of those who call for a sense of proportion about the extent of the social danger posed by the mentally ill:

> More fires are started by mismanaged chip pans, insurance fraudsters and naughty children than by pyromaniacs. More people are killed by drunken drivers than by schizophrenics. More children are hurt by accidents in the home than by aggressive paranoiacs on the street. More children are abused and more women raped by members of their households than by sex maniacs driven by uncontrollable Voices. As a matter of measurable fact, in contradiction to the impression given by our tabloid media, the number of murders committed annually by individuals with a mental health problem is not increasing; it has actually declined as a percentage – because more 'sane' people commit murders.
>
> (Maitland, 2001, p.76)

Maitland is right. The assertion of mental health campaigners and politicians that deinstitutionalisation policies have directly resulted in rising numbers of homicides committed by those suffering from mental illness is simply not borne out by the available evidence.

For instance, Home Office statistics show that in Great Britain, rates of homicide attributed to the mentally disordered rose between 1957 and 1979 (as did homicides in general), which is the period directly *preceding* expansion in care in the community policies (Taylor and Gunn, 1999).

Since 1979, homicides due to mental disorder have fallen consistently while homicides due to other reasons have continued to rise. As Taylor and Gunn (1999, p.9) put it of tabloid reporting on the dangers of mental health care in the community: 'there is no evidence that it is anything but stigmatising to claim that ... [people with mental disorder] living in the community is a dangerous experiment that should be reversed'. Discussing the same official statistics, Large et al. (2008) also point out that the fall in homicide statistics has occurred despite there having been no changes to the official definitions of the defences to murder since the 1950s. Large et al. (2008) also note that one would expect improved diagnosis of mental illness in modern times to have inflated the rates of murder attributed to mental illness and *not have reduced them*. Comparable findings are reported in countries such as New Zealand and Denmark (Prins, 2005).

Maitland's argument is that the tabloid media, like much popular culture, are not simply stigmatising the 'insane' but are symbolically shoring up the boundary between 'us' and 'them', which until recently was concretely manifest in the bricks and mortar of the asylum. Her point is not that schizophrenics do sometimes kill people since this is an incontrovertible fact, but that such killings are widely exaggerated. Consider for instance the news media's headline response to a 2006 report by the National Patient Safety Agency (part of the Department of Health), which includes this finding: 'The Inquiry investigated 249 cases of homicide by current or recent patients, occurring between April 1999 and December 2003, 9% of all homicides occurring in England Wales during this period. This figure translates into 52 patient homicides per year' (Appleby et al., 2006, p.15). The significance of the figures is underlined by the fact that more or less every national newspaper headlined the statistics:

• Mentally ill patients kill one person a week (*Sunday Telegraph*, 3 December 2006, p.9)
• Mentally ill murder 400 (*Sunday Times*, 3 December 2006, p.1)

- One person a week killed by mentally ill (*The Observer*, 3 December 2006, p.1)
- Every week someone is murdered by a mental patient (and a third had just been classed fit for release) (*Daily Mail*, 4 December 2006, p.5)
- One person each week is killed by a mental patient (*The Express*, 4 December 2006, p.29)
- 'One murder a week' by psychiatric patients (*The Independent*, 4 December 2006, p.8)
- Mental patients 'kill one person a week' (*The Times*, 5 December 2006, p.27)

Such scary headlines constitute media distortion not simply for the heightened sense of danger that the headlines individually and collectively convey. Since the figures themselves cannot (and should not) be denied, the more significant distortion lies in the underlying assumptions contained in many of these news reports that suggest mental health care in the community is a 'soft system' for people whose *essential deviancy* ought to be more securely managed. The figure of one person killed a week is hostage to journalistic fortune as the news media post-Clunis, compete to frame the meaning of psychiatric policy as jeopardising public safety:

> The public fear of madness leading to violence, especially unprovoked and gratuitous, remains a driving force. Single events can change public policy: the case of Christopher Clunis ... being an example. Looking back on this I think that it was one of those defining moments that promote a new view of the mentally disordered. Gone was the earlier world-view of the mad as victims of their condition; this was replaced by the mad as predators.
>
> (Bean, 2008, p.162)

The change in public policy that Bean alludes to concerns new safety controls that the community safety lobby sought and has received in the wake of the government enquiry on the Clunis case. As Peter Beresford (2001) points out in his work on populist approaches to welfare policy and ideology, the agenda setting impact of the tabloid press has vastly extended its political influence on government and politicians via promotion of stereotyped images of deviance:

> In the context of mental health policy, for example, at a conference on mental health and the media, David Brindle, editor of *Guardian Society*, stated that while publicly government ministers rejected the association of mental health service users, dangerousness and homicide, at private briefings, they and their spin doctors 'spun a different tune fuelling demands for a more custodial form of mental health care', as advanced by the *Sun* and *Daily Mail*.
>
> (Beresford, 2001, p.504)

Brindle suggests that a combination of opportunistic pressure groups, populist politicians and media hacks have been influential in promoting a policy response aimed at protecting the public from psychiatric patients – despite the evidence noted above that there has been no statistical increase in killings perpetrated by psychiatric patients in the post-asylum era. The role of the tabloids in the sphere of political and public influence has nevertheless led to support for government approaches to psychiatric patients located within a framework of 'public safety', which prioritises protection of the public. For instance, the new Mental Health Act (2007) includes provision for Supervised Community Treatment powers, which will return a patient to hospital if their medication regime is not complied with in the community.

Public anxiety about community psychiatric patients also has real-world consequences beyond psychiatric policy. For instance, a 2007 survey of English public attitudes towards mental illness found an increase in prejudice across a variety of indicators, including not wanting to live next door to someone who has been mentally ill, not believing that people with mental health problems have 'the same right to a job as anyone else' and believing that people with mental health problems are 'prone to violence (TNS, 2007). Similarly, the British mental health charity Rethink has published a report (Stigma Shout Survey, 2008) on stigma and discrimination experienced by community psychiatric patients, which shows that close to nine out of ten service users (87%) interviewed reported some experience of stigma. Two-thirds of respondents said that they have stopped doing things because of stigma, and two-thirds have stopped doing things because of the fear of stigma and discrimination. The figures lend weight to mental health campaigners who equate the abuse of psychiatric patients with recognised forms of 'hate crimes' such as racism or homophobia (e.g. Sayce, 1998; Warner, 2004).

Since the advent of community-care policies in the mid-1990s, numerous commentators have highlighted how, in terms of limited access to good housing, jobs, social networks, as well as loss of social status, people living and coping with a psychiatric condition are among the most excluded in society (see, for example, Repper, et al., 1997; Dunn, 1999; Sayce, 2000; Huxley and Thornicroft, 2003). For instance, the slogan 'schizophrenics go home' was painted in a London street where a psychiatric care home was being readied. As one mental health campaigner notes of this "nimby" (i.e. 'not in my backyard') response, it is ironic that 'people were attempting to set up home but were prevented from doing so by neighbours who appeared to believe that service users belonged somewhere else – preferably in a distant institution. They were not seen as part of the local community' (Sayce, 2000, pp.42–3).

If anything, the social stigma attached to psychiatric patients appears to have worsened in recent years. A recent government-funded survey shows a hardening of attitude among respondents to the proposition, 'We need to adopt a far more tolerant attitude toward people with mental illness in our society' (TNS, 2007). Respondent agreement reportedly decreased by eight per cent: from 92 per cent in 1994 to 84 per cent in 2007. The same government survey also shows:

- One in eight people would not want to live next door to someone who has been mentally ill,
- Nearly six out of ten people describe a person with a mental illness as 'someone who has to be kept in a psychiatric or mental hospital',
- One third of people think that people with mental health problems should not have the same rights to a job as everyone else,
- Only 31 per cent of people think that mental hospitals are an outdated means of treating people.

The relocation of psychiatric services and patients into the community has clearly not been coterminous with a shift in social attitudes towards those with a mental illness diagnosis. Some commentators place the blame for this state of affairs on negative media portrayal of community psychiatric patients as a social menace. For example, in their widely cited work on this issue, Philo, McLaughlin and Henderson (1996) argue that negative media portrayal of psychiatric patients influences social fear of the mentally ill such that they are seen as a preternaturally dangerous and menacing social problem. This is also a generally held view among mental health professionals internationally (see Sartorius and Schulze (2005) for a global programme of work on stigma reduction that identifies journalists as 'peddlers of public fear' (p.5) about psychiatric illness, the corollary of which is that journalists might be usefully harnessed to highlight 'successful outcome' within mental health news stories to begin changing attitudes towards the mentally ill).

This is too simplistic in my view. While segregation in the asylum has been replaced by psychiatric care in the community, official medico-psychiatric language for managing the lives of the psychiatrically ill continues to decide, 'where and how they can participate in the lives of those deemed to be of full mental health' (Phillips, 2001, p.36). In considering the recovery of the psychiatric patient's 'place' in the community, Glass (1989) has written that 'the medical language that exercises such a powerful hold over the patient's sense of identity and liberty, reinforces the self's knowledge of its own separateness, its essential and abiding alienation from the species, from community' (p.77). This view underlines how the politics of madness is the key to unlocking the social consequences of media misrepresentation.

I want to suggest therefore that within the disputed politics of madness are to be found historical and contemporary examples of the cultural silencing of the mad perspective that take us beyond a media-centred view of the problem of (mis)representation of mental illness in the media. I prefer instead to situate mediations of madness that form the core of this book within the context of arguments that our impulse to see the mad as 'suffering' has deprived them of their point of view: 'To think of suffering as the worst thing we suffer from', says the psychoanalyst Adam Phillips, 'can itself be a form of censorship' (Phillips, 2001, p.33). This is not to deny the distress that madness can cause. Rather, it is to say that the mad are taken as socially, culturally and politically dissident and that what they know and think has long been prevented from adding to the stock of available reality.

The politics and terminology of madness

Madness, like its twentieth-century counterpart, mental illness, is an evaluative concept; that madness is a disturbance of *mind* not behaviour. This view is brought out most effectively in Michel Foucault's influential philosophical analysis of madness and reason, *Madness and Civilization* (Foucault, 2001). For three centuries, according to Foucault, madness has stood in opposition to reason, and it is unreason and irrationality that are presumed when someone is identified as 'mad'. In Foucault's estimation, the constitution of madness as 'illness' at the end of the eighteenth century is evidence of a broken dialogue between reason and insanity. Historians of psychiatry have rejected this claim as lacking in historical evidence (e.g. Midelfort, 1980; Porter, 1987a), but are persuaded by Foucault's attendant argument that the history of madness is also a history of power relationships.

For example, while disagreeing with many historically sweeping aspects of Foucault's analysis, Roy Porter (1987a) sees particular value in Foucault's observation about madness as unreason. Porter's view is that the literal 'shutting up' of the insane in institutions did indeed result in a deafness towards the communications of the disturbed, in particular a discounting of the reactions to, and complaints against, the treatment meted out to them. Of course, inmates themselves were all too aware of how power relations outside and inside the asylum obscured their point of view – a fact wryly noted by the Restoration playwright Nathaniel Lee, following his committal instigated by members of his own family to Bethlem Hospital (popularly known as Bedlam) in the mid-sixteenth century: 'They called me mad, I called them mad, and damn them they outvoted me' (Porter, 1991, p.1). Nathaniel Lee's experience of being 'shut up' in the asylum is not merely a historical anecdote however.

In 2008, a British general practitioner, Dr Humayra Abedin, was tricked into flying to Bangladesh with news that her mother was seriously ill. On her arrival, members of her family, including her mother, held her hostage apparently to force her into an arranged marriage. Although she was given sleeping tablets to quieten her complaints she reportedly managed to text message UK friends to alert them that her life was in danger (*The Guardian*, 20 December 2008, p.11). Realising that she had communicated with the outside world, Dr Abedin's family then admitted her to a local psychiatric hospital where she was given anti-psychotic drugs. Under the influence of these powerful drugs Dr Abedin was forced to undergo an arranged marriage to a complete stranger, a ceremony she later reported being barely able to remember. She was shortly afterwards rescued from her ordeal and on her return to the UK testified before a House of Lords committee about the experience of being detained by her family for her 'unruly' behaviour and institutionalised as 'mad' for not wanting to marry. Nathaniel Lee would presumably have empathised with the plight of Dr Abedin.

We can only imagine what Nathaniel Lee might make of subsequent psychiatric developments, which over the past two-and-a-half centuries has consolidated power over the lives of the psychiatrically ill in the hands of the medical profession. This has resulted in the former group being deprived by the latter of their right to be heard on the politics of compulsory treatment, that is, a politically motivated policy responding to public concern about their apparent dangerous condition: 'The symptomatology of mental illness together with the cultural constructs we have placed upon it – especially the prevailing view that "rationality" is key to full humanity – leave the sufferers of these illnesses particularly vulnerable' (Maitland, 2001, p.77). Their vulnerability, Maitland suggests, resides in popular mythology that the mentally ill are a danger to themselves and others, and society therefore has a right and a duty to control them, to force them to 'get better' and to receive treatment without consent.

Maitland's argument is important given that in recent years England and Wales, Scotland, Canada and the US, among other countries, have introduced powers to compel the mentally disordered to submit to treatment regimes in the community. These countries have each passed community treatment laws in the aftermath of homicides perpetrated by schizophrenics. The popular press refer to these as 'Brian's Law' in Ontario, Canada, 'Kendra's Law' in New York and 'Laura's Law' in California, each ruling named after the victim of a homicide by an unmedicated schizophrenic living in the community (Lawton-Smith, 2005). In the context of UK political and policy debates on this issue, psychiatric service users have complained that their political opinions and policy viewpoints have hardly registered in the non-compliance debate (Coleman, 1999; Sayce, 2000; Crepaz-Keay, 2005).

From a mainstream psychiatric perspective, attending or listening to the voice of the mad is pointless since, by virtue of their unreason, their views are worthless. In the context of psychiatry's institution-alised relations with patients, this erasure of the voice of the mad is appropriate since 'psychiatric theory advised that delusion was contagious and that it was foolish to reason with the mad' (Porter, 1987b, pp.235–6). As a historian interested in stories by/of the insane, getting inside the heads of the mad (as it were) is important, Porter advocates, because listening to the pillars of sane society such as psychiatrists, gives only a partial account of madness. I intend to retain the wisdom in Porter's point for our later brush with contemporary voice hearers/mad voices in the public spheres of broadcasting and the Internet (see Chapter 6).

This is not to say that the mad have not had champions vocalis-ing on their behalf. We can for example point to the tragic case of James Norris, who was discovered in 1813 by lunacy campaigners to have been chained by his arms and neck to the wall in his Bethlem/Bedlam cell for more than 12 years (see also Chapter 2 for more detail on the Norris case). Norris was able to converse normally with his rescuers, which included the radical journalist William Hone: 'On each day that we saw him he discoursed coolly, and gave rational and deliberate answers to different questions put to him' (quoted in Wilson, 2005, p.87). Notwithstanding the fact that journalists such as Hone have from time to time spoken up on behalf of silenced and vulnerable mad voices, other so-called mad voices have been lost to psychiatric and social history.

When the writer Maggie O'Farrell began research for her 2005 novel *The Vanishing Act of Esme Lennox*, a story about a vocal and independent-minded 16-year old committed to an asylum in the 1930s and who remains there, ignored and forgotten by her family for 60 years, she discovered that the asylum was for hundreds of women a real-world destination because of them having commit-ted misdemeanours such as being pregnant outside marriage, being overly sexually interested in men or conversely not being interested enough. We shall never now know if any of these 'unruly' women protested their incarceration but it does not stretch us to imagine how difficult it might have been to find anyone to listen let alone take one seriously:

> Once you were put inside, the 'mad' label foisted on you would, in all likelihood, become true, not only from the shock and horror of your new surroundings, but also courtesy of the 'treatments' you received. It must have been hard to retain mental stability in the face of comas induced by insulin injection, or a combination of straitjackets and cold baths, or the more severe, invasive procedures of cliterodectomies and frontal lobotomies. Society's view of you as insane could, in such circumstances, become a self-fulfilling prophecy.
>
> (O'Farrell, 2006, p.18)

In recent years, historians (e.g. Davies, 2001) have drawn on patients' oral testimony to recover the history (perhaps her-story is more appropriate here) of these 'troublesome' women literally and metaphorically silenced in the asylum. This work confirms how once one has been labelled 'mad', their social status is all too easily erased as the ravings or importunings of irrationality (as deviancy theorists might put, e.g. Scheff, 1999). Moreover, appearing 'mad' albeit as a consequence of cold baths and other psychiatric 'treatments', can and does undermine one's credibility to speak publicly on matters pertinent to one's situation. In Chapters 3 and 4 we shall see how the public spheres of non-fictional television and the popular press has constructed images of the mad as symbolically charged 'suffering' characters.

The politics of labelling insanity is not a new concern, however. Writing in 1621 about the blurred line between sanity and madness, Robert Burton, a physician and theologian (the two often went hand in hand), was minded to comment on the difficulties in apprehending the true appearance of the insane from the sane:

> But to see the Madman rage distraught
> With furious looks, a ghastly sight.
> Naked in chains bound doth he ly,
> And roars amain, he knows not why?
> Observe him; for as in a glass,
> Thine angry portraiture it was.

His picture keep still in thy presence;
Twist him and thee, there's no difference.

Burton's instructional poetry is an early recognition that the labelling of human behaviour *as madness* is primarily a social act, a badge that we pin on those displaying in their looks, in their social portraiture, a subjectively defined bundle of traits we recognise as 'difference' (Gilman, 1982). In this sense, Burton presages the criticisms of the so-called anti-psychiatrists by almost three-and-a-half centuries.

The anti-psychiatry movement that emerged in the mid-1960s around the Scottish psychiatrist R. D. Laing took aim at psychiatry's denial of the mad (read: schizophrenic) experience. The popularity of Laing's *The Divided Self* (1965) is partly because it is imbued with concern for revaluing 'schizophrenic' communications as intelligible. Laing's name is often coupled with that of the American psychiatrist Thomas Szasz. Szasz (1974, p.8) argues that 'Mental illness is not something a person *has*, but is something he *does* or *is*'. Szasz does not deny the concept of mental disorder, but attacks the terminology of 'mental illness' as conceptually meaningless, not to say intellectually corrupt. He suggests that people who have 'life problems', such as victims of racism, are thrust into a sick role. While the neurotic embraces the role in order to receive help with problems of daily living, the psychotic may have the sick role involuntarily applied. It acts as a convenient way of labelling objectionable behaviour and helps to justify 'treatment' by incarceration.

Szasz's view roughly tallies with George Orwell's smart quip that madness means being in 'a minority of one'. This is a view with which Nathaniel Lee presumably would have concurred. Indeed, Lee's despair at being 'outvoted' on who is mad could be seen as touching on a fundamental truth about madness: not that it leads one to encounter, say, visions of God, the Virgin Mary or the Devil, but that true madness is where one is alienated from the world. As the seventeenth-century moralising Baptist Thomas Tryon expressed his view of the madness of the world around him: 'To Speak Truth, the World is but a great *Bedlam*, where those that are *more mad*, lock up those that are less' (cited in Porter, 1991, p.3, Porter's emphasis).

The notion that those locked up as mad are less mad than those who lock them up has been a recurrent theme in caustic social commentary about madness and madhouses over the past three centuries (see Kullman, 1985). This theme has been, perhaps not surprisingly, prioritised by the mad themselves over any other issue relating to their condition and treatment (for a potted historical perspective on this topic see an entertaining anthology of US and British 'mad writings' in Peterson, 1982). The possibility that we may be incarcerated in the madhouse while proclaiming our sanity in the manner of Nathaniel Lee brings us to a view that repudiates the idea of madness as a clinical disorder and instead inserts it into a network of power relationships inseparable from wider webs of society and culture.

Here, for example, is David Cooper, the most avowed Marxist of the 1960s anti-psychiatrists (though he was himself a trained psychiatrist). His argument concerns the language of madness; in particular using the word 'madness' to challenge what he sees is the repressive apparatus of psychiatric nomenclature:

> The madness about which I'm writing is the madness that is more or less present in each one of us and not only the madness that gets the psychiatric baptism by diagnosis of 'schizophrenia' or some other label invented by the specialized psycho-police agents of final phase capitalist society. So when I use the word 'madman' here I'm not referring to a special race of people, but the madman in me is addressing the madman in you in the hope that the former madman speaks clearly or loudly enough for the latter to hear. The language of 'madness' means the way that this universal madness is expressed is not only in uttered, audible words, but in a type of action, running across experience, that is 'mad discourse'.

(Cooper, 1978, p.8)

Cooper's radical view of the 'psycho-police' tactics of psychiatry came to a dead end as proponents of psychiatry emerged more or less unscathed from the ideological assault of anti-psychiatry (see the swinging retort to the anti-psychiatry school in Roth and Kroll, 1986). Nevertheless Cooper's view of the communicative potential in the term madness ('the madman in me is addressing the madman in you') offers a conceptual device for analysing the hegemonic net of madness discourse, whether this be the net cast by images of madness in medical, legal and literary texts or that linking representations of madness in film, television, news media, paintings, theatre and cartoons.

However, this is not to argue that contemporary psychiatric nomenclature has no claim whatsoever on cultural representations of madness. For example, ever since the onset on tabloid antipathy towards psychiatric patients in Great Britain in the 1990s, psychiatric professionals have made it a priority to promote public understanding about psychiatric conditions, including its modern treatment regimes in light of what it sees are systematic *mis*representations about psychiatric matters in contemporary media culture (e.g. Byrne, 1999; Hart and Phillipson, 1999; Leff, 2001; Anderson, 2003; Thornicroft, 2006; Benbow, 2007). Rather, I want to make it clear that the psychiatric profession's attendant claim that its members alone can provide the 'correct' representational/terminological criteria for making sense of madness as 'mental illness' is to impose an alien logic on the imprint of mad culture.

This is illustrated in the retrospective medical diagnosis imposed on George III whose periodic bouts of madness left him straightjacketed within his royal apartments. His 'madness' has since been diagnosed as variegate porphyria, a hereditary disease caused by a chemical insufficiency in the production of haemoglobin (Green, 2003). At the same time, this diagnosis cannot dislodge the image of 'mad King George' in Alan Bennett's play *The Madness of George III* (later a successful feature film *The Madness of King George*) or in Sir Peter Maxwell Davies' 1969 mini-opera, *Eight Songs for a Mad King*, in which the King vocalises weirdly as he bemoans his fate and attempts to teach birds to sing. Retrospective diagnostics cannot unpick the cultural net that has secured the ranting and ravings of George III as the 'mad King' in the popular imagination. In this sense, the category 'madness' acts as a cultural reference point for making sense of that which psychiatry has traditionally conceived as unintelligible or non-sense (Foucault, 2001). Because the expression of madness exceeds what is possible to talk about using conventional psychiatric discourse, it is our best tool for coming to terms with images and representations of madness circulating within works of art.

This example steers me to my first justification for using the umbrella term 'madness' throughout this book. As Roy Porter (1991) wisely points out, the term conveys the richest of resonances in everyday parlance since, 'it is widely applied to many people besides the clinically certifiable, and includes all manner of abnormalities and extremes of thought and emotion (I can be mad over you, mad at you, madly in love with you). No synonym or euphemism is half so evocative' (Porter, 1991, p.xi). Indeed, when one also allows Samuel Johnson's dictum (or is it a diagnosis?) that 'no human mind is in its right state', madness stands for more than a derogatory term of abuse; it supremely illuminates the myriad shades of humanity that lie between supposed black-and-white distinctions between the mad and not so mad.

I want to offer a second, more extended political justification for using the term 'madness' in this book. The notion that madness conveys the richest resonances in popular culture has not gone unnoticed by those who understand only too well the impact of social distinctions as to who is mad and who is not. Some of those who live and cope with the impact of a psychiatric label such as schizophrenia or bipolar disorder prefer to use the term 'mad' to distance them from the pathologising implications in the phrase 'mental illness'. Consider this account by someone previously diagnosed as schizophrenic:

> When you receive a psychiatric diagnosis your life changes forever. You live the rest of your days in a box marked 'nutter'. Your life will probably be shorter, your income lower and your opportunities significantly reduced. That is discrimination in action. Alongside this, everything you say is heard as the words of a mad person. In many ways, this devaluation, and sometimes complete removal, of a person's voice is the cruelest discrimination of all. When everyone else tells you that they know what's best for you, and any disagreement or dissent you express is seen as a symptom of your illness, that is when you most need your voice.
>
> (Crepaz-Keay, 2008, pp.8–9)

This writer goes on to say that he now prefers to describe himself as a 'survivor' of psychiatric labelling since for him being marked a 'nutter' is dehumanising and renders him a prisoner of others' stigmatising prejudices.

Others have encountered this problem in very public ways. For example, when in 2003, *The Sun* infamously reported that the former world heavyweight champion boxer Frank Bruno had been 'sectioned' (i.e. legally detained) in a psychiatric hospital, the paper did not pull its punches – pun intended. Its headline 'Bonkers Bruno Locked Up' was a last minute replacement for the original planned headline of 'Loono Bruno'. An accompanying picture of Bruno appearing wide-eyed and with tongue poked out underlined his comic appearance as 'bonkers', and there is also here a racialised dimension to Bruno's appearance as 'big, black and dangerous'. In case any reader was still uncertain about the image that the paper wanted to convey, the report also referred to Bruno as a 'nut'. By the third edition however, the headline 'Bonkers Bruno' was altered to the more subdued, 'Sad Bruno In Mental Home' suggesting (better late than never) that Bruno's public ridicule was perhaps beyond a joke.[1]

The term 'trans-coding' has been applied to the practice of taking the existing meaning of a word or phrase and re-appropriating it for new meanings, as in the reversal of black stereotypes of ugliness with the phrase 'Black is Beautiful' or the reclaiming of the stereotypical notion of 'queer' by gay and lesbians. Words and images carry connotations over which no one has complete control, and these marginal or submerged meanings come to the surface, allowing different meanings to be constructed, different things to be said (Hall, 1997). Organisers of Mad Pride Rallies, modelled on Gay Pride festivals, and the annual 'BonkersFest' Arts Festival held in London have adopted the practice of trans-coding to facilitate public dialogue with those conventionally viewed as 'bonkers'. For example, promotional material for the 2008 BonkersFest event promised it would be 'One Sandwich Short of a Picnic Fayre on the Camberwell Village Greene'. Its aim of celebrating mad people's culture includes reclaiming the stereotypical language and appearance of madness.

BonkersFest borrows the cartoon character Daffy Duck as their tongue-in-cheek motif. The significance of the Daffy Duck image is that it refers to a Warner Brothers 'Looney Tunes' character; 'Looney Tunes' is a recent addition to the vocabulary of comic abuse intended to denigrate anyone reckoned 'loony'. Accordingly, some activists reclaim comic stereotypes of abuse that tend to accompany popular representation of their condition. The strategy is to neutralise the language and imagery of psychiatric otherness and undermine social stigma by draining whatever is spuriously 'comic' about mental illness. 'All this has happened', the writer Jonathan Freedland appreciatively notes, 'while the rest of us have been stuck in the old thinking about nutters and weirdoes. The lunatics have not yet taken over the asylum – but they are raising their voice' (Freedland, 1998, p.28).

But raised voices can and sometimes do also convey an impression of the irrational and the dangerous. In fact we should be wary of assuming that because self-labelled 'loonies' are reclaiming the stigmatising language of madness on their own (and others) terms, they are turning their prison into a fortress and overcoming psychiatry-related stigma. This is not necessarily so. When one is in the midst of mental distress it is difficult to avoid the cultural image of the 'nutter', which as Frank Bruno might testify, *silences* the lived experience of madness (Blackman, 2000, 2007). Thus, it is apposite to note that opportunities to challenge stereotyped images of the 'mad, bad and dangerous' in the public sphere of the tabloids, where critics rightly judge that mad images are at their harshest, is limited because no legal right of reply exists when one has been transformed into their object of vilification.

Restricted opportunities to counter their devalued public image have resulted in the mentally distressed relying on others for advocacy. For instance, Henderson (2007) notes how some mental health charities have persuaded TV soap operas to include psychiatric-related topics in storylines so as to promote 'positive' (whatever that might mean) accounts of mental health recovery. A more familiar form of mental health advocacy prevails, however, such as in SANE's courting of royal and political personalities as patrons to ensure that its agenda is prioritised by journalists reporting on mental health issues. By contrast, the now defunct Schizophrenia Media Agency failed to persuade journalists to draw upon their pool of volunteers willing to talk to journalists about their experiences. It appears that when faced those who are at best ambivalent about psychiatric labels that are applied to them, and who prefer to redefine themselves from outside the psychiatric paradigm (see Chapter 6), journalists find it difficult to stop talking about them and start listening to them (Freedland, 1996).

Nevertheless those with a psychiatric diagnosis are more visible and publicly vocal than they were in the days of the asylum and can be talked to and talk for themselves in a variety of settings. At the same time however, they present a unique conundrum not shared by any other minority group lobbying for greater access to the public sphere. In the case of schizophrenics, for example, their claims to speak authoritatively about their experiences are undermined

by the predominant public perception of them as 'unreliable' wit-
nesses, subject to hallucinations, delusions and violent tendencies.
To publicly declare one self 'mad' or 'bonkers' for political reasons,
as many of those in the 'mad pride' movement certainly do (Curtis
et al., 2000) may well be a witty cultural–political riposte to how
these terms are used beyond mad culture, but does risk those who
use such terms not being taken seriously.

Nevertheless the re-appropriation of 'madness' and 'bonkers' as more
positive terms than, say, 'schizophrenia' or 'bi-polar disorder' does pose
a critical counterpoint to the conventional language and assumption of
the psychiatric and allied professions. But herein lie two problems that
refuse to go away. Firstly, the language of psychiatry more often than not
shapes public discourse on mental health to such an extent that its critics have to rely on it in order to participate. To prefer to use terms such
as 'mad' or 'crazy', as I do, risks appearing less than competent when
discussing psychiatric-related issues in the public sphere. Secondly,
those who use the term 'mad' must navigate popular fears linking madness with violence, and which I have shown, remind us that cultural
imagery about the perils of madness are not easily dislodged.

Conclusion

In this chapter, I have argued that we must consider the resilience of
the lay category of madness in the popular imagination. To somehow
wish away the terminology of madness in favour of, say, a technical
description of 'mental illness' is not the answer to contemporary
concerns about media stigmatisation of the psychiatrically ill. This
goes against the current grain of anti-stigma campaigning, which
is to encourage journalists to take more seriously their role in the
mistreatment of psychiatric conditions, such as reporting schizophrenia as synonymous with violence. My view expressed in this chapter
is that madness is *the* pre-eminent term through which we can best
appreciate that what is at stake in this era of 'negative' reporting is
the more fundamental issue of where we imagine is the place that
schizophrenics and others with a psychiatric history properly belong.
To want to align my argument with those who reject the terminology
of psychiatry is important and matters because it opens up a dynamic
encounter with the cultural history of madness and mad folk, both
real and imagined. This is the theme of what follows in Chapter 2.

2
Illustrations of Madness: Seeing and Reading Historical Images of Insanity

Reading historical images of madness

Why should we read images of madness historically? What value can be derived from this and what would a developed historical perspective provide that is not available from other positions and approaches? Is it not the case that any delving into the past is simply a distraction from analysing and assessing contemporary media representations of madness? Surely it is only those representations that should command our attention.

In this chapter, I want to argue that looking at images of madness historically is indispensable. One of the major benefits of doing so resides in enabling us to negotiate patterns of continuity and change without falling prey to the pitfalls of relativism and presentism. It is these two pitfalls that, more than any others, lie in wait for the unwary cultural analyst (see Pickering, 2009).

The standard view is that there is a straightforward historical continuity in the stereotypical portrayal of the insane. This encourages a presentist view backwards over the centuries, with what we have now being the same as what went before. I want to argue against this by showing that we can only understand continuities in the 'othering' of the insane in relation to changing perceptions of madness. Stereotypes do indeed persist, sometimes quite remarkably over considerable stretches of time. These continuities prevent us from indulging in the temporal solace of relativism and feeling proud of any progress made since then, back in the benighted past. But such continuities are not perceived in the same way from one period to another.

They appear to embody sameness from one time to another but they are always understood within a particular present, which is always historically defined. What appears directly continuous has therefore to be seen against what is historically different. Change becomes the key to unlocking continuity. It is only in this way that apparent continuities across broad swathes of time make any sense at all.

I want to say just a little more about why change is the key to unlocking continuity, and what this means for historical cultural analysis. The early modern period for example is often portrayed as a period of relative continuity compared with the period of turbulent change that followed the French Revolution and the Industrial Revolution. How then does the speed of historical change affect our perceptions of and attitudes to continuity? It is not just a matter of using change to understand continuity because if change were the only temporal coordinate, we would not have any conception of continuity whatsoever. There is always a two-way relation between continuity and change, with that relation being historically contingent and historically variable, which is of course the emphasis we have come to take in modernity and through history itself as a discipline of modernity. This two-way relation between continuity and change is easy to miss when contemporary images of madness are our sole preoccupation.

In Chapter 1 I noted how media images of the mentally distressed as dangerous have become a campaigning issue for psychiatric service users and their advocates. Otto Wahl, a leading American mental health advocate is an example of this. He has been influential both in the US and internationally for documenting the persistence of disparaging and socially harmful images of the mentally distressed, which he argues are consistent across the whole spectrum of the US mass media: from children's cartoons to film and TV drama. Wahl suggests a historical explanation for why disparaging media images persist:

> The images of mental illness that appear in today's mass media reflect conceptualizations and representations of people with mental illnesses that have been around for centuries. The creative professionals of today's media are, in some ways, just carrying on traditional depictions of the past. Many of today's images are repetitions or residuals of long-standing popular beliefs.
>
> (Wahl, 1995, p.114)

Wahl argues that in today's mass media, depictions of people with mental illnesses as dangerous are consistent with the stigmatising images of bestial insanity that are found, for example, in Greek mythology or the Bible. Wahl's assertion that there is direct continuity between historical and contemporary images of mental distress claims to explain why the mass media systematically misrepresent psychiatric patients as dangerous contra to modern psychiatric knowledge, which rejects this view. In some ways, this may seem reasonable, but what I want to argue is that Wahl's claim for continuity between historical and contemporary images of mental illness obscures much more than it reveals.

The problem that Wahl's study of contemporary media images of madness does not address, and that I explore in this chapter, concerns how patterns of continuity in the historical image of madness build up over time. In Wahl's estimation the issue is straightforward enough: older images of madness are a misrepresentation of 'mental illnesses that have been around for centuries'. In other words, historical images of, say, bestial madness assume the representational form that they do because madness was not properly recognised and treated as mental illness. Wahl is not alone in this view. Historians of psychiatry (e.g. Hunter and Macalpine, 1963; Shorter, 1997) also blur the disjunction between past and present by suggesting that those whom history labels mad would today be diagnosed mentally ill.

Consider the case of James Tilly Matthews, a tea-broker imprisoned in France during the Revolution while attempting brokerage of a more dangerous kind. His attempts to secure peace between Britain and the new Republic led ultimately to his arrest and torture. Matthews survived and in 1797 returned to England. Soon after, he wound up in the House of Commons gallery from where he cried 'Treason' at the then Home Secretary, Lord Liverpool, who Matthews blamed for his own political failings in France. Matthews was sent to London's Bethlehem asylum, usually shortened to Bethlem but more popularly known as Bedlam, where for more than a decade John Haslam, Bethlem's apothecary, documented Matthews' insistent claim that he was subject to an 'influencing machine', which he called the Air Loom. Detailed notes made by Haslam have transformed Mathews into schizophrenia's 'Patient Zero' (Jay, 2003) but as Jay notes, such a retrospective diagnosis of schizophrenia is notoriously difficult to recover from history:

> To look back before 1800 is to peer into another world where ... what we would now call mental disorders were often understood as religious ecstasies or diabolic possessions. And historically, of course, no-one was looking for the category of schizophrenia.
>
> (Jay, 2003, p.26)

This has not stopped Haslam's case notes on Matthews and the Air Loom being used to make a retrospective diagnosis of paranoid schizophrenia. But as Jay (2003) points out, Matthews' 'delusions of persecution' or 'ideas of reference' (to use contemporary psychiatric parlance) must be set against the historical record that shows Matthews' *was* some kind of spy travelling between England and France carrying letters of correspondence between the two governments. Matthews had thus been for a time at the centre of world events and had reason to feel paranoid. At the very least, his paranoia seems appropriate in light of the letter that Jay reveals was sent to Bethlem authorities from Lord Liverpool stating his view that Matthews was dangerously insane and should be detained in their hospital in perpetuity.

The case of James Tilly Matthews illuminates how divergent early-nineteenth and early-twenty-first century horizons of perception and of understanding about images of madness are. John Haslam's book *Illustrations of Madness*, published in 1810, was written to prove Matthews was mad. An attempt had been made by Matthews' family to have him pronounced sane and released from Bethlem. A legal enquiry had been held at which doctors gave evidence that Matthews was sane. While the outcome eventually favoured Haslam, he became concerned that his reputation was tarnished by suggestions that Matthews was illegally held in Bethlem. Haslam therefore sought to embarrass the doctors who thought Matthews' sane by publicising the full extent of Matthews' fantastical ideas about how an international gang of criminal operators inserted thoughts into the minds of others (which Matthews memorably termed 'lobster cracking') through the influencing machine.

In fact, Haslam's *Illustrations of Madness* is really Matthews' work since much of the precise information and detail about the Air Loom and its effects were Matthews' own testimony based on notebooks written in Bethlem. Moreover, Haslam included in his book (or should that now be Matthews' book?) a technical drawing of the Air Loom 'made by the lunatic himself' (Haslam, 1989, p.32). The point was to make the patient's insanity visible and concrete. In Jay's view, the diagram might appear to today's onlooker as 'a precise and beautiful image, which at first glance wouldn't be out of place in any scientific or technical journal of the time' (Jay, 2003, p.169). Jay adds that the Air Loom diagram looks not at all like an illustration of madness since we are more used to tortured images of 'frenzied scribbling' and the like. These differing interpretations remind us that perception and understanding are historically based and historically shaped.

The contemporary installation artist Rod Dickinson draws our attention to this point in spectacular fashion. In 2002, Dickinson *built* the Air Loom based faithfully on Matthews' own reported dimensions and specifications documented in Haslam's *Illustrations of Madness*. More than 200 years after Haslam invited the public to consider the meaning of the Air Loom, it reappeared on view for public inspection. The result is a huge piece that fills a gallery space, towering over the spectator, giving some sense of the claustrophobia that the Air Loom imposed on Matthews. On one level it is pure eighteenth-century panelling, brass fittings and tanned leather tubes. On another level altogether its vast scale projects an eerily familiar sense of futuristic technology designed to induce paranoid imaginings. As Dickinson (2005) has noted, among its remarkable features is that it is the prototypical mind-influencing machine, which in relation to our twenty-first century paranoid and apocalyptic imagination might appear plausible rather than insane in its repertory of associations because of our knowledge of failed CIA 'mind-influencing' experiments conducted in the 1950s:

> If Matthews' vision was a precursor to secretive CIA projects, then it also seems fitting that his vision, the Air Loom, was first built in the 21st century. Its natural habitat is a culture riddled with paranoia and driven by the production of fear from the constant, unseen threat of dark and mysterious forces.
>
> (Dickinson, 2005, p.85)

Bringing into contemporary realisation, Matthews' fearful vision of a mind-influencing machine helps us to understand the changing relations between historical texts and historically

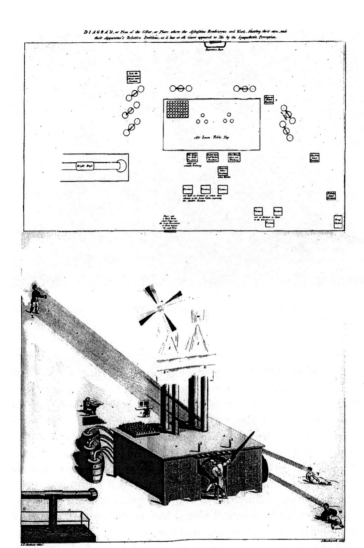

Figure 2.1 James Tilly Matthews' Assassins Air Loom machine, 1810. *Credit*: Wellcome Library, London

Figure 2.2 Image of the Air Loom installed in The Laing Gallery Newcastle, 2006. *Credit*: Rod Dickinson

grounded contexts of vision, which in each case ask onlookers to view what madness means and how it might be seen (perceived/represented/interpreted).

That Jay (2003) says it is now virtually impossible to read the Air Loom illustration in the way that Haslam intended it supports my argument that there is no easy 'fit' between historical images of madness and how we are to read them in a different historical period under different historical conditions. The notion that there is a pattern of continuity in images of madness that run across history raises definite hermeneutical problems because, as the Matthews case illustrates, each historical period has its own understanding of what madness is, how mad folk are to be regarded, and what sort of representational identity madness should adopt vis-à-vis the community for whom the image(s) of madness signify in the first place. While not wanting to undermine the historical explanation suggested by Wahl, I do want to problematise reading *into* historical images of madness evidence of the continuous historical othering of the mad.

Michel Foucault's claim in *Madness and Civilization* (2005, p.12) that, 'from the fifteenth century on, the face of madness has haunted

the imagination of Western man', identified in the medieval imagination the onset of fascination with the cultural image of madness
that has reverberated down the centuries and helped shape our
current era's social fears about madness and dangerousness. As
Foucault puts it: 'Something new appears in the imaginary landscape
of the Renaissance; soon it will occupy a privileged place there: the
Ship of Fools, a strange "drunken boat" that glides along the calm
rivers of the Rhineland and the Flemish canals' (p.5). Foucault reads
Hieronymus Bosch's painting *Ship of Fools* (1498), in which the
medieval insane are depicted searching for their Reason on board
ship, as evidence of the medieval response to madness, that the mad
were not only symbolic but also literal outcasts.

However, the idea that European mariners sailed mad cargo along
the canals of Europe gives a historically false impression of the medieval mad as living symbols of Folly adrift from the shores of rationality. In England, for example, no 'ship of fools' set sail (Midelfort,
1980; Scull, 2006). The mundane historical reality is that where the
medieval mad proved troublesome they were beaten, locked up, left
to rot, or forced to roam and beg. Foucault's dubious historical scholarship also belies the fact that the meanings of madness were matters
of continuous negotiation. By the eighteenth century, for example,
as Roy Porter (1987a) points out in his magisterial study of social and
psychiatric attitudes to madness in England during the period from
the Restoration to the Regency, madness assumed multiple guises,
meanings and symbolism such that it was endowed not only with
clinical but also comic or cosmic understanding:

> It could assume all the solemnity of a clinical diagnosis, or be a
> street-corner insult; now a stigma, next an endearment. It could
> signify rage – *ira brevis furor* (anger is a brief madness) was an
> old saw – but also signal the comic and ludicrous. It could mark
> the passions, especially pride and vanity; indeed it could be passion
> itself (a 'mad' person might simply, *par excellence*, be impassioned,
> like a mad bull); or be a synonym for illogicality, absurdity, reason
> in motley. 'Mad caps', 'mad rogues', 'mad devils', all such idioms
> traded upon the mysteries of liminality, bursting the bounds of
> the workaday – notions which the Renaissance cult of the singular
> Saturnine genius replicated higher up the social scale.
>
> (Porter, 1987a, p.17)

Porter's work is based, contra Foucault, on the actual historical record, which shows that eighteenth-century society experienced and interpreted madness at close hand and in its own temporally specific cultural terms. Thus, rather than literally and symbolically casting madness beyond the boundaries of the community, the range of representations that circulated in the real historical encounter between mad folk and their community reflected multiple sites of clinical or street-corner contact. In short, the mad were not one-dimensional folk devils, as is clearly implied in Foucault's (2005, p.68) claim that from the medieval period 'madness borrowed its face from the mask of the beast', but were configured into various kinds of cultural symbolism including the Renaissance cult figure of the mad genius noted by Porter above.

Of especial significance for my own argument about why we should read images of madness historically is that the social context in which the community engaged in, or conversely, withdrew from day-to-day contact with mad folk, always influences the available cultural imagery about madness and the manner in which they are interpreted. For instance, in the proliferating visual culture of early modern English society, popular views on mental disturbance focused on the image of Bethlem/Bedlam, which 'seemed to open a window onto the dark side of nature, to ask troubling questions about the human condition, and to compel the sane to band together against it to assert their own identity' (Jay, 2003, p.30). Bethlem was a small institution (until the mid-nineteenth century it never housed more than one hundred patients at any one time), but loomed large in the public imagination as 'Bedlam', embodied in a range of mad figures, mad images and mad stereotypes. This demands that, while we examine patterns of continuity in the historical image of madness, we need also to consider important changes in its visual form and mediation. That is why in this chapter I attempt to keep continuity and change in twin view of each other.

Having made the argument about *why* we should read images of madness historically, I now want to ask *how* we should read them historically. There are three dimensions that I pay attention to in the remainder of this chapter. Firstly, I identify *visual stereotypes* of madness that are historically perpetuated. Secondly, I examine the *visual form* in which they are historically mediated. Thirdly, I consider how the *visual reading* of the image changes when one moves between, say, looking at a painting to viewing a photograph of madness. Paying attention to these analytical dimensions shows that, while historical images of madness appear fixed, ways of *seeing* (representing/perceiving) the 'insane' are not immutable. Because historical images of madness appear across a range of symbolic forms and cultural practices I shall interrogate distinctions between types of images not exclusively visual. This enables me to consider shared conventions in the changing representation of madness.

Seeing Bedlam: Change and continuity in images of madness

I now want to move on from seeing continuity in historical images of madness primarily through change, to develop a dialectical reading of historical images where *we can see change/continuity through each other*. This reading strategy will allow me to highlight and emphasise specific differences in the mediation of mad images and stereotypes over time. As Pickering's (2001) work on the historical process and practice of stereotyping shows, it is, in the end, always a matter of seeing sameness through difference, and difference through sameness. I shall pursue this dialectical mode of reading historical images of madness beginning with the visual form in which early modern stereotypes of Bethlem Hospital were mediated.

Established in 1247 as a monastic foundation, Bethlem has been continually involved with the care of the mentally distressed since 1377 when the first Bethlem lunatics are recorded (Andrews et al., 1997). In 1676 Bethlem moved from a dilapidated site at Bishopsgate to a new building at Moorfields. Robert Hooke's palatial design for the new Bethlem was literally and figuratively intended to render its charitable work strikingly visible (Stevenson, 2000). Despite the palatial façade however, Bethlem became a byword for all things mad and mindless. It is important to note however, that Bethlem became the Bedlam of our popular imaginings not because of anything that went on inside the institution since the daily grind was largely uneventful (see Allderidge, 1985), but because it took on a life of its own.

In early modern England, as Roy Porter (1997) notes, Bethlem and Bedlam played off each other in the culture of madness. For example, from the 1680s, visitors to Bethlem passed between two lifelike statues, known as 'raving' and 'melancholy' madness, which adorned the main gates to the institution. Sculptured by Caius Gabriel Cibber, their bald, naked, chained forms were immortalised in Pope's

Dunciad (1729), as 'brainless brothers'. The statues gave symbolic confirmation that Bethlem was a portal to Bedlam, a world given over to madness. Thus, in 1815, when Bethlem was scandalised by allegations of mistreatment of patients (see below), the statues were covered by curtains and hidden from public view. It is tempting to give this literal cover-up of Cibber's statues a metaphorical reading, in terms of the familiar adage about the psychiatrically disturbed being hidden away 'out of sight, out of mind'. In Bethlem's case this would be inaccurate in more senses than one.

Firstly, in the period between the 1570s and the 1700s it was standard for Bethlem to discharge inmates after one year if they were diagnosed as incurable (Andrews et al., 1997). A popular (though false) view was that Bethlem licensed ex-patients to beg without fear of arrest. While some ex-Bethlemites no doubt sang songs and recounted tales of their time inside Bedlam, counterfeit madmen who pretended to have suffered in or escaped from Bethlem in order to solicit alms amplified the actual numbers of 'Bedlam beggars' in the community. The 'Bedlam beggar' might appear historically specific with no contemporary relevance. However, like today, early modern folk wisdom feared the mad for its dramatic violation of social norms, behaviours and practices (MacDonald, 1981). Thus, by the mid-seventeenth century the most notorious subgroup of lunatics in England were known as 'Toms o'Bedlam'.

The 'Bedlam' nomenclature reflects the impact of the mythical Bedlam on the mental landscape of early modern England, as well as the diffusion of generally understood stereotypes of insanity. For instance, in the mid-seventeenth century, Daniel Pearce, a Salisbury Corporation Mace-bearer, also known as Dowdy, took on the role of escaped Tom o'Bedlam in his spare time, preying on unsuspecting visitors to the city inns. Dowdy's joke depended upon him donning the accoutrements of madness, which included 'the tatter'd garment, decorations of straw, rattling chains, visage stained with blood, and deportment of the most desperate lunatic; in which he was assisted by a most frightful tone of voice and articulation' (Ingram, 2005, p.151). Dowdy's antics bring me to my second point about how Bedlam was perceived visually.

In early modern England, the figure of Mad Tom was a widely accepted embodiment of Bedlamite insanity. Thus, when real or counterfeit ex-Bedlamites tramped the highways begging for their supper, 'they were expected to busk, singing Bedlamite ballads for their bread' (Porter, 2004, p.33). Such mad music, which include a corpus of songs about Mad Tom o'Bedlam as well as his female counterparts, Mad Bess or Mad Maudlin (see MacKinnon, 2001), mediated the popular stereotype:

> For to see Mad Tom of Bedlam,
> Ten thousand miles I've travelled
> Mad Maudlin goes on dirty toes
> For to save her shoes from gravel

> *Chorus:*
> It's well that we sing bonney boys
> Bonney mad boys
> Bedlam boys are bonney
> For they all go bare, and they live in the air
> And they want no drink nor money

> I went down to Satan's Kitchen
> For to break my fast one morning
> And there I got souls piping hot
> All on the spit a-turning

> A spirit howled as lightning
> Did on that journey guide me
> The sun did shake and the pale moon quake
> Whenever they did spy me

> My staff has murdered giants
> And my pack a long knife carries
> For to slice mince pies from children's thighs,
> From which to feed the faeries

> Tonight I'll go a-murdering
> The man in the moon to a powder
> His dog I'll shake and his staff I'll break
> And I'll howl a wee bit louder

> To see Mad Tom of Bedlam,
> Ten thousand miles I've travelled
> Mad Maudlin goes on dirty toes,
> To save her shoes from gravel

These lyrics to the song 'Mad Tom of Bedlam' (known also as 'Boys of Bedlam', among other titles) appears to confirm the stereotype of madness parading its dangerous nature. However, I want to suggest that this is not a straightforward case of stereotyping madness since the idea that Mad Tom has 'murdered giants' or that he carries a knife to 'slice mince pies from children's thighs' paradoxically *subverts* the conventional stereotype of madness as dangerousness. Why do I make this claim and how is it achieved?

Far from offering an alternative portrayal or counterweight to the image of madness as dangerousness, the song glorifies the stereotype of dangerousness to such an extent that it confirms it a hundred-fold. It is in this extension that the subversion takes place because it works to render the stereotypical dangerousness absurd, or mythical. Indeed, 'Mad Tom o'Bedlam' is preoccupied with wild fantasies of adventures among the gods of classical mythology (Wiltenburg, 1988). Thus, the song lifts Mad Tom to superhuman proportions as in the preposterous notions of going bare, walking on gravel to save shoes from wear and tear, or murdering the man in the moon. Thus, while we cannot regard the figure of Mad Tom as a mirror image of how madness was perceived in early modern England, we can view it as an *image in reverse* illuminating a historically grounded sense of the urban danger precipitated by the antics of the violent insane. Does this mean that we can view the figure of Mad Tom as a forebear of the contemporary tabloid stereotype of the murderous schizophrenic abroad in the community? I suggest not because we cannot ignore subsequent historical change in the performance and meaning of 'Mad Tom o'Bedlam'.

For instance, it is initially surprising that despite Mad Tom's historicality as a sixteenth- and seventeenth-century wandering beggar, songs under the name of Tom o'Bedlam were sung in theatres and music hall as late as the 1840s (Carroll, 2002). In this changed historical and popular entertainment context, the social conditions of the song's early modern performance were lost as Mad Tom, once emblematic of poverty, suffering, displacement, even histrionic counterfeiting, assumed a different guise as a music-hall entertainer. Such continuity *and* change in the figure of Mad Tom is less surprising if we consider that until the 1840s, when a national programme of asylum building began to be implemented, Bethlem was still England's only public receptacle for the insane. Mad Tom's transformation into a music-hall entertainer reflects the appeal of singing about the Bedlamite across two-and-a-half centuries. I do not suggest however, that the musical appeal of Mad Tom is trans-historical.

To the contrary, the appeal of singing about Mad Tom is historically variable and in the early- to mid-Victorian period it resides in fascination and popular appeal with the grotesquerie. Thus, according to one historian of Victorian song, 'Mad Tom of Bedlam' achieves longevity within the popular tradition because, 'To startle, horrify, or terrorize the audience, with or without excuse, was the height of the Victorian baritone's ambition. And since people did not walk out on him, we must conclude that to be startled, horrified, and terrorized was the height of the audience's ambition' (Disher, 1955, p.36). Thus, another mid-Victorian song about madness, Henry Russell's 'The maniac' (written in 1840), was sung alongside songs with overt moral messages such as 'The Gambler's Wife' and 'The Drunkard's Child'. Why does this juxtaposition of Victorian morals and maniacs matter?

For the Victorian period at least, singing about madness must be seen in relation to the attractions of melodrama, fairy tales, gruesome murder ballads, penny dreadfuls and so on. Thus, when Disher notes that Victorian pleasure in singing about 'Mad Tom' or 'The maniac' reveals a 'relish for insanity', there is a danger of losing sight of the figurative specificities of 'Mad Tom' but at the same time we can recognise the song's relation to popular tradition and popular aesthetics. The practice of singing about Mad Tom appears to exit the music hall stage after the 1840s, though it is not the final curtain call for the song 'Mad Tom o'Bedlam'.

In the late twentieth- and twenty-first centuries, singers sensitive to English traditional song include songs about Mad Tom in their repertoire. Notable examples include, firstly, 'Boys of Bedlam' performed by the folk-rock group Steeleye Span on their 1973 *Please to See the King* recording. Secondly, Maddy Prior, an occasional member of Steeleye Span, performs a version of 'Boys of Bedlam' on *Year*, her 2003 recording. Another interpretation of 'Mad Tom of Bedlam' appears on American singer Jolie Holland's 2004 *Escondida* recording. Tom o'Bedlam therefore now 'belongs' within a contemporary 'folk music' idiom, which is to say that these songs' aesthetic is recognisably 'folk' in vocal and acoustic tonalities.

Mad Tom's transformation from early modern street ballad through Victorian theatre and musical hall grotesquerie to late twentieth- and twenty-first century folk song illustrates the change/continuity argument that I have been promoting in relation to seeing and reading historical images of madness. Thus, in its contemporary folk manifestation 'Mad Tom o'Bedlam' is not intended to 'startle, horrify, or terrorize' the audience, which we have seen was the Victorian baritone's ambition. Similarly, we can contrast the Victorian music hall performance of 'Mad Tom of Bedlam' with early modern performances that construct Mad Tom as the embodiment of insanity.

The dynamics of this transformation in the figure of Mad Tom means that a modern recording or performance of songs about Mad Tom only partly conveys through the musical arrangement and choral accompaniment, how the song mediated Bedlamite madness in past times. We must therefore find some way to imagine the mediation of Mad Tom in early modern musical performance. Fortunately, we can turn to historians of popular musical culture such as William C. Carroll (2002), who explains that in the largely non-literate culture of early modern England songs about Tom o'Bedlam were enhanced by grand symbols, histrionic gesture and especially, a terrifying voice:

> Some made a horrid noise hollowly sounding, some whoop, some holler, some show only a wild distracted ugly look, uttering a simple kind of *maunding* [begging] .... Then he will dance and sing or use some other antic and ridiculous gesture, shutting up his counterfeit puppet-play with this epilogue or conclusion: 'Good dame, give poor Tom one cup of the best drink!'
> (Dekker, 1608, quoted in Carroll, 2002, p.84, emphasis in the original)

The sound of whooping and hollering, coupled with a 'distracted ugly look', would have left illiterate and literate hearers in no doubt that this is 'madness' that is being represented. Laughing at the antics of Tom o'Bedlams, which is one among other intentions of Bedlam ballads, remind us that our own failure to 'get' this kind of joke today should alert us to the problem of historical understanding (see Darnton, 1984).

How are we to read change/continuity in the stereotypical figure of Tom o'Bedlam? Rather than interpreting songs about Mad Tom as benighted compared with our own enlightened times, since this limits recognition of our own culture's use of mad stereotypes for popular entertainment, we can think about the continuity of the Tom o'Bedlam figure over two-and-a-half centuries in relation to relatively little change in the social and psychiatric construction of madness up to the 1840s. When, in the 1850s, a programme of social and psychiatric change emerged in the form of public asylums housing the lunatic poor, Tom o'Bedlam diminished not only as social commentary but also in its visual potency. This was quite unlike Bedlam itself, which has proven a more fluid and flexible image of madness and mindlessness.

What I now want to illustrate is how we can read change/continuity in the image of Bedlam as a place wholly given over to *craziness*. As I noted in Chapter 1, terminology such as 'crazy' is today interpreted as derogatory to the lived experience of mental distress. I disagree. I want to show that using 'craziness' to describe the real and imagined interior of Bethlem/Bedlam is multi-layered, essential for historical cultural analysis of a place that became both the mask and mirror of madness (Fuller Torrey and Miller, 2001).

At the start of the eighteenth century, Bethlem's palatial façade was one of the sights of London, and its governors seized a market opportunity by allowing the paying public entry to the hospital to view the inmates. 'The true lure of Bedlam, says Roy Porter, was "the *frisson* of the freakshow"' (Porter, 1987a, p.122). For example, reporting on his visit to see the freaks in Bethlem in 1700, the Grub Street hack Ned Ward tells what can be seen and heard describing, 'such drumming of doors, ranting, holloaing, singing and rattling, that I could think of nothing but Don Quevedo's vision, where the damn'd broke loose, and put Hell in an uproar' (quoted in Porter, 1991, p.42). Ward, like any modern-day hack, tickles his readers with the image of Bedlam that they would expect any *normal* spectator to observe. But as Ingram (2005, p.171) points out, it is 'an image, albeit an oblique one, of the mind that viewed'.

Thus, Bedlam was represented through ingrained stereotypes to a public familiar with its reputation as a place for 'crazies'. Over time however, who exactly is crazy in relation to Bedlam was begged. For instance, in the eighteenth century, Bedlam was mined as a rich seam of social satire and ridicule. In Jonathan Swift's *A Tale of a Tub* (1704), Bedlam became a metaphor for a topsy-turvy world:

Is any Student [Bedlam is here imagined as a kind of college] tearing his straw in piece-meal, Swearing and blaspheming, biting his Grate, foaming at the Mouth, and emptying his Pispot in the spectator's Faces: Let the Right worshipful, the Commissioners of Inspection, give him a regiment of Dragoons, and send him into Flanders among the Rest.

(Swift, 1966, p.26)

Given most empire builders and religious and political leaders had been clinically mad, Swift went on to argue, he asked if it would not be worth appointing commissioners who would select Bedlamites to command regiments or partake in political elections. Thus, two-and-half centuries before R. D. Laing popularised the idea of madness as a sane response to a mad society, Swift (while not the first to use Bedlam to satirise the state of the nation, but widely acknowledged to be the wittiest) imagined Bedlam's inmates as far less mad than politicians and generals.

It is in the tradition of social satire that we also read the final, eighth frame of William Hogarth's *The Rake's Progress*, which has defined the image of Bedlam for generations (painted 1732, set of engravings 1735).

Above all artists, Hogarth seized upon the visual potency of Bedlam and its incurable ward where lying semi-naked and bald among the incurables we see feckless Tom Rakewell, sent mad after frittering away his inherited fortune. Porter (2002) summarises Hogarth's Bedlam scene:

> Finally, demented and dumped in Bethlem, he lies naked, a brutalized wreck, surrounded by his fellow crazies: a mad lover ('love sickness' had long featured in the roster of insanity), a mad bishop, a mad king (a *pretender?*), sitting with make-believe orb and sceptre on his close-stool of a throne, a popish religious enthusiast, a mad tailor, and a crazy astronomer, gazing up to the rafters through a rolled up paper 'telescope'.
>
> (p.74, emphasis in the original)

Hogarth's nightmare vision of Bedlam also panders to his audiences' understanding that this is the place where spectators come to view the self-deluded antics of the Bedlamites. Thus, Hogarth includes in his Bedlam scene two women voyeurs, one well to do, the other her

Figure 2.3 Engraving by H. Furnell taken from Plate VIII of William Hogarth's Rake's Progress series, 1735. Now insane, Tom Rakewell sits on the floor of the long gallery at Bethlem hospital, London, surrounded by his fellow lunatics. *Credit*: Wellcome Library, London

maidservant, who have paid to see the freaks in the human zoo but who have themselves become part of the attractions on offer. Who is really crazy here? Those on display or those who make play of the display?

According to Catherine Arnold, author of a recent popular history of Bedlam, the question has contemporary relevance in the context of television talk shows. She makes the connection in relation to the crowds who thronged to see an exhibition dedicated to Hogarth at Tate Britain in 2007: 'Scores perused the fate of poor Tom Rakewell, and gawped at his eventual breakdown and incarceration, surrounded by mad stereotypes. A more cynical commentator might add that reality television programmes serve the same purpose, as millions examine and comment on the public spectacle of helpless, and often it seems senseless, individuals, losing their dignity on screen' (Arnold, 2008, p.275). I disagree not only because I was one among the scores that attended the Tate's exhibition of Hogarth's work and 'gawped' at his entertaining vision of Bedlam. I disagree more so because Arnold's facile comparison is so nakedly rhetorical that Hogarth and his satirical vision of Bedlam are altogether drained of historiographical value. This is precisely where the pitfalls of relativism and presentism lie in wait for the unwary cultural analyst.

Arnold's comparison between Hogarth's vision of Bedlam and din of the contemporary TV talk show, where pandemonium appears to rule on-screen while the feckless audience are presumed to gawp because, like the benighted Bethlem/Bedlam spectator, they are unfeeling about the freaks on display, obfuscate continuities between eighteenth- and twenty-first century visual stereotypes of insanity, which make sense only in relation to differences in the visual culture of madness between then and now. For instance, Swift's biting satire on the madness of normative environments and the sanity of the cuckoo's nest is echoed in a 2007 photographic essay for, somewhat improbably, the international fashion house Vogue.

Employing the style of contemporary paparazzi photography, the photographic images entitled 'Supermods Enter Rehab', parody contemporary celebrity magazine and tabloid obsessions with hurriedly taken shots of fashionable celebrities attending 'rehab' in equally fashionable private psychiatric clinics such as London's The Priory. After entering what looks like a sanatorium, models dressed in asylum-grey/brown chic, run amok conveying in their wild conduct the mindless abandon typically associated with Bedlam. Attendants stand guard in some images but none figure for example in the photograph featuring a model shaving her head. The image perhaps pays homage to paparazzi images of pop star Britney Spears' recent apparent display of mental distress in hair shaving but which owe iconographic allegiance to Cibber's sub-human Bedlam statues and Tom Rakewell's final shameful appearance.

The change/continuity dialectic in the image of Bedlam is also apparent in contemporary television drama. For example, when viewers watched BBC TV's mid-90s drama *Taking Over the Asylum* or Channel 4's more recent 2008 drama *Poppy Shakespeare*, they saw a modern-day 'bedlam' in which notions of 'care' are a secondary consideration. The Swiftian satire of bedlam-society relations turned on its head is apparent in both dramas when psychiatrists, nurses, patients, visitors, indeed the psychiatric system itself appear crazy. Thus, when the maverick Glaswegian psychiatrist in *Taking Over the Asylum* (stereotypically chiselled from the same anti-psychiatric rock as R. D. Laing) is revealed to be a manic-depressive who hates taking medication to control his condition, we read his empathy for his patients thus: 'you don't have to be mad to work here, but it helps'! As we shall see, Bethlem/Bedlam can also lay claim as the original source material for this standard office witticism.

I want to conclude my reading of change/continuity in the historical image of madness through the figure of another Bedlamite, this one historically real. James Norris, detained in Bethlem for 15 years, was propelled into the national consciousness in the early decades of the nineteenth century as a symbol of all that was corrupt in the management of the insane. Thus, in 1814, a self-appointed committee of lunacy reform campaigners, which included the radical journalist William Hone and the politically well-connected philanthropist Edward Wakefield, visited Bethlem and to their horror discovered men and women chained to the wall. Among the inmates was James Norris who had reportedly attacked his keepers at some point in the past and ever since had been chained in the following manner:

> A stout iron ring was riveted round his neck, from which a short chain passed through a ring made to slide upwards and downwards on an upright massive iron bar, more than six feet high, inserted into the wall. Round his body a strong iron bar about two inches wide was riveted; on each side of the bar was a circular projection; which being fashioned to and enclosing each of his arms, pinioned them close to his sides.
>
> (quoted in Porter, 2002, p.107)

Norris had spent around 12 years of his detention in Bethlem pinioned in this custom-built harness. What made it all the more shocking was that Norris could apparently converse rationally with his visitors. On a further visit to Bethlem, Norris' visitors included an artist who sketched Norris in his iron structure. Shortly thereafter, the image of Norris in chains was transformed into an engraving, and became news.

The image of Norris in chains formed part of a portfolio of evidence for the House of Commons Sub-Committee on Madhouses Enquiry

Figure 2.4 James Norris (wrongly named as William) restrained by chains at the neck and ankles in Bethlem hospital, London. Coloured etching by G. Arnald, 1815, after himself, 1814. *Credit:* Wellcome Library, London

of 1815. The focus was almost entirely on Bethlem, whose officials, including its physician Dr Thomas Monro and James Tilly Matthew's old nemesis, the apothecary John Haslam, gave evidence. In the case of Norris, they defended the manner of his restraint arguing that he was double-jointed and thus normal restraint was useless. They also claimed weakly that they were about to release him just as the lunacy campaigners knocked on their door. For his part, Norris was released from his mechanical torment only to die shortly thereafter of a ruptured bowel caused by his years in a static position.

Around the time of the 1815 Parliamentary scrutiny of Bethlem, William Hone's role in exposing the institution was shamelessly sidelined by the political manoeuverings of Edward Wakefield (see Wilson, 2005). Today, Wakefield is credited as the single driving force behind the campaign to expose conditions inside Bethlem and other private madhouses. This is incorrect because Hone was both instigator and main driver in what was by any standard a remarkable example of public action, fully in keeping with Hone's career campaigning for 'lost causes'. Surprisingly, even the standard history of Bethlem (Andrews et al., 1997) contains no mention of Hone's key role in publicising abuses inside the hospital. I stress this point both for historical accuracy and to pre-empt my discussion of the role that journalists have played campaigning on lunacy reform, which I shall further develop in Chapter 3.

The House of Commons enquiry led to the disgrace and resignation of Monro and Haslam. Bedlam's apparent craziness was compounded when Parliament learned that three generations of Dr Monro had run Bethlem like a private fiefdom (Thomas Monro was duly replaced with his son Edward, the fourth Monro to take charge in Bethlem). Thomas Monro and Haslam tried unsuccessfully to shift blame for what had happened to Dr Bryan Crowther, the former surgeon to Bethlem, who had conveniently died in 1815. It was revealed that Crowther was an alcoholic who often ended up straightjacketed among the incurables that he was supposed to attend. It is not stretching the point to suggest that herein lays the source of the wisecrack that psychiatrists are madder than their patients. When in 1835 Bethlem again moved premises, this time to Lambeth, the legacy of abuse relocated. The image of Bedlam, by this time fast becoming stock-in-trade of 'sensation' writers such as Wilkie Collins, conjoined the sinister and corrupt with the monstrous and the depraved.

It is tempting to read into the nineteenth-century image of James Norris pinioned in Bethlem as the template for twentieth- and twenty-first century fictional stories of patients abandoned to the megalomania of asylum doctors and keepers. There is no need. Modern psychiatry has its own repository of real-life torments with which we can see change/continuity in mad-doctors' delusions that their techniques of therapy are really torture. Thus, we can point to extreme physicalistic treatments for mental disorder including frontal lobotomies, insulin coma therapy, malaria therapy (the rationale was to induce fever so that the resulting heat would fry the disease), transplantation of endocrine organs, surgical removal of large parts of the small intestine, renal dialysis and metrazol-convulsion therapy (see Clare, 1980).

Amid this panoply of mental treatments/torments, two figures stand out as twentieth-century equivalents to mad-doctors like Monro and Haslam, their similarity seen through their different techniques. Firstly, there is the American Dr Henry Cotton, who from 1907 pioneered the use of surgery in the bacteriological treatment of mental disorder (Scull, 2007). His surgical intervention killed hundreds of patients, but was praised by his profession for advancing psychiatric science. When he died his colleagues initiated the 'Cotton Award for Kindness'. The second is the Portuguese psychiatrist Ugo Cerletti, who in 1938 introduced electroconvulsive therapy (ECT), which he developed after observing the electric slaughtering of pigs in the slaughterhouse (Klein, 2007). Over the twentieth century, thousands of psychiatric patients had their bodies and brain worked upon by psychiatrists convinced that slicing the brain or producing electrical currents did their patients good.

While I see change/continuity in the image of the madhouse as a useful counterpoint to Whiggish notions of psychiatric progress, in truth, the historical record shows that Bethlem itself was no more corrupt than any other contemporary private madhouse housing for the mad (Andrews et al., 1997). Ironically, while mad-doctors became stigmatised, Bethlem's medical appointees following the 1814–15 scandal were at the cutting edge of scientific research into the causes of mental disorder. For example, Dr Alexander Morison (1779–1866) published his pioneering study of psychiatric illustration, *Physiognomy of Mental Diseases* in 1840, three years after his appointment to Bethlem. Morison's visual studies of the insane coincided with a deepening aestheticisation of madness in the second half of the nineteenth century, a development related to a combination of older physiognomic theories combined with new technologies of illustrating the clinical features of insanity.

Seeing and reading historical images of female insanity

I now want to show that how continuities and changes are read into historical images of madness depend on three interconnecting factors. They are media technologies, cultural forms and historical consciousness. In the nineteenth century, these factors interconnected in visually significant ways when the development of photography and a changing pictorial aesthetic of madness fused with new theories of mental disorder. Through close analysis of three exemplary, historical forms of representations of madness, that is, clinical photographs, lithograph engravings and portraiture in oils, I show how they produce certain constructions of madness, with different truth-claims and forms of visual rhetoric being involved, each with attendant consequences for certain historically based epistemological positions.

In the nineteenth century, the popular assumption that says, 'you know a lunatic when you see one' became a professional concern for mad-doctors; for artists it remained as ever an aesthetic judgement. A case in point concerns paintings of monomaniacs produced between 1821 and 1824 by the French portrait painter Theodore Gericault (1791–1824). They were commissioned by Dr Etienne-Jean Georget (1795–1828) to educate his students at the Ivry asylum about the typical facial features associated with the condition. But as Gericault himself acknowledged, the appearance of the insane looked to him no more unusual or bizarre than the average person and he deferred to Georget's expertise that what he (Gericault) was seeing was insanity (MacGregor, 1989). What were needed were *objective* images of insanity.

It was with the introduction of photography that a fully objective portrait seemed to be accessible. The breakthrough came in 1839 with W. H. Fox Talbot's calotype process of fixing photographic images as negatives. Psychiatry was the first medical field to exploit the technological potential of photography. Thus, by the 1850s, the combined psychiatric and photographic work of Dr Diamond, superintendent of the Female Department of the Surrey Lunatic Asylum, made him celebrated among both professional groupings for pioneering the use of clinical photography in the diagnosis and also in the treatment of the insane. As Dr Diamond put it in an address to the Royal Photographic Society in 1856 entitled, 'On the Application of Photography to the Physiognomic and Mental Phenomena of Insanity':

> The Photographer ... needs in many cases no aid from any language of his own, but prefers rather to listen, with the picture, before him, to the silent but telling language of nature – It is unnecessary for him to use the vague terms which denote a difference in the degree of mental suffering, as for instance, distress, sorrow, deep sorrow, grief, melancholy, anguish, despair; the picture speaks for itself.
>
> (Diamond, 1856/1976, p.19)

In his address Diamond also highlighted how photography provides a comprehensive, objective and truthful representation of the image of insanity 'free altogether from that painful caricaturing which so disfigures almost all the published pictures of the Insane as to render them nearly valueless either for purposes of art or of science' (Diamond, ibid., p.21). Gericault's portraits of monomaniacs exemplify the tradition of 'caricaturing' mental suffering that Diamond is distrustful of.

Diamond enumerated the ways in which photographs could advance the diagnosis and treatment of the insane: firstly, photographs provided accurate and objective records of insanity, in the sense of how we might see criminal mug shots; secondly, they enabled alienists to catalogue psychopathologies; thirdly, they revealed to the patients their own pathological state. In terms of the latter third benefit, Diamond's claim is that the act of looking at the photograph of one's mental suffering encouraged insight into their insane condition when doctor and patient came together to read the image. Diamond's approach to securing the patient's 'insight' from reading the photographic image also implies a historic change *in sight*, in the sense that the photographic image reveals the patients' true condition through some physical stigmata. This begs the question as to what can be seen in clinical photographs.

To answer this question I want to consider one of Diamond's clinical photographs taken in 1856. The photograph is of a young woman looking directly into the camera lens. She is seated in front of a curtain presumably to aid Diamond in illuminating her image. She is posed head slightly tilted, resting her elbow on a bureau with the palm of her hand resting against a cheek. By contrast, her other arm hangs down at her side hidden behind her ruffled skirt. Her attire is unremarkable except for the crucifix that hangs from her neck over her clothes (partially obscuring a medal, probably religious, pinned to her dress). The crucifix is the centrepiece of her outfit and almost the centre-point of the photograph. In sum, and regardless of the

Figure 2.5 Photograph of female patient taken by Dr Hugh Welch Diamond in the Surrey County Lunatic Asylum, 1856. *Credit*: Royal Society of Medicine, London

asylum context in which the photograph was taken, it appears entirely typical of Victorian photographic conventions.

What else is there to say about this photographic image, this woman? In my reading she is as enigmatic as the Mona Lisa. Is this because we do not know her name? I see a half-smile, yet what has she to smile about? After all, she is an inmate of a mid-Victorian lunatic asylum. The half-smile may equally be resignation to the time-consuming process of being photographed. At this point, I must confront the historical reality that Diamond photographed her because she is identifiably insane, that is, suffering from 'religious melancholy'. For the twenty-first century viewer/reader of the image however, there is no clinical evidence of this in respect of the photograph since science and society now scorn the notion that one sees evidence of insanity in portraiture. Yet such was the appeal of photographic objectivity to the nineteenth-century scientific imagination that no less a figure than Charles Darwin became involved with one of England's leading supporters of clinical photography.

Inspired by Diamond's photographs of the insane, James Crichton Browne, Superintendent of the West Riding Lunatic Asylum, became involved in a 'picturing' enterprise to support Darwin's studies on human expression (Browne, 1985). However, Crichton Browne's attempts to involve Darwin proved fruitless, 'because Darwin simply could not *see* any differences' (Browne, ibid., p.161, emphasis in original). Dr Isaac Kerlin came to the same conclusion when in 1858 he took photographs in the Philadelphia Asylum to raise funds for the institution. He circulated photographs of his patients to emphasise that his charges' were not just normal but *appeared* normal (Browne, ibid.). Why could Diamond *not* see? How did his ideas about clinical photography come to exert professional influence?

The answer is that Diamond's proclaimed objectivity of the photograph was a timely blending of positivist aesthetics combined with an revival of interest in the physiognomy of insanity – a combination caught up in nineteenth-century attitudes concerning the transparency of photography to procure a new kind of psychiatric knowledge or 'proof' value. I have also noted that professional photographers were influenced by Diamond's pioneering photographic work in the asylum. For instance, the Parisian photographer Ernst Lacan writing in 1856 not only praised the quality of Diamond's photography, but also embraced the clinical reading of the photographic image, including the one I have been discussing of religious melancholy:

I have before me a collection of fourteen portraits of women of various ages. Some are smiling, others seem to be dreaming [here, according to Gilman, Lacan is referring to the photographic image of 'religious melancholy' that I have been discussing]. All have something strange in their physiognomy: that is what one sees at first glance. If one ponders them for a longer period of time, one grows sad against one's will. All these faces have an unusual expression which causes pain in the observer. A single word of explanation suffices these are portraits of the insane.

(quoted in Gilman, 1976, p.13)

Lacan's notion that there is something 'strange' in the physiognomy of the insane, which he sees at first glance, is a reminder of the hermeneutical problem that I raised earlier in this chapter. As I noted above, each historical period has its own understanding of what madness is, how mad folk are to be regarded, and what sort of representational identity madness should adopt vis-à-vis the community for whom the image(s) of madness signify in the first place. In the case of clinical photography, the portrait of insanity is fully bound up with the ideology of photographic objectivity.

From a Foucaultian perspective, the art historian John Tagg (1988) has contextualised Diamond's photography as a tool of psychiatric knowledge production in which the female lunatic is subject to the institutional power nexus within which she is codified as 'insane' in medical texts. Thus, Diamond's understanding of how 'religious melancholy' *looks* illustrates how physiognomic rules operated 'at the point where discourses of psychiatry, physiognomy, photographic science and aesthetics coincided and overlapped' (Tagg, 1988, p.80). From a feminist perspective, Showalter (1987) has noted the cultural–political paradox that follows, which is that while we have been bequeathed remarkable photographic pictures of nineteenth-century madwomen, the *power of seeing* insanity always rested with a male doctor.

The power of psychiatric seeing would eventually reach its apotheosis in the photographic records of hysterical women patients taken in Paris' Salpêtrière Hospital in the 1880s and 1890s. Produced under the direction of the great French clinician, Jean-Martin Charcot, the diagnostic visualisation of hysteria was a fusion between artistic and medical representations of insanity. As Sander Gilman (1982, p.203) explains: 'The complexity of even the relatively subjective depiction of the hysteric through the camera's eye was too great to present the desired schematic nature of the appearance of the hysteric'. This led Charcot's colleague Paul Richter to reproduce engravings from photographs illustrating the composite features of hysteria. Ironically, the desire for scientific precision in the visualisation of hysteria marked a return in artistic representations of the insane in medical iconography to especially standard poses derived from works of Renaissance and Baroque art (Kromm, 2002).

In Britain, too, the reproduction of engravings taken from photographs had proven invaluable for purposes of psychiatric seeing. For instance, Dr John Conolly, writing in the *Medical Times and Gazette* of 1858 and 1859, followed Diamond's thesis on clinical photography, arguing that photographs were virtual copies of nature, possessing a truthfulness, and preserving minutiae, which could not easily be perpetuated by older pictorial (read: *aestheticisation*) methods. Unfortunately for Conolly, 'his argument was hardly enhanced by the fact that Diamond's originals could not be commercially printed, and his case notes were poorly illustrated with lithographs' (Browne, 1985, p.157). That Conolly was forced to illustrate his ideas with lithographs taken from Diamond's original photographs does not appear to have undermined their veracity as scientific documents. How then are we to read the lithographic reproduction of the photograph of the insane woman that I have discussed above?

My approach to analysing two nineteenth-century images of the same subject borrows from Patrizia Di Bello's (2005) illuminating analysis of a wood engraving of Queen Victoria and her daughter Princess Beatrice, and the photographic carte-de-visite that was its likely original. The wood engraving, which was published on the front page of an 1863 edition of the *Lady's Newspaper and Pictorial Times*, shows Queen and Princess gazing downwards at a photograph they hold of Prince Albert, who had died two years earlier. Di Bello's analysis goes beyond conventional analysis of the meaning of the image to take into consideration the role of the ordinary readers of the illustrated magazine, whose hands hold the magazine's reproduction of the royal image. Di Bello's point is that the readers' touch, and here she means a *gendered touch*, is just as crucial to reading the image as sight because women are both the subjects of the image as well as readers and users of the image.

Commenting on the value of Di Bello's work for reading historical images, Pickering (2009, p.206) has noted how her approach to a tactile female gaze is 'quite different to the distancing, mastering effect of the male gaze'. This is my starting point for reading the lithograph of 'religious melancholy' that appeared in the *Medical Times and Gazette* of 1858.

Figure 2.6 Lithographic engraving of 'religious melancholy', *Medical Times and Gazette*, 1858. Lithograph taken from original photograph by Dr Welch Hugh Diamond. *Credit*: Wellcome Library, London

Consider the following condensed extract from Conolly's diagnostic account of the engraving intended to educate the reader/viewer:

> We discern the outward marks of a mind which, [sic] seemingly, after long wandering in the mazes of religious doubt, and struggling with spiritual niceties too perplexing for human solution, is now overshadowed by despair. The high and wide forehead, generally indicative of intelligence and imagination; the slightly bent head, leaning disconsolately on the hand; the absence from that collapsed cheek of every trace of gaiety; the mouth inexpressive of any varied emotion; the deep orbits and the long characteristic eyebrows; all seem painfully to indicate the present mood and general temperament of the patient. The black hair is heedlessly pressed back; the dress, though neat, has a conventional plainness; the sacred emblem worn round the neck is not worn for ornament. The lips are well formed, and compressed; the angle of the jaw is rather large; the ear seems well-shaped; force of character appears to be thus indicated, as well as a capacity of energetic expression; whilst the womanly figure, the somewhat ample chest and pelvis (less expressed in the engraving than in the photograph) belong to a general constitution out, which in health and vigour, may have grown up some self-accusing thoughts in an innocent and devout, but passionate heart. For this perverting malady makes even the natural instincts appear sinful; and the sufferer forgets that God implanted them.
>
> (Conolly 1858/1976, pp.27–8)

To the modern viewer/reader of this image, Conolly goes far beyond what we would expect from a clinician, bestowing a moral and gendered reading of 'religious melancholy'. This seems strange to us now, but Conolly's status as one of the pre-eminent alienists of his time (see Scull, 1989) underlines that what is being offered to the mid-Victorian reader of *Medical Times and Gazette* is a masterly descriptive account of what the internal psychic state of 'religious insanity' looks like and *means* in its external appearance. Thus, while Conolly's reading of the lithograph for the purpose of psychiatric *seeing* exemplifies Foucault's (1980, 1982) arguments about disciplinary techniques that produce scientific knowledge about individuals as psychiatric 'types', I think that there is more to be said on the interrelations between mid-Victorian lithographic engraving and the cultural construction of female insanity.

In the extract above, Conolly makes particular reference to a difference between the engraving and the photograph, in which the viewer loses sight of the 'somewhat ample chest and pelvis'. I want to bring both photograph and engraving into colloquy so as to consider other significant changes in the subject. For instance, the most immediately noticeable change is that the subject of the engraving no longer looks towards the camera lens/viewer but *downwards* giving the impression of indifference to the process of being photographed. The appearance of indifference might suggest why the woman's hair appears swept back untidily whereas in the photograph it is parted in keeping with contemporary fashion. This adds to a change in her facial expression. Whereas in the photograph there is (to my eye) a hint of a smile, the edges of her lips now appear to sink downward bearing the trace of unhappiness we associate with melancholy. The downward tilt of her head suggests that her eyes, which we can no longer see because they are replaced by shadows (further visible evidence of her melancholy), are not looking to the floor. Where then is she looking?

If we follow her gaze downward she appears focused on the crucifix. There is also something changed about the crucifix. It is moved from the centre of the photographic image to accommodate the shift in position that the engraved subject now takes. These changes to mouth and eyes tally with Conolly's case notes: 'the mouth inexpressive of any varied emotion; the deep orbits and the long characteristic eyebrows; all seem painfully to indicate the present mood and general temperament of the patient'. The palm that was resting on cheek now appears to prop up the head, that is, her head has sunk into hand rather than her hand coming upward to meet the head (as it appears in the original photograph). In turn, books prop up her elbow as if to emphasise that she is incapable of using them for normal purpose. In the engraving we also see her other arm and hand resting on her lap. Both arm and hand tilt downward adding visual confirmation to what we now see is her compositional and literal *depression*, to give melancholy its contemporary catch-all label.

I am not the first to note how insanity is constructed in the transition from photograph to engraving. The French cultural historian Didi-Huberman (2003) has pointed out how Diamond's

1856 photograph of a female patient taken in the asylum courtyard changes in the engraving that appeared in *Medical Times and Gazette* of 1858. In the engraving the woman's dress loses its multicoloured pattern and becomes 'uniform' – in the sense of an asylum uniform. The curtain behind her is also lost having the effect of making the woman gaze into space. Asks Didi-Huberman: 'how could her gaze not appear insane, drawn without space or destination?' (p.39). In a second pairing, Didi-Huberman notes another change between a photographic image and its engraved version. A female patient's posture is straightened in the engraving to provide the reader of the image with more convincing meanings: for example, in the original photograph her hands are clasped but in the engraving appear symmetrical, in prayer, illustrating that this patient suffers from 'religious madness'.

My reading of mid-nineteenth century clinical photographs and engravings shows how media technologies and the cultural forms they produce are implicated in the aesthetic construction of insanity, which is at the same time an expression of the social power of mid-Victorian mental medicine to *self*-represent as the arbiter of knowledge about madness. Thus, visual images such as that of 'religious melancholy' produce truth-claims with attendant forms of visual rhetoric that give the silent image a vocabulary through the reading of the skilled physician. Photographs, as well as lithographic reproductions, were not only available for scientific study but were incorporated into medical textbooks and journals for the express purpose of accurately visualising the insane. In this context, these mediating technologies have come to shape and embody the myth of photographic truth where concepts of positivist science held sway. The ideology of photographic objectivity did not mean that the photographic image replaced painted depictions of the insane, however.

On the contrary, paintings and photographs of the insane co-existed from the 1850s. For instance, Shakespeare's famously suicidal Ophelia was a compelling figure for Victorian artists who painted her again and again. Among them was the pre-Raphaelite artist Dante Gabriel Rossetti who painted Ophelia in 1858 and 1864. Rossetti's 1864 painting, 'The First Madness of Ophelia', was produced in the period after clinical photography 'fixed' the appearance of female insanity and begs the question how we read the painted image of female insanity in the era of clinical photography. Thus, one way to read Rossetti's image of Ophelia is that it is romantic or perhaps quaint, a reading that tallies with the popular image of the pre-Raphaelites as themselves romantic figures seeing only tragic beauty in female insanity. Such a conventional reading in fact misses how the painted image of Ophelia supports and visually reinforces a historically grounded theory of female insanity, which functions in parallel with the photographic and lithographic constructions of madness.

In *The Female Malady*, Elaine Showalter's (1987) account of cultural–historical representations of women and madness, we encounter the complexity of gender politics in the nineteenth-century cultural and psychiatric arenas. Thus, cultural ideas about women situated them 'on the side of irrationality, silence, nature and the body, while men are situated on the side of reason, discourse, culture and the mind' (Showalter, 1987, pp.3–4). The feminine 'stands for the irrational in general' and means that 'madness, even when experienced by men, is metaphorically and symbolically represented as feminine: a female malady' (1987, p.4). In this gendered nineteenth-century cultural milieu, Rossetti's Romantic conceptualisation of Ophelia exemplifies renewal and reconfiguration in the Victorian's image of madness; from a masculine portent of violence typified in Sir Charles Bell's images of bestial madness (see Gilman, 1988, pp.30–2) to that of a young, beautiful, female image.

This was also reinforced by new psychiatric ideas and theories of 'love madness' proposed in 1825 by Alexander Morison in his *Outlines of Lectures on Mental Diseases*. 'Love', says Morison 'produces febrile symptoms, and increased sensibility ... when hopeless – sometimes insanity' (quoted in Small, 1998, p.33). In 1848, Morison elaborated on his theory and noted that 'disappointed love' had caused 25 recent admissions to Bethlem Hospital. Writes Morison: 'According to Zimmerman, the passion of love makes girls mad; jealousy, women mad; and pride, men mad. The former passion that of love, has been a fruitful source of insanity in all ages, and jealousy and ambition not less so' (quoted in Small, 1998, p.33).

The fusion of the Romantic cult of love-mad women, reflected in Rossetti's 'The First Madness of Ophelia', with gendered psychiatric theories put forward by Morison and others, meant that the lovesick madwoman was part of 'a fascinating traffic between cultural images and psychiatric ideologies' (Showalter, 1987, pp.13–14). Thus, while Rossetti's depiction of Ophelia being gently led away after revealing her insanity is clearly not intended to illustrate psychiatric theorising, as in Gericault's portraits of monomaniacs four decades earlier, it did reinforce contemporary psychiatric theories of women's mental breakdown in adolescence, a period of sexual instability which the Victorians regarded as risky for women's mental health:

> As Dr John Charles Bucknill, president of the Medico-Psychological Association, remarked in 1859, 'Ophelia is the very type of a class of cases by no means uncommon. Every mental physician of moderately extensive experience must have seen many Ophelias. It is a copy from nature, after the fashion of the Pre-Raphaelite school'. Dr John Conolly, ... [i]n his *Study of Hamlet* in 1863 ... noted that even casual visitors to mental institutions could recognize an Ophelia in the wards: 'the same young years, the same faded beauty, the same fantastic dress and interrupted song'.
>
> (Showalter, 1985, pp.85–6)

How do we *now* read Rossetti's painting of Ophelia? Do we still see it as quaint or romantic? What of the photographs of the insane taken in the asylum in the same era? Romantic seems inappropriate when one sees asylum mug shots.

Thus, in the same decade that Rossetti painted 'The First Madness of Ophelia', some of the larger European asylums began to photograph patients as part of its admission procedure. In cultural as well as temporal–historical terms, we can ask what the painted depictions of Ophelia such as by Rossetti are doing alongside these hospital mug shots? I ask this question because we can begin to see a huge semantic difference opening up between, on the one hand, Rossetti's romantic image of Ophelia and, on the other, photographic portraits of hundreds of female patients taken for instance in the San Clemente hospital in Venice, which produced an immense clinical and administrative record of madwomen (see Didi-Huberman, 2003, pp.42–3). There are certainly no Ophelia-like images in the sample of 40 photographs of female inmates that Didi-Huberman reproduces from San Clemente's 1873 registry.

In the second half of the nineteenth century, then, we find competing visual discourses of female insanity in the same historical period. In her tracing of the multiple ways in which the image of Ophelia has been appropriated across the nineteenth- and into the twentieth-century cultural arena, Showalter suggests that the representation of Ophelia 'depends on attitudes toward women and madness' (Showalter, 1985, p.92). This obvious but decisive point underlines how, contemporaneous with mug shot-like images of insanity that eventually peaked in the 1890s, the image of female insanity became used and confused in the gendered interrelations between reality, psychiatry and representational convention.

A final case in point concerns a photograph taken in a British asylum sometime in the 1850s. It jars awkwardly with Diamond's thesis on the objectivity of the photographic image discussed above because the photographer posed one of his female patients in the guise of Ophelia. Clad in convention she appears dressed in a shawl with a garland of flowers and leaves it placed in her hair. As Showalter (1985) sardonically notes of this photographic image, the fictional character and the real madwoman have become one. In fact, none other than Hugh W. Diamond himself took the photograph. Diamond's desire (here a purposefully loaded term) to picture Ophelia clearly overrides his own stated view that the objectivity of photography reveals the truthful appearance of the insane. His status as all-powerful asylum superintendent, coupled with his obvious desire to represent the figure of Ophelia, was too much for him to ignore. The point of course is that he did not have to ignore his desire. He could and did see the image of female insanity that he wanted.

Conclusion

This chapter has promoted the argument that we need to investigate historical images of madness analytically to see how mad images, mad figures and mad stereotypes change and perpetuate in myriad forms of seeing and reading. In doing so, I have sought to pay close attention to complex interplay between historical media and cultural forms, historical consciousness and the characteristics of visual change. The notion that stereotypes of madness are the same now as they were at some point in the past is not sustainable either empirically or analytically. This is why I have argued that we can only properly understand continuity in patterns of stereotyping in relation to change. Seeing historical images of madness entails reading and interpreting them historically so as to illuminate the changing historical conditions in which they gave meaning to the historical subjects that viewed them. We, too, are historical subjects and this means that our own twenty-first century engagement with past images of madness brings our own historical consciousness to bear on their reading.

3
Bedlam in Mind:
Campaigning Journalists
and Insane Conditions

Introduction

In almost every Western country, bricks and mortar remnants of
the public asylum system litter the countryside. Once the jewel in
the crown of a lunacy reform movement that swept Europe and
North America in the first half of the nineteenth century, the asylum is now a monument to a failed policy of segregating the insane.
In Great Britain, for example, scientific optimism that the asylum
would yield new treatments for insanity gave way to public concern
that such places were harmful to those they purported to cure. As
one historian of psychiatric policy sees it: 'The rise of the asylum is
the story of good intentions gone bad' (Shorter, 1997, p.33).

How psychiatry's 'good intentions gone bad' are mediated in public accounts of psychiatric arenas, from the segregated world of the
asylum to the current wide-open spaces of 'the community', is my
main focus in this chapter. Among the protagonists telling this story
are journalists. Indeed, general histories of psychiatric policy in Great
Britain (e.g. Rogers and Pilgrim, 2001; cf. Busfield, 1986) and the US
(e.g. Grob, 1991; cf. Shorter, 1997) give tantalising acknowledgment
that alongside mental health campaigners, journalists have also
played an important role in alerting the public to mistreatment taking place 'out of sight, out of mind'. At the same time however, these
histories glide over the *detail* of what journalists reported.

In what follows, I draw on a century of US and British reporting
and reportage on the asylum, the psychiatric hospital and 'the community' as emblematic of broad paradigm shifts in ways of seeing

mental disorder and its appropriate place in our world. The politics of mental health in modern societies such as Great Britain and the US is an outcome of historically complex, nationally contingent, political and policy deliberation, the long-term dynamics of which are normally absent from public discourse. However, notwithstanding national differences in psychiatric politics and policies what US and British reporting on places of insanity share is that they illustrate the *human consequences* of psychiatric policy-in-practice.

I do not want to imply that journalistic interventions helped reformulate psychiatric politics and policy. While not causal agents in historical changes in psychiatric policy, journalists are indirect variables shaping public discourses of sympathy and antipathy towards the recipients of psychiatric care. From illicit encounters in the asylum, through observations sanctioned by hospital authorities, to criticism of apparently uncontrolled care in the community, journalists have reported on the *place of insanity*. While this chapter illustrates emblematic 'moments' in journalism's advocacy on behalf of the mentally distressed, I want to examine how advocacy has been mediated in and through the image of the *suffering* patient.

As I noted in Chapter 2, William Hone's now largely forgotten role advocating on behalf of the voiceless inside madhouses such as London's Bethlem hospital in the early years of the nineteenth century played a major role in bringing insane conditions (in the double sense of the term) in that institution to public attention and reforming action. A campaigner on many unfashionable social issues (reform of madhouses being a classic example), Hone recognised that the harrowing sketch of James Norris, shackled and cruelly tormented in his cell, could be used to embody in the public imagination, the urgent need for lunacy reforms. In practice, however, support for the expensive proposition of humanely caring for the mentally distressed has never really figured prominently in political circles (Scull, 1979) albeit for those occasional 'moments' when journalists and other campaigners have found imaginative ways of propelling insane conditions to the fore of public attention.

Breaching the walls

Enclosed in asylums, the mad became invisible and voiceless, consigned to the imaginary landscape of Bedlam, a region populated by shadows and punctuated by unsettling sounds. By the mid-nineteenth century, the locked doors of the asylum marked the boundary between rationality and derangement; one could not easily step through to see at first hand what gothic horrors lay 'on the inside'. If fame counts for something however, then it must surely be the access it gives to normally restricted places and experiences. Charles Dickens no doubt understood this point when, on his lecture tour of the US in 1842, he asked to inspect the Boston and New York asylums. His impressions of the Boston asylum were favourable and he garnished it with the highest praise. Of the newly opened New York asylum located on Blackwell's Island he painted a dismal and disheartening picture:

> everything had a lounging, listless, madhouse air which was very painful. The moping idiot, cowering down with long, dishevelled hair; the gibbering maniac, with his hideous laugh and pointed finger; the vacant eye, the fierce wild face, the gloomy picking of the hand and lips, with munching of the nails: they were all there, without disguise, in naked ugliness and horror. In the dining-room, a bare, dull, dreary place, with nothing for the eye to rest on but the empty walls, a woman was locked up alone. She was bent, they told me, on committing [sic] suicide. If anything could have strengthened her in her resolution, it would certainly have been the insupportable monotony of such an existence.
>
> (Dickens, 2001/1842, p.104)

Dickens goes on to say that he was so shocked by conditions in the asylum that he made his excuses and left. However, what is also revealing about this particular episode is that no local journalist considered Dickens' observations worth pursuing; as we see below, it would be almost five decades before another journalist ventured into the 'madhouse' on Blackwell's Island. The blunt reality is that journalism only slowly came to recognise the plight of those incarcerated in asylums.

Consider Dickens' account of inspecting a lunatic asylum closer to home. On Boxing Day 1852, Dickens took up an invitation from London's St Luke's Asylum to visit the institution and to publicly report on his findings. St Luke's was a sister institution to Bethlem Hospital, and its management was keen to distance itself from scandal that had once again attached itself to that institution. In 1851, lunacy inspectors discovered that a number of female patients had died as a result of abuse and that their deaths had been covered up (see Andrews, et al., 1997, Chapter 25). The secrecy that surrounded the lives and deaths of inmates in Bethlem is the counterpoint to what Dickens reports is the transparency that he found in his visit to St Luke's.

Dickens' account of visiting St Luke's Asylum begins by reminding his readers that in the Bethlem/Bedlam of just a few decades back, 'lunatics were chained, naked, in rows of cages that flanked a promenade, and were wondered and jeered at through iron bars by London loungers' (p.88). Dickens' eye for character then goes on to describe the inmates whom he found attending the asylum's Boxing Day dance:

> There was the brisk, vain, pippin-faced little old lady, in a fantastic cap – proud of her foot and ankle; there was the old-young woman, with the dishevelled long light hair, spare figure, and weird gentility; there was the vacantly-laughing girl, requiring now and then a warning finger to admonish her; there was the quiet young woman, almost well, and soon going out. For partners, there were the sturdy bull-necked thick-set little fellow who had tried to get away last week; the wry-faced tailor, formerly suicidal, but much improved; the suspicious patient with a countenance of gloom, wandering round and round strangers, furtively eyeing them behind from head to foot, and not indisposed to resent their intrusion. There was the man of happy silliness, pleased with everything. But the only chain that made any clatter was Ladies' Chain, and there was no straiter [sic] waistcoat in company than the polka-garment of the old-young woman with the weird gentility, which was of a faded black satin, and languished through the dance with a love-lorn affability and condescension to the force of circumstances, in itself a faint reflection of all Bedlam.
>
> (Dickens, 1968/1852, pp.89–90)

The contrast with the physical and mental appearance of patients that Dickens encountered on Blackwell's Island a decade and another continent away could not be greater. The image of St Luke's patients at home (as it were) in the asylum, and thus not in need of 'chains' or other such constraining device, paints a picture of domestic contentment. Dickens was not alone in reporting the asylum dance as a 'good news' story.

The coming together of inmates, staff and visitors for the asylum dance epitomised the modern alternative to Bethlem/Bedlam. And Victorian asylum doctors were keen on what we now call media 'spin' to popularise their new therapeutic initiatives. Thus, Gilman (1982) points out the promotional value of the asylum dance that appeared in many mid-nineteenth century newspapers: 'The asylum becomes the extension of society through dance. Among the dancers were to be found not only patients but also the staff, who no longer consisted of the sadistic torturers of the old asylum but had become an extended family' (p.149). In our modern interpretation of the Victorian asylum as brutalising places, Dickens' characterisation of the 'asylum dance' as happy event appears a curious, even perverse, interpretation. But at the time it perfectly expressed the Victorians' conviction that in music making, a medicinal therapy for normalising and pacifying the insane (music that is used to 'sooth the savage breast', as it were) had been found (see MacKinnon, 2003).

Dickens' visit to St Luke's took place in the same decade that asylum-building in Great Britain reached its crusading zenith (see Scull, 1979). Asylums were then still a cause for hope and optimism, for cures and treatments yet to be discovered. Dickens' visit to St Luke's should therefore be interpreted as a shrewd *public relations* manoeuvre by its management. Indeed, so pleased were they with Dickens' sanitised and sanguine reportage that they sought and were given permission to use his report as publicity for their institution (which they continued to use for more than three decades). Issues relating to patient's rights, needs and dignity are not addressed; only later do these become social concerns in psychiatric care.

While doors were opened to public figures like Dickens, asylum inspection was beyond the purview of most journalists. In the US, occasional exposes of psychiatric mistreatment had been published including allegations that perfectly sane people were confined in asylums (Deutsch, 1937/1967). Without independent verification such reports had an air of myth about them. A solution eventually presented one enterprising newspaper editor with a scoop. Colonel John Cockerell, managing editor of Pulitzer's *New York World*, decided to breach the asylum walls.

Cockerill's opportunity to investigate came in the form of Elizabeth Jane 'Pink' Cochrane. Recently arrived in New York, Cochrane had cut her teeth as a reporter at the *Pittsburgh Dispatch* using the pen

name 'Nellie Bly'. She impressed Cockerill and was rewarded with
an assignment that would test her journalistic and theatrical skills.
Cochrane's remarkable brief was to feign insanity and to report
first-hand what it was like to be committed into the women's insane
ward in Blackwell Island.

Cochrane practiced her performance as a lunatic before checking
into a boarding house as 'Nellie Brown', where she soon exhibited signs
of distress and memory loss. This led to examination by doctors who
diagnosed Miss Brown as suffering from 'dementia with delusions of
persecution'. She was then committed to Blackwell's Island. Cochrane,
writing as Nellie Bly, later explained how, '[f]rom the moment I entered
the insane ward on the Island I made no attempt to keep up the assumed
role of insanity. I talked and acted just as I do in ordinary life. Yet strange
to say, the more sanely I talked and acted, the crazier I was thought to
be' (Bly 1887, p.3). Cochrane's experience has direct resonance with the
famous experiment conducted by the Stanford University psychologist
David Rosenhan (Rosenhan, 1973), who in 1972 fabricated insanity to
illustrate how once inside the psychiatric system, normal behaviour
begins to take on the appearance of abnormality. I shall further discuss
Rosenhan's experiment later in Chapter 6.

'Pink' Cochrane was to spend ten days in the asylum and the
dramatic manner of her subterfuge rendered her the most famous
investigative reporter of her era. During her incarceration, the story
of 'Nellie Brown' became a *cause celebre*; press reports speculated that
she was a victim of a jilted wedding proposal and that her fiancé
had sailed for Europe sending her insane. The *New York World* kept
its own council of course, before dramatically securing her release
through the timely arrival of her 'brother', in reality the *New York
World's* lawyer. Within twenty-four hours of her release the first
account of Cochrane's subterfuge appeared in the *New York World*:

INSIDE THE MADHOUSE
Nellie Bly's Experience in the Blackwell's Island Asylum ...
How the City's Unfortunate Wards are Fed and Treated
The Terrors of Cold Baths and Cruel, Unsympathetic Nurses
Attendants who Harass and Abuse Patients
And Laugh at Their Miseries

(quoted in Winston, 2005, p.108)

Later headlines revealed the true story of the mysterious Nellie Brown. They included 'Feigning Insanity in Order to Reveal Asylum Horrors' followed by 'Trying Ordeal of the *New York World's Girl* Correspondent' (Deutsch, 1937/1967, p.307). Each issue detailing Cochrane's subterfuge sold out, leading to re-publication (in time for the Christmas market) of Nellie Bly's exploits in book-length format: *Ten Days in a Mad-house: Or, Nellie Bly's Experience on Blackwell's Island* created a national scandal with the added sensation of a first-hand portrait of institutional abuse:

> What, excepting torture, would produce insanity quicker than this treatment? Here is a class of women sent to be cured. I would like the expert physicians who are condemning me for my action, which has proven their ability, to take a perfectly sane and healthy woman, shut her up and make her sit from 6 A.M. until 8 P.M. on straight-back benches, do not allow her to talk or move during these hours, give her no reading and let her know nothing of the world or its doings, give her bad food and harsh treatment, and see how long it will take to make her insane. Two months would make her a mental and physical wreck.
>
> (Bly, 1887, pp.33–4)

Cochrane's reportage combines reportorial analysis (such as the extract above) with subjective testimony. Her account of receiving an ice-cold bath remains vivid:

> My teeth chattered and my limbs were goose-fleshed and blue with cold. Suddenly I got, one after the other, three buckets of water over my head – ice-cold water, too – into my eyes, my ears, my nose and my mouth. I think I experienced some of the sensations of a drowning person as they dragged me, gasping, shivering and quaking, from the tub. For once I did look insane.
>
> (p.28)

In Cochrane's experience, and who now could doubt otherwise, Blackwell's Island Asylum made female inmates 'look insane'. The physical and mental transformation of Miss Tillie Mayard is a case in point. Miss Mayard, who arrived at the asylum in the same batch of new admissions as the mysterious 'Nellie Brown', is initially described as 'not appearing crazy'. Miss Mayard apparently confirms that she is suffering from 'nervous debility' as a result of recent physical illness but she quickly succumbs to the asylum's practice of rendering the sane *insane*:

> Insane? Yes, insane; and as I watched the insanity slowly creep over the mind [of Miss Mayard] that had appeared to be all right I secretly cursed the doctors, the nurses and all public institutions. Some one [sic] may say that she was insane at some time previous to her consignment to the asylum. Then if she were, was this the proper place to send a woman just convalescing, to be given cold baths, deprived of sufficient clothing and fed with horrible food?
>
> (p.8)

Cochrane's empathic narrative has considerable rhetorical force and she later gave evidence to a Grand Jury investigation into conditions in the asylum. Of course, *Ten Days in the Madhouse* is empathic only in so far as Cochrane acknowledges that patients like Miss Mayard are just like her, that is, sane individuals who really do not belong in the asylum and who succumb to insanity simply by the sheer misfortune of ending up in such a place.

There is no sense that Miss Mayard or any other female inmate are 'casualties' of a gendered psychiatric system; this kind of critical analysis would have to wait many decades and would eventually come from feminist cultural historians rather than journalists. I make this point not to undermine the exploits of Cochrane and the *New York World*, but because it is worth remembering that what is driving their expose of Blackwell's Island Asylum is popular fascination with the grotesque and the melodramatic. On both sides of the Atlantic, each was an important driving force in the development of 'New Journalism' (Salmon, 2000), especially where they could be married with the enormously popular style of 'personal journalism', at which 'Pink' Cochrane and the *New York World* excelled. In this sense, Blackwell's asylum is conceived as a rhetorical space, much like the archetypal Bedlam, onto which can be inscribed all sorts of pliable assumptions about the kinds of madness one can expect to see and hear within.

Thus, *Ten Days in the Madhouse* is above all a *voyeuristic* narrative – after all, Blackwell's Island asylum is where one would expect to find *dangerous* female lunatics isolated and confined for good reason. For instance, in a chapter memorably titled 'Promenading With Lunatics', Cochrane melodramatically describes walking the grounds of the asylum when she suddenly encounters the grotesques on the 'rope gang', composed of 'the most dangerous and most suicidal women' on the island:

> A long cable rope fastened to wide leather belts, and these belts locked around the waists of fifty-two women. At the end of the rope was a heavy iron cart, and in it two women – one nursing a sore foot, another screaming at some nurse, saying: 'You beat me and I shall not forget it. You want to kill me', and then she would sob and cry. The women 'on the rope', as the patients call it, were each busy on their individual freaks. Some were yelling all the while. One who had blue eyes saw me look at her, and she turned as far as she could, talking and smiling, with that terrible, horrifying look of absolute insanity stamped on her. The doctors might safely judge on her case. The horror of that sight to one who had never been near an insane person before, was something unspeakable.
>
> (p.41)

On one level, we can see in this particular passage about the 'rope gang' that Cochrane's critique of the asylum on Blackwell's Island did not extend to suggesting that the whole concept of sequestration was wrong. To the contrary, her concerns were focused on the *terms of incarceration* rather than the issue of incarceration itself. On another level, we can also see in the 'horror' of the rope gang how popular assumptions about the asylum and its inmates were embedded in a journalistic rhetoric that traded on the same kinds of 'sensation' narrative that made Wilkie Collins' fiction writing, for example, internationally famous for its horror and pathos in imaging and imagining 'mad women' as *beyond normal* characterisation.

Today, Elizabeth Jane 'Pink' Cochrane is a largely forgotten figure in the history of popular tabloid journalism but her remarkable abilities as the investigative journalist Nellie Bly deserves continuing recognition. While Cochrane's expose of abuses on Blackwell's Island eventually helped secure $2 million extra funding for New York's insane, her revelations did little over the long term to bring about permanent gains in the institutional treatment of the insane.

This was not Cochrane's remit of course, but it would later become the motivating force for other campaigning journalists on mental health both in the US and in Great Britain.

Opening the doors

By the mid-twentieth century, American publicly funded mental hospitals, like their British counterparts, had become the tattered undergarment of the otherwise well-dressed modern health care system. Ever the financially poor relation of the general hospital, the psychiatric hospital system in both these countries had limited financial resources to attract let alone sustain a supply of well-trained personnel. For this reason, during the Second World War several thousand conscientious objectors in the US and Great Britain were required to work in psychiatric institutions. Following the end of hostilities, some of those who had been pressed into psychiatric service began to publicly comment on the conditions that they found. For instance, *Life* magazine in the US agreed to publish Albert Q. Maisel's article 'Bedlam 1946', a photographic essay documenting the terrible abuse of psychiatric patients:

> Court and grand-jury records document scores of deaths of patients following beatings by attendants. Hundreds of instances of abuse, falling just short of manslaughter, are similarly documented. And reliable evidence, from hospital after hospital, indicates that these are but a tiny fraction of the beatings that occur, day after day, only to be covered up by a tacit conspiracy of mutually protective silence and a code that ostracizes employees who *sing too loud*.
>
> Yet beatings and murder are hardly the most significant of the indignities we have heaped upon most of the 400,000 guiltless patient-prisoners of the over 180 state mental institutions .... Hundreds – of my own knowledge and sight – spend 24 hours a day in stark and filthy nakedness. Those who are well enough to work, slave away in many institutions for 12 hours a day, often without a days rest for years on end.
>
> (Maisel, 1946, p.2, emphasis in the original)

Maisel's photographic essay powerfully reinforced the point that social and therapeutic infrastructures inside US mental hospitals had decayed. *Life* magazine readers, still reeling from images of death camp survivors in Nazi Germany encountered harrowing images of naked and demoralised humanity close to home.

Maisel's report appeared in the same year that Mary Jane Ward published her fictional account of a woman who goes insane and is institutionalised. *The Snake Pit* became a national best seller (later turned into one of the most popular films of 1949), which further highlighted social concerns about US mental hospitals. It then became a campaigning issue when taken up by a journalist whose interests straddled 'mental hygiene' reform and investigative reporting. Albert Deutsch's reports for *PM* magazine investigated conditions inside US psychiatric hospitals. His reports, later published as *The Shame of the States* (Deutsch, 1948), graphically illustrated the need for reform of psychiatric facilities. Consider his account of Philadelphia State Hospital (known as Byberry) and referred to by Deutsch as 'Philadelphia's Bedlam':

> The male 'incontinent ward' was like a scene out of Dante's Inferno. Three hundred nude men stood, squatted and sprawled in this bare room, amid shrieks, groans and unearthly laughter. These represented the most deteriorated patients. Winter or Summer, these creatures were never given any clothing at all. Some lay about on the bare floor in their own excreta. The filth-covered walls and floors were rotting away. Could a truly civilized community permit humans to be reduced to such animal-like level?
>
> (p.49)

Deutsch's description of the incontinent ward is vivid. But what scandalised the American public were photographs of seemingly abandoned patients:

> This 16-year-old girl [whose picture appears in Deutsch's book] might have been sent home cured were she afforded active psychiatric treatment. At Byberry she faced a dismal future, a potential candidate for one of the dreaded 'back wards' where the forgotten men and women await a merciful death. She wore a ribbon-tied cloth for shoes.
>
> (p.50)

Deutsch's book also presented a blueprint for reform in his outline of the 'Ideal Mental Hospital'. His proposals included provision of well-funded psychiatric hospitals housing a maximum of 1000 patients sited in urban centres where public monitoring of such places could more easily take place. Deutsch thus suggested that mental hygiene campaign groups could 'stimulate local newspapers to cover the mental hospital beat' (p.187) and raise morale among patients by frequent spot-check visits from concerned outsiders. This was not to be Deutsch's legacy, however.

I want to suggest that Deutsch's legacy lies precisely in the inter-section between investigative journalism and social campaigning on behalf of forgotten mental patients. As the eminent US psychiatrist Karl Menninger wrote of Deutsch in the foreword to *Shame of the States*: 'As a professional writer, a columnist in a New York daily and a con-tributor to many national journals, he has probably done more than anyone else to keep before the eyes of the American people the abuses that are perpetrated in their name in public psychiatric hospitals .... He combines the skill of the reporter and the training of the scientist with the deep feeling of a man of compassion and vision' (Deutsch, ibid., p.19). Praise indeed for a journalist inextricably associated with discred-iting the US psychiatric profession in the eyes of the nation.

While Deutsch's own preferred Ideal Mental Hospital would be replaced by an even grander vision of psychiatric care in the com-munity, his efforts did much to stimulate action research and policy debate on hospital care. Indeed without his efforts it is difficult to imagine how Erving Goffman's celebrated indictment of the insti-tutional care of mental patients could have been written. Goffman's book *Asylums: Essays on the Social Situation of Mental Patients and Other Inmates* (1961/1984) documented how a single US psychiatric hospital 'stripped' patients of individuality leading inexorably to their social atrophy. However, this is precisely Deutsch's argument in *Shame of the States* and his campaigning journalism deserves recognition for paving a route into a closed world for social researchers like Goffman.

Voluntarily entering the closed world of psychiatric hospitals is traditionally seen as risky, especially when one considers the standard psychiatric joke: 'If you're not already mad when you enter the asy-lum, you soon will be!' This is an underlying theme in the pulp film *Shock Corridor* (d. Samuel Fuller, 1963), in which a journalist seeking a scoop on a murder suspect has himself committed to a mental hospital where inmates have information on the culprit. To maintain his disguise, the journalist undergoes electrical shock treatment whereupon latent monomaniacal urges (usually a more common affliction among editors!) are released and he becomes genuinely insane. However, the real-world encounter between social expose and psychiatry presents other kinds of occupational perils.

A case in point concerns Frederick Wiseman's 1967 film *Titicut Follies*, a fly-on-the-wall documentary about Bridgewater, a Massachusetts' prison-hospital for the criminally insane (see also my discussion of Wiseman's film in Chapter 5). Images in Wiseman's film include a highly disturbing sequence in which we see a patient who has apparently been kept naked in solitary confinement for seventeen years. Guards are seen taunting him about his dirty cell and later complain that when they control such patients with tear-gas, fumes cling to *their clothes*. Another Bridgewater inmate is shown being force-fed through a tube into his nose while the doctor in charge casually smokes a cigarette (as a result of the feeding the man later dies). So challenging was Wiseman's film that the Commonwealth of Massachusetts censored it for 25 years.

This response is a far cry from New York state authorities' response to Nellie Bly's expose of abuses on Blackwell's Island. Though not a journalist, Wiseman subsequently defended his right to report these images citing a journalist's First Amendment (free expression) rights to report on conditions in a prison (see Benson and Anderson, 2002). The legal ban on *Titicut Follies* was finally overturned in 1991 and was broadcast on US and British public service channels in 1993, 26 years after it was first completed. At that time, Bridgewater's authorities stated that the institution had long since changed practices of containment shown in the film (Szasz, 2007). We have no independent confirmation however, since legal complexities that dogged Wiseman rendered Bridgewater and other similar psychiatric/prison institutions off-limits to journalists and film-makers. It remains the most contentious example where access to a psychiatric hospital was granted and then declined.

British journalists also gained access to the asylum. Historically, access was restricted on privacy grounds and understandable uncertainty about what went on behind the institution's locked doors prevailed. (For this reason, some nineteenth-century local newspapers did feature official annual asylum inspection reports; see Bartlett and Wright, 1999.) Expansion of current affairs television from the 1950s meant that British TV journalism responded to matters of serious moments including scrutiny of conditions and psychiatric treatment services inside Victorian-built asylums. New 'open door' policies meant that journalists were able to visit such places, and even film reports on the institutional conditions they found.

Consider British television's earliest current affairs series on psychiatry and psychological medicine, the BBC's *The Hurt Mind* (1956–7). The series included a first-person account of conditions inside a Victorian-built asylum. Presented by Christopher Mayhew (a serving Member of Parliament), the opening of the episode, entitled 'Put Away', sets the scene by showing film of the hospital exterior: 'This is a mental hospital. Does it fill you with foreboding? I know it did me. What's really going on inside there? Hopeless misery? Raving? Violence? Weird, uncanny behaviour? I thought I'd find out.' Mayhew's report then documents how the place historically occupied by insanity (i.e. the asylum) has been transformed, symbolically – if not concretely – into the epitome of the modern psychiatric hospital.

This is achieved via a sequence in which Mayhew's favourable view of the hospital ('This particular hospital is one of the best in Britain, despite having been built 50 years ago' – a statement that immediately follows on from his introductory comments above) is contrasted with an older psychiatric regime. It includes a series of vignettes illustrating modern 'scientific' psychiatric treatments including electro-convulsive therapy (ECT), insulin coma therapy and occupational therapy (the cumulative success of each therapy is personified by interviews with patients whom we are told are on the verge of discharge) contrasting with human casualties of an older asylum system. For example, Mayhew introduces a ward for 'chronic cases':

> Though the staff are splendid, I thought this was the worst ward in the hospital. These are the hard core of chronic patients. They are all very seriously ill. Most of them became ill before modern treatments became available .... Many of these patients didn't notice our camera or the lights at all. Their minds were elsewhere, withdrawn quite outside our world.

Reminiscent of Dickens' visit to St Luke's, Mayhew is at pains to contrast an old asylum regime with the modern psychiatric environment: 'Take away the nurses and this might be a hostel or a private hotel'. The contrast with the asylum system also forms the basis for Mayhew's interview with a male nurse, who describes the former prison-like regime in which patients were incarcerated behind locked gates:

Mayhew: And this made the patients frustrated I suppose, and violent?

Nurse: Well naturally, particularly on wet days when they couldn't get their two hours exercise in the morning and two hours at night. They did tend to get irritable.

Mayhew: And then the nurses I suppose had to retaliate a bit?

Nurse: Well on the whole, they were a very tolerant staff but of course the circumstances under which we were living and the anxiety and the tension we were experiencing made it almost inevitable that sooner or later there would be retaliation.

Mayhew: You hit out because you were frightened, was that it?

Nurse: Often in self-defence, yes.

Mayhew: Well now, Mr Ralph, when was the last time that a patient hit out seriously against you or a member of your staff? Was it this year for instance?

Nurse: No, no, I wouldn't say this year or last year. I shall have to go back a long way.

Mayhew: And what do you attribute it to Mr Ralph?

Nurse: Well, I should attribute it to several factors. Of course drugs and various treatments like ECT, insulin, and of course the open doors have taken away the air of a prison and they have given a good relationship between the staff and the patients.

Mayhew: Thanks very much.

A central feature of Mayhew's reportage in 'Put Away' is that efforts by staff on behalf of their patients are nothing short of honourable, even heroic. Thus, the remaining vestiges of Dickensian sanguinity can still be traced more than a century later (not least in Mayhew's anodyne interview with the nurse, which appears to miss the latter's admission that violence is used *against patients*!) However, such a gentle approach to reporting conditions inside psychiatric hospitals could not last.

In Britain, the policy of using Victorian-built asylums was seen as an irredeemable state of affairs even by government. In a 1961 speech, Conservative health minister Enoch Powell spoke in uncompromising terms about their reactionary status: 'There they stand, isolated, majestic, imperious, brooded over by the gigantic water tower and chimney combined, rising unmistakable and daunting out of the countryside – the asylums which our forefathers built with such immense solidity. Do not for a moment underestimate their power of resistance to our assault' (Jones, 1993, p.160). Powell's assumption was to prove correct; a 'paralysis' in psychiatric policy (Porter, 1991) meant that it took more than three decades to close the asylums, during which time allegations of patient abuse surfaced leading to accusations in the media that psychiatric institutions were tainted with scandal (see Martin, 1984).

Powell's 'water tower' speech also proved to be a significant trigger for media critique of asylums during the 1960s. For example, Granada Television's *World In Action* (*WIA*) investigation of 'Ward F13' (broadcast 20 May 1968), which documented the plight of psychiatric patients housed in unsanitary wards, led to calls in the press for such places to be closed (I return to this programme below). Like Kuhn's (1970) model of scientific change conceived not as a cumulative acquisition of knowledge, but as a series of peaceful interludes punctuated by violent revolutions, older forms of institutional psychiatric care receded slowly only after successive UK governments accepted fiscal arguments that psychiatric hospitals were too expensive to maintain and that care in the community offered a cheaper option (Jones, 1993).

The Kuhnian model of science also posits that one conceptual scientific world-view is eventually replaced by another. This is the case in the mental health field since the policy of 'community care' is now in ascendancy in a majority of Western countries (Micale and Porter, 1994). The core of the policy involves profound changes in psychiatric theory and values, including the principal of restoring patients back to society. In Britain (unlike the US, where debates on psychiatric care mobilised by campaigning journalists like Albert Deutsch garnered public interest more quickly than the UK), the slow-paced demise of the public asylum system underlines the limited impact that campaigning/investigative journalism per se had on reform of psychiatric policy (a point that Deutsch himself was all too aware of having already written a definitive history of American psychiatric care – see Deutsch, 1937/1967).

Bedlam in the streets

In this section, I want to discuss more recent reporting on psychiatric care in the community in modern Britain. (In the US, the functional equivalent of psychiatric 'care in the community' had different policy momentum, see Scull, 2006, pp.92–106.) In keeping with earlier sections, I focus attention on images of psychiatric patients, which are embedded in reporting on the spillage of mental disorder into new spaces and places of post-asylum psychiatry: 'the community'. By focusing exclusively on the British psychiatric policy context, I can more adequately explore interplay between investigative reporting on psychiatric patients in the community and journalists' accounts of human suffering as manifestations of policy *gone awry*.

In the segregated environment of the madhouse reported on by 'Pink' Cochrane, those sent insane by the institution are to be pitied, if not understood. Similarly, in reporting on psychiatric hospitals by campaigning journalists like Albert Maisel and Albert Deutsch, psychiatric patients are not only pitied for their 'Bedlam-like' existence, but also found to be in urgent need of care that might see them return to take up their place in the community. It is a genuine irony then that in the era of mental health care in the community, psychiatric patients are feared as 'mad, bad and dangerous to know'. Sympathy has been replaced by hostility and fear, while *empathy* has remained largely absent from reporting.

Sympathy for psychiatric patients is not a *conditio sine qua non* of journalism, however. A case in point concerns the reporting of a journalist-turned-campaigner on psychiatric policy. Marjorie Wallace produced a series of award-winning articles in *The Times* and *Sunday Times* on the theme 'The Forgotten Illness' (16, 17 and 18 December 1985; 20, 23 January and 17 February and 3 March 1986). Referring exclusively to schizophrenia (defined by Wallace as not meaning split personality: 'a better definition is bouts of mental anguish or insanity', *The Times*, 17 December 1985, p.8), Wallace drew attention to the reality of care in the community for individual families' caught up in the day-to-day problems of the new policy:

For some ex-patients, this prospect [of homelessness] is too much. Michael became a schizophrenic at 23, throwing up his career as an artist. He spent several turbulent years in and out of hospital and terrorized his family. 'He used to line up the knives and point them in my direction wherever I moved', his mother recalls. 'He even threatened us with an axe'. He was admitted to Friern Hospital but discharged because it was no longer hospital policy to retain people who were unlikely to improve.

Six weeks later his mother heard that his body had been found in a river not far from the house where the family had lived when he was a child.

(p.8)

Leaving aside the thorny question why such a representation of an axe-wielding schizophrenic is necessary to criticise community care policy, Wallace presents 'The Tragedy of Schizophrenia' (a sub-headline in each of her reports) in terms of the policy of closing mental hospitals and summed up in her phrase, 'An Open Door to Despair' (*The Times*, 17 December 1985, p.8). As she subsequently put it in a retrospective account of being *the* front line of investigating and reporting on psychiatric hospital closures in the mid-1980s, Wallace, perhaps reminiscent of Albert Deutsch, scandalised an emerging British-style programme of care in the community:

I was taken to Dave's Guest House in Portsmouth .... Dave summoned his guests for my inspection. All of them were recently patients in a psychiatric hospital. 'Ladies and gentlemen', he said, 'I want you to tell this lady: do you have a good breakfast here?' They all said 'Yes!', and that was the end of that; but upstairs, there were poor soiled mattresses on the floor, no clean linen, no towels, no means of washing as far as I could see. Yet Dave was getting paid about £50 a week for each 'guest' from Social Security .... They had been deposited there: social workers had driven them straight to Dave's place to be officially 'looked after' as soon as they were discharged from a psychiatric hospital.

So this was community care, the promised land of the libertarians. Even worse than the physical deprivation was the emotional emptiness. Those who were lucky enough to be in perfectly clean accommodation, still received a minimal level of care.

(Wallace, 1992, p.28)

By the time Wallace delivered the latter reflections (reworked from her original reporting) as a speech to a professional Conference on

'Community Care and Schizophrenia' (Nuffield College Oxford, July 1990) she was no longer a journalist but Chief Executive of SANE (Schizophrenia – A National Emergency), the charity that she founded while reporting on care in the community for *The Times* and *Sunday Times*. The apparent 'emergency' reflected in the charity's name promoted the notion that community care policy was failing the families of schizophrenics. As Wallace goes on to explain, her priority as a reporter was to sympathise with the latter:

> As an investigative reporter ... my task was to find what was happening to people who were mentally ill, day by day, hour by hour. It was then that I discovered the real tragedy. It was not the misery and hopelessness of the people in those awful doss-houses, nor the privations and neglect of people on the streets, but the pain and desperation of families struggling to care for sons and daughters whose lives have been blighted by mental illness.
>
> (Wallace, 1992, p.28)

Expressing sympathy for families caring for mentally ill loved ones is a legitimate expression of a journalist's ethic of care, of course. But also embedded in Wallace's account can be found a more troubling expression of personal–professional antipathy towards the cause of the carers' 'tragedy': the mentally ill. But we need not worry too much about them since (in light of the latter extract, and as the popular adage says), 'where there's no sense there's no feeling'. Thus, the 'misery and hopelessness of the people in those awful doss-houses' is secondary to the 'pain and desperation of families' whose struggle to care for loved ones presumably renders them *compos mentis* to the harsh realities of community psychiatric care. Wallace then makes explicit the psychiatric policy problem by drawing on the familiar public image of the mentally ill as harbouring a *non-compos mentis* state of mind(lessness):

> Like many others I started out with starry-eyed acceptance of the ideology of community care. I had already campaigned to get mentally-handicapped people, especially children, out of hospital, and seen it work. When children and young people were removed from the cloying illness-oriented ethic of the hospital, they bloomed: the quality of their lives improved and they were

able to gain confidence and exploit their potential. What I had
not realised is the fundamental difference between people with a
mental illness and those with a mental handicap. The difference
is not yet fully recognised by many of our policy makers, and certainly not the general public.

(Wallace, 1992, p.28)

Here, Wallace's account of the inappropriateness of community
care 'for people with a mental illness' policy failure is manifest in
the notion of a 'fundamental difference between people with a
mental illness and those with a mental handicap'. What the 'fundamental difference' referred to actually means is not forthcoming,
however. Wallace presumably feels that 'the difference' is obvious
to her professional audience (though not to 'policy makers' and the
'general public').

Wallace subsequently became a campaigner opposing care in the
community policies. By contrast, other mental health campaign
groups welcomed the new policy (Crossley, 2006) while being mind-
ful that it has brought new problems and controversies. For example,
with reform has come criticism that patients are no longer in receipt
of drug treatments and are not monitored by psychiatric professionals (see Sayce (2000) for an outline and rejection of this argument).
Consequently, community-care policy has resulted (so the argument
goes) in dangerous individuals left to roam the streets becoming
at the very least a public nuisance and, at worst, a threat to themselves and/or others. Notwithstanding the accuracy of such claims,
two heavily reported incidents became synonymous with apparent
failure of the policy.

Firstly, the murder in December 1992 of Jonathan Zito, a passenger
on the London Underground, attracted national media attention
when he became a random victim of Christopher Clunis, a diagnosed
schizophrenic. I have already noted the significance of this tragedy
in Chapter 1. I will simply add here that following Clunis' conviction for murder, the background events leading to his unprovoked
attack on Zito continued to attract significant media interest because
Zito's widow Jayne and Clunis *together* pursued a joint legal challenge
against Camden Mental Health Trust for failing to provide Clunis
with treatment. Their claim for damages was subsequently rejected
by the High Court but kept the policy of care in the community

high on the political and news media agenda. The second incident to define care in the community as a 'failing policy' involved Ben Silcock, the schizophrenic who climbed into the lion's enclosure at London Zoo (see Chapter 1).

It will be recalled that Silcock's mauling was captured on amateur film and became emblematic of visible failings in mental health care in the community. The Silcock case set in train policy debate about care in the community. This included a current affairs investigation by Granada Television that used journalistic subterfuge reminiscent of Nellie Bly's pioneering stunt journalism. Broadcast in Granada's *Disguises* current affairs strand in 1993, 'A Place of Safety' investigated the social impact of mental health care in the community. Series reporter Adam Holloway acted the role of a homeless schizophrenic to investigate provision of psychiatric care in the community at more or less the moment of its implementation in law. Using a combination of hidden and fixed camera techniques, Holloway begins his report in the grounds of an abandoned asylum:

> Powick Hospital, empty and overgrown was once the scene of a documentary by Granada television 25 years ago. Filming took place in this very ward where mentally ill people were stored without modern medication for decades of their lives.

As he moves through the ward, Holloway 'views' footage from Granada's *World In Action* episode noted above now superimposed on to dilapidated ceilings and walls. An amplified soundtrack gives a ghostly impression of the noise and chaos popularly associated with Bedlam, the implication being that patients evidently suffered here. We then see Holloway leave the asylum as he explains:

> The idea was to empty huge old institutions like Powick and put patients in small concentrations of good housing. The plan was called care in the community but not all the money for this has been provided. And when the act becomes statutory in April [1993] still more of the seriously ill will be homeless. I've now arrived in Birmingham.

Hidden camera footage then offers brief vignettes of the apparently 'seriously ill' among the city's homeless: a woman gesticulates wildly for no apparent reason; a man exhibits dramatic jerk-like movements of his body; another man plays a pipe, which we are told, 'endlessly fails to produce any sound'. What we are witness to is a visual topography of what mental pathology looks like beyond the *cordon sanitaire* of the asylum. The unspoken assumption embedded into this sequence is that Hogarth's nightmarish vision of Bedlam has relocated into *our* communities.

Reminiscent of 'Pink' Cochrane's performance as Nellie Brown entombed in the 'madhouse', Holloway's own subterfuge also includes a first-person expose of conditions inside a 'guest house' (read: madhouse) in which former psychiatric patients have been housed. For one week, Holloway lives in the guest house/madhouse to document conditions and he, like Nellie Bly, duly casts fellow residents as victims of a system that does not care. For example, Holloway introduces 'Eric, the schizophrenic who talks to his own voices':

Holloway: How many times have you seen a doctor since you've been here?

Eric: I'm all right, I get by without it I'm all right. I'm all right. Are you a social worker are you?

Holloway: No I'm a resident.

Justification for Holloway's concern about whether Eric has seen a doctor is not immediately recognisable as grounded in popular assumptions about voice-hearing schizophrenics being in urgent need of medical help, since it is presented as sympathy for his *suffering*. We may or may not be able to understand why Eric hears voices and harbours the belief that he is 'alright', but that is beside the point. In the context of a investigation exposing the failing policy of psychiatric care in the community it is enough to know that Eric is a schizophrenic, hears 'voices', and *has not seen a doctor*. Sympathy and antipathy are bedfellows in Holloway's reportage.

Granada, the television company that produced *Disguises*, promoted it as a series that 'gets to parts of a story others can't reach' (Granada TV publicity material for *Disguises*, March 1993). But when journalists wear a mask to unmask others, the best that we can hope for is perhaps a voyeuristic thrill in thinking that we are seeing something of the experience of the insane other. Though separated by more than a century, the dramatic similarities between Nellie Bly's and Adam Holloway's use of subterfuge nevertheless tells us much about journalism's continuing inability to enable psychiatric patients to speak for themselves about their experiences of living and coping with the day-to-day impact of psychiatric policies and practices.

Conclusion

This chapter has drawn on three important examples of intervention by journalists seeking to draw public attention to failings in psychiatric policy and practice. Although spread over 100 years of US and British newspaper reporting and reportage, each of the illustrative exemplars that I have discussed has had immense significance on public perceptions of psychiatric policy, and patients as victims of policy. Thus, what I have emphasised here is not so much historical reporting and reportage on the locus of psychiatric care, but some key moments of representational continuity – recurring tropes – in journalist's accounts of psychiatric policy gone awry. Psychiatric policies may well have moved beyond Bedlam, but in reporting psychiatric patients as emblematic victims of policies, journalistic assumptions about disorderly psyches have proven much more entrenched and less mobile.

4
Mad, Bad and Dangerous: Psychiatry and Criminals in the Popular Press

Introduction

The categories of sickness, madness and badness are in constant flux because they are evaluative, socially constructed categories with imprecise boundaries. This poses problems for those who have jurisdiction over these boundaries, and those who seek to undermine their established authority. This is not just an academic point. For instance, a British schizophrenic named Peter Coonan changed his name after tabloid reporting of his case became intolerable. Coonan is a convicted murderer held in Broadmoor high security hospital. Even after noting this morbid fact I suggest that it is possible to find some degree of sympathy for Coonan's plight because psychiatrists who gave evidence at his trial confirmed to the court that his criminality occurred as a direct consequence of his paranoid schizophrenic condition: voices told him to kill.

The case of Peter Coonan might well elicit even more sympathy if I also point out that despite *three* psychiatrists testifying that he was suffering from schizophrenia, this diagnosis was rejected by the jury who found him guilty of murder rather than the less culpable option of manslaughter on grounds of diminished responsibility. Coonan was sent to prison and eventually transferred into the forensic hospital system some years later when his disturbed mental state became impossible for the prison authorities to ignore. Why was he not sent to hospital in the first place? Why did the jury reject the arguments of not one but three psychiatrists? It will help to know that Peter Coonan's former surname is *Sutcliffe* and he is also known as the

Yorkshire Ripper, the notorious serial killer of 13 women in the late 1970s and 1980s.

Can we still find some vestige of sympathy for the sickness of Peter Coonan? I suspect that few of us can. Yet the fact remains that Peter *Sutcliffe* committed his crimes as a consequence of his paranoid and delusional state thinking that God wanted him to kill women. The flip side of this point is that Sutcliffe would not have thought himself God's appointed assassin had it not been the tragedy of his schizophrenic condition. This surely demands some degree of sympathy for the mental sickness that caused him to commit terrible murders. Yet why is it so difficult or even impossible for us to imagine feeling *sorry* for Peter Sutcliffe? Why do anti-stigma campaigners for example, not demand an end to ongoing tabloid newspaper coverage of Peter Sutcliffe as a 'crazed killer' or 'mad murderer'?

Such a possibility appears ludicrous because the press and public opinion reject Sutcliffe's schizophrenic diagnosis. The basic line is this: Sutcliffe has managed to con government, prison authorities and psychiatry into believing that he is mentally ill. Sutcliffe is not alone in pulling this con apparently, since many of the criminals/patients who reside within the high security hospital system including Broadmoor are also involved in duping the authorities for an easy alternative to the harsh prison existence. The fact that it is the popular press and not psychiatrists who have grown wise and report this scandal underlines the diminishing influence of psychiatry as the preliminary mediators of madness. This is where I shall begin my journey across the shifting sand on which resides the expertise of the psy professions.

Criminal minds and the preliminary mediators of madness

Psychiatrists and psychologists usually deal with mental distress in conditions of privacy. Increasingly though, practitioners in the psy professions are public commentators on mental distress. In Britain, for example, Dr Raj Persaud, until recently a consultant psychiatrist, was also a popular writer and broadcaster on mental health topics. However, in communicating with media audiences on psychiatric matters, psychiatrists and psychologists are reflexively conditioned by their pursuit of media attention, and the need to get their message across. This led in 2000, to criticism that psychologists working on Channel 4's *Big Brother* reality TV show were unethical by publicly commenting on stress placed on its participants by the demands of the show (Milmo, 2000). The criticism implied that psychologists were not identifying implicit features of mental distress but *complicit* in its manufacture.

Ironically, this was also the outcome of a 2008 reality-style TV programme entitled 'How Mad Am I?'. It showed how a psychiatrist, a psychologist and a psychiatric nurse 'diagnosed' volunteers as the latter carried out a series of tasks. The three psy professionals had to identify which volunteers they thought had mental health problems including eating disorder, depression, bi-polar condition, social anxiety disorder and obsessive-compulsive disorder. Ostensibly, the theme of 'How Mad Am I?' was to challenge the stigma of a psychiatric diagnosis. The professionals correctly 'diagnosed' two volunteers and incorrectly 'diagnosed' three others with no history of mental health problems. One woman was incorrectly 'diagnosed' twice, giving the clear impression that they were determined to diagnose her with some or other disorder.

I want to suggest that the psychiatric profession, which secured its legitimacy as the preliminary mediators of madness in the segregated world of the public asylum, is now involved in shoring up its legitimacy in the open arenas of the public sphere. In making this argument I want to borrow from Melucci's approach to analysing social movements, which he says, can themselves be theorised *as media* since collective action, 'by the sheer fact of its existence represents in its very form and models of organisation a message broadcast to the rest of society' (quoted in Cottle, 2008, p.854). Melucci's approach also signals how the actors within social movements bring issues to the fore within and through the media, to claim wider public support and legitimacy for their political and policy campaigns. If this is true of new social movements then it is certainly true of psychiatry's recent public efforts to be the predominant professional 'voice' on mental health in an era of post-asylum psychiatric politics.

The Royal College of Psychiatrists (RCP), the body representing the professional and political interests of UK psychiatrists, notes on its web home page (www.rcpsych.ac.uk) that it has a database of more than 200 experts across UK who will speak to journalists on a wide range of topics and mental disorders, ranging from addiction to women's problems. The site also houses RCP press releases and information on interventions made by the RCP in its promotional work to Parliament. In other words, the broad orientation of this self-promotional work is a tripartite navigation between psychiatric professionals, publics and policymakers. Thus, between 1998 and 2003, the RCP mounted a five-year 'Changing Minds' campaign (see Crisp, 2000, 2004) against media stigmatisation of mental illnesses with the especial aim of encouraging journalists and other media commentators (including the medical press) to replace the popular discourse of 'psychos', 'loonies', 'schizos' and so on, with accurate and apparently more sensitive psychiatric terminology.

However, as all journalists know, the 'news story' is at the core of their professional activity and 'narrative', that is, storytelling is the central factor structuring news work (Cottle, 2003). This means that 'news stories, like myths, do not tell it like it is, but rather, "tell it like it means"' (Cottle, 2003, p.15). Approached in this way, psychiatry's effort at countering the discourse of 'madness' with 'mental illness' is hampered by the fact that when psychiatrists and psychologists participate in the public sphere of news making (for example) they necessarily make accommodation to what Altheide and Snow (1979) discern is a generalising 'media logic'. Thus, the conventionalised formats of news produces a standardised template that condition how stories are scripted. This very different script to that of the lecture theatre or consulting room/hospital ward means that psychiatrists must trade professional narratives of 'mental illness' for culturally determined definitions of 'madness'.

To illustrate how psychiatrists publicly go about being the preliminary mediators of madness I now want to recall the circumstances when two of Britain's most hated criminals, Myra Hindley and Ian Brady, popularly known as the 'moors murderers', stepped out from the shadows of their prison cell (as it were) to speak for themselves in the public sphere. These were two quite separate media events but symbolically connected because of Hindley and Brady's past joint criminal enterprise in torturing and murdering children. Ever since their convictions in 1966, Hindley and Brady have been constant topics of media debate and vilification rendering them iconic figures in the British popular imagination. With this in mind one can perhaps understand the moral indignation when they each contributed publicly to debate on the individual psychology and personality leading a person to become a killer.

The circumstances by which the moors murderers were seared into the national consciousness rest not just on the murder of five children but also on an audio recording of the torture of one victim. This has been deemed a moment when the country's tolerance of the immorality of the 1960s 'permissive society' reached breaking point. Certainly, morality (or indeed the lack of it) played a key part in media framing of Hindley and Brady during and after the original trial (Cameron and Frazer, 1987). Over time, Hindley's iconic status as the antithesis of caring femininity has led to argument about her actions: is she mad or is she bad to have willingly facilitated torture and murder of children. There are some who claim to understand her motivation. Consider the following passage from *A Mind to Crime* (1995), a popular science book written by journalists on the links between crime and mental disorder:

> There is a suggestion that women psychopaths seek out their male equivalents to commit crimes – like the child-killing duo of Myra Hindley and Ian Brady, who tortured their victims before killing them and burying them on the Yorkshire Moors. Even after years of imprisonment, and a concerted campaign to prove to the public that she represents no danger to them, Hindley is capable of joking, 'I don't know why they call me the Moors Murderer – I've never murdered a Moor.' Such insensitivity to the families of her young victims is a classic psychopathic trait. Brady accepts his fate and acknowledges his condition.
>
> (Moir and Jessel, 1995, p.163)

When extracts of *A Mind to Crime* appeared in the *Guardian*, Moir and Jessel's 'diagnosis' of Hindley did not go unchallenged. In a letter to the same newspaper, one particularly well-informed reader on Hindley's state of mind criticised their 'casual' application of a psychopathic diagnosis, which in her view placed Hindley's actions in the 'mad' not 'bad' category. That reader was Myra Hindley herself. 'To be casually labelled a psychopath by two people who have never met or spoken to me flies in the face of reason,' wrote Hindley. 'In my 30 years in prison I have met, spoken with and been examined by psychiatrists and, in particular, a senior psychologist with whom I did a series of tests, the results of which ruled out psychopathy, schizophrenia, manic depression, episodic dyscontrol and any form of psychosis or neurosis. In a word, there was no evidence of a mentally disordered mind' (*The Guardian*, 4 October 1995, p.18). I shall shortly return to the implication of Hindley's point about having long been examined by psychiatrists and psychologists.

Firstly though, *The Guardian* newspaper invited Myra Hindley to further explain why she chose to participate in the procuring, torture and killing of children and teenagers. In a 5000-word essay subsequently published by the paper (*The Guardian*, 18 December 1995, pp.10–11) she discussed her familial and social background culminating in her view that because Brady is now diagnosed as having a predisposing mental illness, she is the more culpable. She also acknowledged personal regret that she is not able to explain her own actions in a psychiatric context:

> I've so often wished that I had suffered from some affective disorder and been diagnosed accordingly. This would have provided some kind of explanation for my actions. As it is, what I was involved in is indefensible. I wasn't mad, so I must have been bad, became bad by a slow process of corruption (certainly there was a strong element of fear) which eroded many of the values I'd held and my latent strength of character obviously enabled me to resolutely cast aside my beliefs in order to identify myself completely with a man who had become my god, who I both feared and worshipped.

Hindley concludes her essay with these words:

> I have said that I believe it is a fact of human nature to apply labels to help us make sense of something, anything incomprehensible, and it reinforces my belief that 'broader society' should take care in defining the word psychopath. It can lead to so many misunderstandings and misrepresentations – as in my own case by David Jessel and Ann Moir – when detailed psychiatric reports from several sources have firmly ruled out any forms of psychopathy.
>
> (*The Guardian*, 18 December 1995, pp.10–11)

Hindley's comment that, 'several sources [psychiatrists and a senior psychologist, according to her original letter to *The Guardian*] have firmly ruled out any forms of psychopathy', is her reminder to the public that psychiatrists and psychologists have ruled out mental illness in her case; she has been certified *sane* (as it were). This of course is intended to cast doubt on the labelling action of the journalists who 'casually' diagnosed her as a psychopath without having met her. Not surprisingly, given public interest in Hindley, virtually every other national newspaper condemned her *Guardian* essay as another attempt to gloss over her crimes and curry public sympathy for her long and unsuccessful (she died still a serving prisoner in 2005 after spending almost 40 years behind bars) attempt to gain her freedom.

Among the many commentaries critical of Hindley's *Guardian* essay was an article in the *Daily Mail* written by Dr Raj Persaud headlined, 'Clever words but not a hint of remorse: a top psychiatrist on Hindley's plea for freedom' (19 December 1995, p.8). In his article (which for sake of brevity I have condensed), Dr Persaud recognises Hindley as a psychopathic personality:

> Her fellow Moors Murderer, Ian Brady, has certainly manifested symptoms of severe mental illness while in custody, but Hindley apparently never has. The very rationality of her interview, coupled with her ability to complete an Open University degree in humanities, are testaments to her mental stability.
>
> So is she in fact too stable and rational? The advantage of madness (if it ever can be an advantage) as opposed to badness is that mental illness is usually temporary and most sufferers can make recoveries. Badness is more intractable because of the difficulty in developing a conscience if it was never established during childhood.
>
> The scientific term for such ingrained badness is psychopathy. And one of the chief characteristics of this personality type is pathological lying accompanied by a lack of remorse or guilt and a failure to accept responsibility for one's behaviour. ...
>
> Another feature of psychopathy, a lack of empathy for others, is possibly revealed when she appears, a full 25 years after the crimes, to have been devastated by a letter from one of the victim's mothers, leading as late as 1987 to her first confession of her part in the murders of Pauline Reade, John Kilbride and Keith Bennett.

Seen in this light, this confession is not the example of remorse her supporters would claim, so much as further evidence of her lack of conscience. Hindley's interview therefore appears to rule out madness, but leaves the disquieting possibility of ingrained badness, in which case expressions of remorse and guilt have to be inspected closely for evidence of attempts to manipulate parole boards. But how can we ever know when someone says they are genuinely sorry that they mean what they say? ...

It would therefore appear that Hindley has offered this interview in the belief that a display of sophisticated rationality is the antidote to the image of the raving Moors monster. But the thoughtful are often more dangerous than the thoughtless, and the change we should be looking for in her is not more reason, but more emotion.

For the crucial difference between psychopaths and the rest of the population is not their lying or manipulation, something we are all guilty of from time to time, but their lack of any emotional feeling for those who are suffering at their hands. That is why they lack the inhibitions which might otherwise prevent such heinous crime.

While the tabloid press and psychiatrists 'diagnose' individual *ills* in very different professional terms, which often means that a psychiatric diagnosis contradicts 'common sense' views favoured by the media, this is not always so, as Persaud's identification of Hindley as a morally aberrant psychopath clearly shows.

I now want to develop this idea further using Hindley's former partner in crime, Ian Brady. Like Hindley, Brady is an iconic hate figure for the tabloids. Some 20 years after being sentenced to life imprisonment, however, Brady was in the mid-1980s transferred into the high security 'special hospital' system. In recent years, his legal fight to be returned to prison where he might be allowed to starve himself to death underlines his media persona as a killer obsessed with killing – even himself. So long as Brady remains a psychiatric patient his suicidal intent is interpreted as the action of a mentally disturbed individual incapable of determining his own interests. In 2000 Brady lost a legal battle with Ashworth Hospital Authority over this issue of his force-feeding. The court concluded that his diminished mental condition meant that he was not in a position to decide his fate and he is fed daily via a plastic tube.

In 2001, following another legal ruling in the High Court, Brady was given permission to publish a book on the theme of serial killing written while a prisoner in Ashworth high-security hospital. No UK publishing house would agree to publish *The Gates of Janus: Serial Killing and its Analysis*, though eventually an independent American publisher eventually did. The British press responded with predictable moral opprobrium not least for Brady's *chutzpah* in 'analysing' psychiatrically disturbed serial killers including Peter Sutcliffe, the 'Yorkshire Ripper'. For instance, Brady's 'diagnosis' of Peter Sutcliffe's mental state leading up to the killings leads to his 'diagnosis' that 'Sutcliffe was in the disorganized, psychotic killer bracket':

> It is my opinion that Sutcliffe was in the sub-category of schizo-phrenia. In the grip of schizo-affective psychosis, and suffering from paranoid delusions of grandeur and persecution. His mission direct from God in actuality being symbiotic revenge for some real or imagined injury at the hands of a prostitute, or a female he ret-roactively deemed a prostitute or to be immoral in some way. His paranoid condition, in the early stages, was probably exacerbated by involutional psychosis or abuse of alcohol, which served as a catalyst to homicidal urges. The satisfying of those urges helped to substantiate and neutralise the threat posed by the psychic schism.
>
> (Brady, 2001, p.71)

What is important about Brady's display of quasi-psychiatric knowledge in *The Gates of Janus* is that it renders psychiatrists vulnerable to the charge that given time anyone embedded in the mental health system (even a psychopath like Brady) can psychiatrically 'diagnose'. However, in a review of (in fact more a riposte to) Brady's book entitled 'Inside the Mind of a Monster' by the writer Thomas Dalrymple (the pen name of Dr Anthony Daniels, a prison psychiatrist), he suggests that Brady's 'diagnosis' of the serial killer's state of mind when he (it is invariably a 'he') killed is instructive not for what it says about the killer's disturbed mental state but, paradoxically, for what it reveals about Brady's own state of mind:

> I have noticed in the prison in which I work that the more con-
> scienceless the prisoner with regard to his victims, the more prickly
> he is about wrongs he believes to have been done to him, however
> slight or trivial they might be. A man who won't hesitate to stab
> a complete stranger if he feels like it, will call down anathema on
> the world if his tobacco ration arrives but 10 minutes late.
> Of such company is Brady. His book is lucid and shows no signs
> of madness. He believes himself to be a victim. He believes he is a
> man of the utmost intellectual and moral integrity. He shows no
> remorse and is utterly unrepentant. He has learnt nothing in the
> intervening years. He believes himself to be the centre of the uni-
> verse, superior to all. I meet his kind every day.
>
> (Dalrymple, 2001, p.1)

This, then, is a message about the institutionalised power of a
psychiatrist to diagnose not madness but *badness* (of Brady: 'I meet
his kind every day [in prison]'). Thus, Dalrymple/Daniels, like Persaud
earlier, provides less of a psychiatric and more a *moral diagnosis*
on Brady and 'his kind'. Whatever we may think of psychiatrists'
moralising-at-a-distance, I want to suggest that each succumbs to the
logic of the tabloid format in which new definitions of the 'psychopath' are traded for an older, cultural discourse of madness and badness. I also want to stress that this is not a question of psychiatrists
falling victim to media templates, but rather accommodating them
for their own broadcast message. This professional mediation of
madness in the public sphere is distinct from but overlaps with com-
muniqués on 'mental illness' such as those emanating from Royal
College of Psychiatry anti-stigma campaigns, where lay notions of
madness are typically frowned on as unscientific and derogatory.

Murderers and the mediation of the
mediators of madness

In this section I examine the mediation of the preliminary mediators of madness. Here I include psychology as well as psychiatry
within my frame of reference since from the late-nineteenth century,
psychological explanations began to exert influence on ideas about

the 'dangerous mind' (Foucault, 1977, 2003). In fact, by the 1930s psychoanalytical ideas about the psychology of the dangerous 'other' had begun to mesh with criminological ideas. I also adopt a broadly historical perspective on the mediation of the mediators of madness to show that the print media's interest in popularising psychological responses to the topic of mental distress is not a new development, as some claim (e.g. Pilgrim and Rogers, 1999).

My analytical focus is on the mediation of psychologists and psychiatrists in the *Daily Mirror*, which for much of the twentieth century was considered a 'paper of record'. In the 1930s, a period that saw fierce circulation wars between national newspapers, the *Daily Mirror* cut by half the proportion of its news devoted to political, social, foreign and industrial news and substantially increased its amount of human-interest features and stories aimed at women readers (Curran and Seaton, 1997). For instance, in January 1938 the paper's correspondent Cyril James reported his 'search for secrets of child happiness' including accounts of 'bad' children. The popularising of psychology in this era also tallies with interest in new psychoanalytic theories for manipulating 'mass society' (Blackman and Walkerdine, 2001).

My approach is not to sample by convenience. Rather, I have identified 'positive' and 'negative' articles where psychiatric knowledge is at the forefront of public debate. My sampling of emblematic articles from the *Mirror* archive has three advantages. Firstly, it identifies where psychological/psychiatric discourse meets populist discourse on madness, criminality and dangerousness. Secondly, *Mirror* reporting on criminals who are/have been psychiatrically ill but discharged from institutional care shows how the paper has extended its news reach into the politics of mental health care. A third advantage is that it allows us to see how the paper over time has mediated the preliminary mediators of madness.

I want to consider two relevant news stories. The first from the 1930s is sensationally entitled 'THIS WOMAN WILL COMMIT A MURDER THIS YEAR' (*The Daily Mirror*, 1 July 1938, p.14) (Figure 4.1). The 'discourse moment' that prompted this particular news feature is the 1938 policy announcement that 'The Home Office has appointed a committee to investigate the causes of juvenile crime – crime at its very beginning'. The item is a personal opinion piece in which 'A Famous Psychologist Says ...', of the Home Office: 'It is throwing

Figure 4.1 'This woman will commit a murder this year', *The Daily Mirror*, 1 July 1938, p.14. *Credit*: Mirrorpix, London

millions of the public's money down a drain' and that 'I venture to prophesy that this committee will discover nothing that is not already known'. It is an all too familiar criticism that the politics and polices of criminal justice are not working properly.

What is notably different though, is how the *Mirror* trades on a 'scientized' stereotype of the 'fallen woman'. Having been thrown out of her father's 'Puritan' home, she then drifts into a life of petty crime and (future) murder. This is the stuff of detective as also *science* fiction – the idea that one can detect crimes before they happen will later become a theme of the Philip K. Dick short story, *The Minority Report*. It is not too fanciful to imagine the 'famous psychologist' (here there are also connotations of the fictional detective, Sherlock Holmes) searching for and illuminating facts in the darkened recesses of the disturbed criminal mind:

> Lets take a case I know of. Call her Amy.
> She's a criminal only in a small way.
> She's been either going to – or coming from – gaol, for the last five years.
> Regularly she has too much to drink. Then she gets into trouble for being 'disorderly', 'immoral' or associating with crooks.

Thus it is that the textual elements of the headline and photograph begin to make sense: they are borrowed from the popular detective pulp fiction of the era. The expanding capital type of the headline phrase culminating in the 'chalked' type-effect of 'MURDER' is reminiscent of, say, Hammett's Mickey Spillane novellas. The posed image of the 'fallen woman', head in arms aside a beer bottle and empty glass, illustrates that this is a story of degeneracy, of mental and moral collapse:

> Now, she has no control over this [drink and immoral] craving which always lands her in trouble. She is in despair and thinks that only a doctor might help her ....
> Obviously, it's treatment she wants – not punishment.

We can now also begin to understand what the quote adjacent to the photograph means ('It would save your money and mine if the nerve kinks that turn a crook into a murderer, were searched for and corrected before he [sic] committed that murder'): the science of psychology – not a Home Office committee – will not only detect the 'criminal type', but help it be 'corrected'. The item gives due deference to six 'conclusions' emanating from the work of a 'brilliant woman psychologist [who] has spent five years studying the psychology of 200 criminal women'. Cumulatively, they promote the conclusion, which is that

> Somebody trained in the problems of the mind and character should be available in every court.
> And prison!
> It would pay a thousand times! It would save your money and mine!

The squandering of public money on criminals is another contemporary tabloid refrain, of course. With the media politics of criminal justice in mind, the headline phrase, 'This woman will commit a murder this year', adds the weight of a scientific prognosis now not so much directed towards 'Amy' the future murderer, but towards existing government policies that do little to steer people from prison. This is how popular discourse in the late 1930s uses the science of psychology as a stick to beat the government and to moralise against the degenerate 'criminal type'. For the Institute for the Scientific Treatment of Delinquency, which is identified in the final paragraphs, it is also evidently something of a public relations coup for their work.

My second item from the 1930s is entitled, 'A TRIP ROUND HITLER'S SKULL!' (13 September 1939, p.6) (see Figure 4.2).

Published less than two weeks after Britain's declaration of war against Germany, this item ridicules and pokes fun at Hitler:

> Is Hitler a normal man? Does he know what he's doing? Does he really believe he can win, or is he driven onward by something stronger than himself? THE DAILY MIRROR PSYCHOLOGIST takes you on ... A TRIP ROUND HITLER'S SKULL!

That the *Mirror* appears to have retained its own psychologist to explain the malfunctioning of Hitler's war-mongering mind is not without significance and I will return to this point presently. First, though, the *Mirror* psychologist begins with the value of a psychological assessment of Hitler for understanding the outbreak of war:

> SOMETHING turns one man's brain into a seething, bubbling cauldron of mad hate, and the world is plunged into war.

Figure 4.2   'A Trip Round Hitler's Skull!', *The Daily Mirror*, 13 September 1939, p.6. *Credit*: Mirrorpix, London

To the psychologist, the writing on the wall is clear, for, out of his own mouth, Hitler stands condemned as a paranoiac, a pathological case, backed by a nation which he has attempted to infest with his own disease.

But, behind this madness, these hysterical screams, these fits of anger, lurks, as with all abnormal men – FEAR!

It soon transpires though, that Hitler's 'madness' is broken down into multiple psychological/psychiatric problems (not surprising given the recent outbreak of hostilities) that render his personality degenerate *in extremis*:

> Megalomania, hysteria, hate and anger are his stock-in-trade.
> His delusions of grandeur spring automatically from his delusions of persecution.

Of Hitler's use of exaltation and low pseudo-humility in his speeches:

> This ... is a recognised symptom of manic-depressive type, the man who is alternately excited and depressed. ...
> To women's meetings, Hitler will shout, 'I am yours and you are mine'.
> Thus he rids himself of his sexual energy – in a manner familiar to those who deal with the dark borderland of men's minds and the dim twilight that separates sanity from the chaos of the insane. ...

Later the popular image of psychoanalysis and schizophrenia make their appearance:

> In his childhood, Hitler loathed his father and adored his mother.
> As a result, he has acquired repressions which have affected him psychologically, so that he must spend his life trying to stifle them.
> Since the war, and his rise to power, this has become intensified into schizophrenia – split personality – which interprets any action, however innocent, as a deep-laid plot menacing his very existence.

This is hugely entertaining stuff. A bowdlerised version of psychoanalysis is conjured up to claim that Hitler hated his father and loved his mother: world war because he was mummy's boy! The familiar stereotype of schizophrenia as split personality seems weak by comparison with such a powerful yet craftily effeminate image for why the world has been plunged into hostilities. What is readily apparent here then, is that *Mirror* psychologist packs just about every popular psychiatric and psychological stereotype into Hitler's skull, which is a brilliantly realised comic metaphor for an asylum of terrifying incurables. But of course it is not just any old asylum.

The psychologist's trip round Hitler's brain trades on three enduring images of Bedlam noted in Chapter 2. Firstly, we glimpse William Hogarth's terrifying final frame of *The Rake's Progress*, a place of mad types, now relocated inside the Bedlam that is Hitler's skull. Secondly, we glimpse Ned Ward's chronicle of one of his many trips to Bethlem/Bedlam, a place where we imagine inmates rattling their chains and banging on the doors of their cell. In other words, our *Mirror* psychologist/tour guide is a modern mediator of Bedlamite madness; equivalent to the attendants to whom Bethlem/Bedlam visitors once paid a penny to gawp at inmates. Thirdly, we glimpse Jonathan Swift's brutally witty satire that England (now relocated to Germany) is a literal *mental state* ('At the end of the last war Germany was a starved, beaten nation. Hitler was typical of this suffering'). Swift, it will be recalled from Chapter 2, suggested that politicians, generals and empire builders be recruited from Bethlem, as they could not be any more insane than the ones currently in charge. Quite.

I now want to propel forward in time to the 1970s. This was an era when the psychiatric system per se was under great scrutiny as a result of a series of hospital-based scandals involving mistreatment of patients. They were not the only psychiatric scandals in this period, however. Between 1972 and 1975, the *Daily Mirror* reported on scandals concerning the release of psychiatric patients who went on to commit further serious offences including murder. Front-page *Mirror* news stories include the following:

- 'SCANDAL OF THE 'CURED' KILLER' (30 June 1972, p.1), which reports on the case of serial poisoner Graham Young released from Broadmoor who went on to carry out further mass poisonings and murders.
- 'WHY DID MANIAC GO FREE TO KILL?' (13 November 1975, p.1) on the case of serial rapist Bryan Knight.

- 'MAN WOMAN MONSTER' (13 October 1975, p.1) on the 'Cambridge rapist' Peter Cook released from Broadmoor hospital and who quickly reoffended.
- 'LET LOOSE TO SLAUGHTER' (22 November 1975, p.1) on Bryan Knight released from hospital and subsequently convicted of killing three elderly people.
- 'RELEASED TO STRIKE AGAIN' (26 November 1975, p.1) on the case of Jack Dunlop released from Broadmoor hospital and who immediately repeated his sexual offending against young boys.

In the latter case, the *Mirror* quotes a QC (Queens Council) saying of Dunlop: 'It's like letting a mad dog loose and expecting it not to bite.' The full weight of the historical stereotype of the mad as wild beasts is exemplified in a mug shot of Dunlop (captioned 'MANIAC') replete with wild hair and facial growth. The stereotypical template here is Charles Bell's 1806 sketch 'Madness', which served as a dark portent of masculine violence. The common sense implication at work is that the animal-like cunning of 'mad dogs' like Dunlop renders them beyond 'cure' suitable only for restraint. Significantly absent in the *Mirror's* reporting on the Dunlop case, indeed in each of the headline stories noted above, is criticism of the diagnostic process by which psychiatrists determined the patient/offender was safe to be released. Such criticism there is is levelled at the *system* that allows dangerous patients to be released into the community. The Dunlop front-page reproduces the front-page stories down the side of the page and refers to them as 'tragic errors'. Such a restrained approach would not last, however.

Consider a contrasting case from the mid-1990s when public concern about psychiatric care in the community was an established issue for the tabloid press. Reporting on the case of Jason Mitchell, who was discharged from a psychiatric hospital and a short time later killed three people including his own father, *The Mirror* named Mitchell as the 'Silence of the Lambs Killer' (8 July 1995, pp.4–5) (see Figure 4.3).

Further reference to one of the most popular films of the mid-1990s included the well-known image of Anthony Hopkins in his role as Hannibal Lecter, replete with straightjacket and bars over his mouth. The subheading renders use of the image clear: 'Psycho struck three times but couldn't eat his victims "because they're too old"'. The paper's coverage includes three separate stories in which the diagnostic actions

Figure 4.3 'Silence of the Lambs Killer', *The Mirror*, 8 July 1995, pp.4–5. *Credit*: Mirrorpix, London

of Mitchell's psychiatrist are increasingly emphasised. The main story detailing the full horrors of Mitchell's attacks on his victim's notes how

> The tattooed strangler launched his killing spree after being released early by a mental hospital – and only seven months after being declared fit to live in the community.

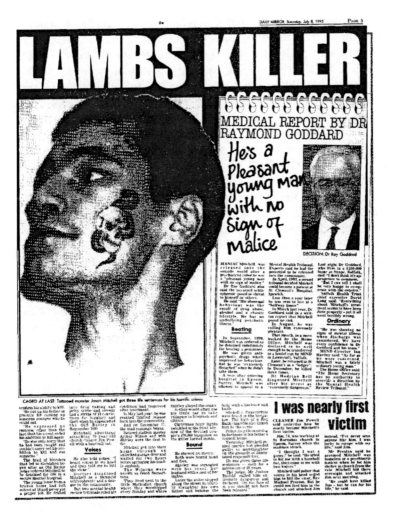

Figure 4.3 Continued

One psychiatrist described him as 'a pleasant young man with no sign of malice'.

Yesterday, 24-year-old Mitchell was jailed for life for crimes that shocked the nation.

As I noted in Chapter 1, the issue of dangerousness has come to predominate tabloid reporting on the contested policy of community care. Within this media frame, psychiatrists are targets of tabloid criticism when their patients kill members of the public. Thus, in a 'news special' positioned directly underneath the Hannibal Lecter image, is an item headlined, 'Bungle led to bloody horror'. This details the timetable of Mitchell's legal moves to end his compulsory detention in hospital for 'battering a pensioner'. The impression is one of inexorable movement from his rightful detention to wrongful release. The item culminates in the political endorsement by the Home Secretary of Mitchell's release based on a psychiatric assessment by Dr Ray Goddard.

Dr Goddard is the main actor featured in the paper's third report. Directly adjacent to a photograph of Mitchell replete with facial tattoo, is a report entitled, 'MEDICAL REPORT BY DR RAYMOND GODDARD'. The subheading reads: 'He's a pleasant young man with no sign of malice.' The latter sentence is printed as if this was Dr Goddard's own handwriting. The handwritten effect is also slightly overlying a photograph of Dr Goddard, signalling that he is being held to account for his benign assessment of Mitchell. Indeed, what we are viewing on the page is an *ironic* visualisation of medical notes complete with punctured holes as if this was Dr Goddard's own contemporaneous medical assessment at the time he was treating Mitchell. Details of Dr Goddard's psychiatric assessment are then presented:

> MANIAC Mitchell was released into the outside world after a psychiatrist ruled he was a 'pleasant young man with no sign of malice'.
> Dr Ray Goddard also said the paranoid schizophrenic posed no threat to himself or others.
> He said: 'His abnormal behaviour was the result of drug abuse, alcohol and a chaotic lifestyle. He has no underlying psychotic illness.'

The 'medical report' then continues with a further recap of the timetable noted above before juxtaposing Dr Goddard's assessment noted above with the following:

> Dr Hadrian Bell diagnosed Mitchell after his arrest as 'extremely dangerous'.
> Last night Dr Goddard, who lives in a £250,000 home at Snape, Suffolk said: 'I don't think it's appropriate to comment'.

In the Mitchell case, the psychiatric *diagnosis* itself, as well as the attendant notions of 'cure', is now part of the media story. The implication is that Dr Goddard is extremely well paid and yet is not able to diagnose that which is obvious not only to Dr Bell but *to the rest of us*. In this sense, there is here a return to an older trusted form of lay knowledge noted in Chapter 1 that says, 'you know a madman when you see one'. One only has to look at the tattooed face of Jason Mitchell to come to *any other* conclusion but that he is 'a pleasant young man with no sign of malice'.

In an era when psychiatric patients are typically viewed by the tabloids as launching unprovoked attacks on strangers without warning, then headlines such as, 'VIOLENT.. PARANOID.. SCARED.. **DANGEROUS**..,' (*The Daily Mirror*, 20 May 2005, p.11; original emphasis used red print to emphasise 'dangerous') reinforce that we have to rely on our own common sense prognosis about the likely outcome of a psychiatric condition. In the latter case of Earl Butler who murdered a policeman, the story recounts how his medical notes were not kept updated, that there was 'a five-year "black hole" in his medical notes'. Furthermore, because of care in the community, psychiatrists no longer see or hear what the rest of us can now see and hear:

> The court heard that over three years the consultant psychiatrist in charge of his case Dr Thilak Ratnayake had seen him just four times, for a total of two hours.
> Dr Thilak told the court: 'I thought he was taking his medication, progressing well, living a good life and we didn't have any concerns, even though he had a serious underlying condition'.
> But one of Butler's neighbours Iris Rose, told the court: "I would hear banging doors, swearing and him talking to himself.
> "Even when I knew no one else was in his flat, I would hear him scream, 'leave me alone, leave me alone'".

While the reporting of the cases of Jason Mitchell and Earl Butler might be viewed as damning indictment on the diagnostic limitations of the individual named psychiatrists, these examples are emblematic of a crisis of trust in expert knowledge. In the era of community care, psychiatric accounts are contested, part of a generalised collapse of trust in the authority of experts and expert systems of knowledge (see Giddens, 1990). For some, the declining faith in expertise is part of a post-modern condition in which lay knowledge is now valorised over expert knowledge. However, this grand narrative ignores how the intellectual enterprise of the mind sciences is much less secure and among the agents of psychiatric change are the tabloids.

In recent years, the tabloid press has not simply reported on mental health care in the community but has gone further, directly challenging psychiatry's authority over the diagnostic process, and how they use diagnostics to predict or assess risk of violence. Although tabloid editors and journalists may well not know it, there may be good statistical evidence for doing this, because as Monahan and Steadman (1994) point out, research reported in the 1970s and 1980s indicated that psychiatrists were consistently found more wrong than right when they predicted violence. Beyond the closed doors behind which psychiatric risk assessments take place, the tabloids are not only reporting on the limits to accuracy in psychiatric diagnostics but to some extent have encroached upon psychiatry's role as primary definers of what is or is not 'mental illness'. Tabloid ridiculing of politicians, policymakers, lawyers, scientists and other professional elites now including psychiatrists is rife, and an important constituent feature of contemporary tabloid logic, which is to reject 'what those in authority know' and bunker down instead on the side of 'what ordinary people know'.

Criminals, patients and the tabloid press

I now want to examine emblematic cases, past and current, where reporting on criminals who are also psychiatric patients reveals how tabloid logic in recent times has influenced their own primary definitions of madness and badness. The question of whether murderers diagnosed as psychiatrically ill are more mad than bad (or vice versa) is contested not only in legal and medical arenas but also in the tabloids. We shall see in the next section that the question ignites the tabloid press' own evaluative adjudications on the porous boundaries between madness and criminality. By the mid-nineteenth century, formal jurisdiction over these boundaries was handed to the nascent psychiatric profession (see Smith, 1981). By the late twentieth century, the tabloids make this determination on behalf of their readers. In so doing they mediate their own images and accounts of sickness, madness and badness.

The tabloid press is the section of the British media that has mobilised most vehemently against/on murder and moral culpability (Williams, 1997). The logic of the tabloids is to sensationalise murder (famously reflected in Alfred Harmsworth's instruction to his journalists when launching the *Daily Mail* in 1896, to 'get me a murder a day') while also demanding strict governance of murderers including over those whom it is claimed are legally beyond personal responsibility for their sins. While the tabloids do not directly influence either penal or psychiatric policy (however much they might like to claim they do), they certainly can and do set the agenda on moral issues, especially in murder cases. As we shall see, however, asserting moral governance over murderers is thwarted when killers end up not in prison but in *hospital*.

The historical roots of moral governance of the insane are not located in the organs of the popular press, however. They are instead to be found in the York asylum, which opened in 1797 to care for Quaker lunatics. Its founder William Tuke saw prison bars as sending the wrong moral-religious message to inmates and banned them from his institution. The large public asylums that were built from the mid-nineteenth century onwards were directly modelled on Tuke's moralised use of architecture (see Stevenson, 2000). This includes the Broadmoor criminal lunatic asylum built in 1860 in Crowthorne, Berkshire, and still a hospital housing the criminally insane. Broadmoor is a serviceable institution in more than one sense.

For example, one autumn afternoon in 1896, Dr James Murray, editor of the Oxford English Dictionary, arrived by train from London at Broadmoor Hospital. A distinguished-looking gentleman whom he presumes is Dr William C. Minor, a man who he has collaborated with for nearly 20 years, though they have never met in person before, greets him. He is then informed that he is quite mistaken and that he has just shaken hands with the Superintendent of Broadmoor Asylum for the Criminally Insane. His astonishment is complete when he is told that the man he has come to meet, the one person beside himself who has done more to further production of the Oxford English Dictionary is a Broadmoor patient: 'He committed a murder. He is quite insane.'

Though the two men did meet in Broadmoor, Murray was in fact aware of the criminal act that had led to Minor's incarceration. The entirely fabricated story of their meeting, Simon Winchester notes in *The Surgeon of Crowthorne*, his entertaining tale of murder, madness and the Oxford English Dictionary, is the product of a tabloid journalist's imagination. That a man so deranged as to be a murderer could also be a savant was too good a story *not* to tell. Thus, in 1915, an opportunistic American hack named Hayden Church sensationalised the encounter between Minor and Murray ('scholarship in a padded cell', to borrow Winchester's phrase) for US newspaper readers. As Church's lurid headline for the *Sunday Star* in Washington, DC, puts it:

MYSTERIOUS CONTRIBUTOR TO AN ENGLISH DICTIONARY PROVED TO BE A RICH AMERICAN SURGEON CONFINED IN BROADMOOR CRIMINAL LUNATIC ASYLUM FOR A MURDER COMITTED WHILE HE WAS IN A DERANGED CONDITION.

(Winchester, 1998, p.151)

The sensationalised story of Dr Minor's detention in Broadmoor illustrates that while the tabloid image of the deranged killer rarely matches the reality, the mentally disturbed do commit serious crime including acts of murder.

What Hayden Church clearly understood is that the figure of the criminal lunatic is the embodiment of the conflated categories of sickness, madness and badness. For example, when London's Whitechapel murderer began his killing spree in 1888, early press reports 'diagnosed' him a homicidal lunatic able to conceal his true nature and blend into the crowd (Walkowitz, 1992). This narrative has allowed at least one contemporary Ripperologist to identify James Kelly as the 'the madman who was Jack the Ripper' (Tully, 1997). Kelly was indeed a real-life criminal lunatic sent to Broadmoor in 1882 for murdering his wife. He escaped the institution in 1888 some months before the onset of the Whitechapel murders. Nothing more was heard from him until 1927 when, astonishingly, Kelly reappeared at Broadmoor asking to be admitted! Kelly conveniently fits the profile of the mad, bad and dangerous killer.

At this juncture, let me propose a thought experiment. Imagine that a Broadmoor patient escapes the institution. What do we anticipate to be the tabloid response? What about 500 escapees? In 2006, *The Sun* imagined such a scary possibility in its story of 500 foreign prisoners 'set free' from mental hospitals, which was picked up widely and reported other press, TV and radio especially when the Home Office failed to refute it (Brindle, 2006). According to the paper, 'Dangermen who have gone free are believed to include murderers, rapists and child-sex perverts' (*The Sun*, 27 May 2006, p.8). That the *Sun* story was a fabrication need not detract from the narrative pleasures of reading about the police 'desperately hunting' for 500 'dangermen' at large in the community.

With this *Sun* story in mind, I submit that it does not take much effort to imagine the moral and political outrage that would ensue if we further imagine a grisly scenario in which a Broadmoor escapee kills a child. What do we now imagine to be the media response? The scenario I have imagined of a patient's escape from Broadmoor followed by a child-killing *did* in fact happen. In 1951, John Straffen murdered two girls and was sentenced to death. He was subsequently reprieved on grounds that he had a mental age of nine years and was diagnosed by psychiatrists as being 'feeble minded'. Straffen was then sent to Broadmoor, from where less than eight months later, he escaped by scaling the wall. For four hours, Straffen was free during which time he strangled a five-year-old girl. What is remarkable by contemporary media standards is the *lack* of media coverage of this tragic event.

To be sure, on the day following Straffen's escape, the *Daily Mirror* asked questions such as: 'WHY was Broadmoor escape so easy?' and 'WHY no alarm of "lunatic at large"?' (*The Daily Mirror*, 1 May 1952 p.1). The case of John Straffen then simply *disappears*. The next major reference to Straffen in the *Mirror* is in 2002 when the same paper reports that he is now Britain's longest serving prisoner and plans to appeal his sentence. Only then is Straffen morally censured as 'evil' (*The Daily Mirror*, 13 May 2002, p.8). Today, tabloid reaction is guaranteed to be intense and is certain to include sustained scrutiny of a wide variety of issues including that of control by the hospital and the Home Office, his diagnosis, medication and so on. It will also more than likely be accompanied by demands that personnel responsible for the patient, perhaps even the Home Secretary, the politician with overall responsibility for Broadmoor's security, take *moral responsibility* and immediately resign from their post.

A similar case to Straffen concerns that of another Broadmoor patient, on this occasion released with the institution's blessing. In 1962, 14-year-old Graham Young was sentenced to 15 years in Broadmoor for poisoning his family and friend. A *Daily Mirror* headline read, 'FANTASTIC MIND OF A 14-YEAR-OLD POISONER' (6 July 1962, p.3). As in the earlier case of Straffen, the reporting makes no demand for Young to be held morally culpable. This remains the case when nine years later, Young once again begins to poison people around him. Having spent nine years in Broadmoor, psychiatrists had concluded that Young was cured and the Home Secretary duly ordered his release. Young then found work in a photographic factory where with access to chemicals, he resumed his activities as a poisoner. Within weeks he had murdered two colleagues. The consequences of Young's release from Broadmoor lent itself to the headline, 'Scandal Of The "Cured" Killer' (*The Daily Mirror*, 30 June 1972, p.1).

The scandal of Young's release from Broadmoor was certainly high profile news but like the Straffen case, there are no calls for any of the major political and psychiatric actors involved to be held accountable for their decisions. Remarkable by contemporary media standards, both these cases are not reported on in terms of, say, psychiatric or political incompetence in releasing dangerous offenders into the community so that they can repeat the very same offences. Clearly, this was a more deferential mediated environment. The Straffen and Young cases can be usefully contrasted with today's thoroughly mediatised environment in which the tabloids are doing more than mediating an issue but are *actively defining what the issue is.*

Consider recent tabloid reporting on the case of Robert Napper convicted for the 1994 killing of Rachel Nickell on Wimbledon Common. Napper has been incarcerated in Broadmoor since 2003 for other sexual crimes including rape–murder. The day following his plea of guilt for Nickell's murder, the Napper case featured heavily in every UK broadsheet and tabloid. Headlines included: 'NAILED 16 YEARS ON.. THE SCHIZO WHO REALLY DID BUTCHER RACHEL' (*Daily Star*, 19 December 2008, p.4); 'PSYCHO KILLER.. AND POLICE COULD HAVE STOPPED HIM' (*The Daily Mirror*, 19 December 2008, p.1); 'Ripper who loved to butcher blonde mothers in front of their children' (*The Sun*, 19 December 2008, pp.4–5). *The Sun* is especially interesting for its use of photograph taken of Napper apparently walking in the grounds of Broadmoor hospital having just fed hens. An adjacent editorial is headlined, 'Cosy life of a twisted killer', and puts the issue thus:

> Hens clucking at his heels, a balding man enjoys a stroll in the fresh air through a vegetable garden. But this is no gardener pottering on his allotment. This is butcher and rapist Robert Napper, a monster whose crimes stand comparison with Jack the Ripper. And the question The Sun asks today is this: Can it be right that a man who has so savagely taken the life of others is allowed to live such a cosy life himself? ...
>
> The Sun accepts that Napper is severely mentally ill. But he has done terrible things. *Common decency demands that the way our justice system treats him reflects his crimes.* Yet he passes his days pleasantly in an institution that seems to have become a cross between a country club and a variety theatre.
>
> (19 December 2008, p.8, emphasis in the original)

This particular tabloid-reporting example exemplifies what I see is a twofold interest in criminals who are also mentally ill. On the one hand, tabloid interest in the criminal resides in their human interest and sensationalist news values; their interest in the patient however, is an expression of general authoritarian/anti-liberal proclivities. These create logical tensions in their responses – the more insane a person is, the more their actions confound mainstream moral codes, the bigger the story is; but the consequence of this is that tabloid thirst for repressive judicial retribution is potentially thwarted. A convenient solution to the tension I have described is for the tabloids to act as their own primary definers on the question of criminal insanity.

The original model of 'primary definition' developed by Hall et al. (1978) explains how news media give definitional priority to those sources that enjoy 'accreditation' by virtue of being representatives of powerful institutions or of having expert knowledge. Hall et al.'s model also posits that the media are 'secondary definers', passively subordinate to the flow of definitions and interpretations emanating from accredited sources. But as Schlesinger and Tumber (1994, p.12) point out in their challenge to Hall et al.'s model, 'Within this conceptual logic, there is no space to account for the occasions on which the media may themselves take the initiative in the definitional process.'

Since Hall et al. published their original study, numerous studies of the criminal justice field have shown that the battle for primary definition is contested with no one group commanding the field (Curran, 2002).

This is a shift that has been especially noted in the sphere of 'mediatized politics' (e.g. Mazzoleni and Schulz, 1999). Media proliferation and competition have changed everything. Journalists are now inclined to adopt a 'pragmatic' disposition (Blumler and Gurevitch, 1999), to the newsworthiness of any particular story. For this reason, Hargreaves (2003) has remarked that the media are now the first, rather than the fourth estate of democracy. Thus, I want to suggest that this 'media logic' (Altheide and Snow, 1979) is more prevalent and that public discourse is more 'mediatized' than mediated. In a strange way (and contra Hall et al.) the media have become the primary definers of social and political issues. This chapter has provided examples of what I call the mediatization of madness with regard to the psychiatric profession.

In this highly competitive media context, psychiatry and mental health is a contested field with groups competing for political and public attention on the politics of mental health. Historically, this contest is most prominent in trials of the homicidal insane where public opinion on madness and badness matters. In such trials, the sharp battles between medicine and the law increased the publicity given to such cases. In courtrooms, where legal and medical opinion is vulnerable to what jurors themselves might conclude, lawyers and psychiatrists do not command primary definition. This loss of definitional power is also evident in the courtroom of public opinion. When the tabloids act as their own primary definers of madness and badness, their logic is to be *querulous* not questioning. To further develop this point, I now consider the most contentious case of madness/badness in British criminal and psychiatric history.

The case of Peter Sutcliffe, known as the 'Yorkshire Ripper', is unique for the enormity of his crimes as well as the complexity of psychiatric evidence presented to the courts. Between 1975 and 1980, Sutcliffe murdered 13 women (from 20 attempts) making him a *quantitatively* different kind of serial killer. Prior to his arrest, the Yorkshire Ripper was an iconic figure in the mould of Jack the Ripper. Unlike in 1888, the unmasking of the Yorkshire Ripper as a 35-year-old married man able to hold down employment as a lorry driver while going about the sordid business of murdering 13 women gave lawyers and psychiatrists opportunity to persuade the public that Sutcliffe was either mad or bad, but *not both*. As it turned out, as well as Sutcliffe, the doctors and their diagnoses were also put on trial in the courtroom.

Before his trial began, Sutcliffe had entered a diminished responsibility (manslaughter) plea, which the prosecution and defence councils accepted. However, on the opening day of the trial the judge rejected Sutcliffe's plea, arguing that the question of his mental state would be a matter for a jury to decide. Three psychiatrists who had previously been called upon to assess Sutcliffe's mental state attended the court and told the jury that, in their opinion, Sutcliffe was a paranoid schizophrenic. This then led to the spectacle of prosecution lawyers rejecting the findings of the psychiatrists with whom they had previously agreed with that Sutcliffe was a highly dangerous paranoid schizophrenic. The jury, however, clearly felt that they too knew a schizophrenic when they saw one, and in Sutcliffe's case he was bad *not* mad:

> Like many previous insanity trials, the Sutcliffe trial exposed the incompatibility of legal and medical discourses on insanity, organized as they were according to opposing categories of sanity/ insanity, mind/body, will/passion, nature/reason, free will/determination, responsibility/irresponsibility. Although in the end, the prosecution's legal case triumphed and Sutcliffe was found guilty of multiple murders, both law and medicine found their discourses 'severely tested' by Sutcliffe's example.
>
> (Walkowitz, 1992, p.231)

Philosophical categories are not the only interpretative frames available when it comes to judging on purported cases of criminal insanity. As Holloway (1981, p.35) notes of the media (notably the press) ridiculing the psychiatrists involved in Sutcliffe's trial, it reflects society's deep ambivalence about the intervention of psychiatry in matters of criminal behaviour. The black-and-white nature of the criminal law, unlike the murky grey area that psychiatrists normally deal with in their day-to-day work, lends itself to the adversarial choice of 'bad' not 'mad', which the jury eventually decided upon with a 10 – 2 majority verdict as an explanation of Sutcliffe's killings: 'Whereas "bad" is a label which requires an understanding of the moral, that is social, content of the acts, "mad" is a label which is used as if it were a self-sufficient explanation' (Holloway, ibid., p.36). In Sutcliffe's case, the bad not mad dichotomy remains important to the tabloids even while he is now a patient in Broadmoor hospital, subject to the discussions and deliberations of psychiatrists.

At his trial, Sutcliffe was accused of having said to a prison officer while on remand that a deal had been accepted for him to go not to prison but to a secure mental hospital, and that 'I will only spend 10 years in the loony bin' before being released (Bilton, 2003, p.502). Conveniently then, a recurring tabloid theme is that the Yorkshire Ripper might have fooled his doctors into thinking he is mentally ill, but he cannot fool the canny public. Thus, Sutcliffe's longevity as the Yorkshire Ripper has modified the question, 'is he mad or is he bad', around a new question: what now motivates the mind of the Yorkshire Ripper? A typical example is a *Daily Mirror* article entitled, 'Ripper: I Faked Insanity For Good Life in Jail' (13 November 1995, pp.6–7), the paper quotes Frank Mone, Sutcliffe's former primary nurse in Broadmoor:

> He killed because he enjoyed it. He is an evil man, it's as simple as that ...
> Peter did not show any of the signs of schizophrenia.
> His original diagnosis when he came to Broadmoor talked about the voice in his head which led him to commit murders, but he told me there was no voice.
> He was on no medication, did not suffer hallucinations, and did not show any of the classic signs of a schizophrenic.
> You would walk into a schizophrenic's room and it would be dis-organised, clothes all over the place, with bizarre pictures on the walls.
> Sutcliffe looks after everything himself – his clothes and washing – his room is neat and tidy and his paintings show flowers and portraits.
> Schizophrenics get confused, but Sutcliffe could remember every single detail of his crimes ...
> This voice would reappear again if he was being re-assessed and then mysteriously disappear.
> You have got to ask whether it is real.
>
> (p.6)

Notwithstanding the point that the nurse's description of a schizophrenic's 'disorganised' room might also describe any typical teenager's bedroom, what the quote is intended to do is to get us close to what is really going on *inside Sutcliffe's mind*, that is, he is feigning schizophrenia to enjoy Broadmoor's 'good life'. The notion that madness not badness motivates Sutcliffe's actions remains intolerable.

The tabloid assertion that Sutcliffe is bad not mad resides in the paradoxical problem of psychiatric otherness and accountability, which I shall term *crazed culpability*. If the psychiatrists' diagnosis of Sutcliffe's paranoid schizophrenia is accepted it thwarts the resolution of accountability inherent in tabloid journalism's news values. In the tabloids, psychiatric otherness matters as part of the framing of murderous characters and events, but what also matters is accountability, that is, the insane are not *like* 'us' but when they commit a crime there will be a reckoning *to* us.

In Chapter 1, I noted that Leudar and Thomas's (2000) analysis of broadsheet newspaper representations of voice hearers implied that they cannot be held morally responsible for their actions when influenced by voices. Drawing on the work of Bauman, they point out that this is not the full story when it comes to press reporting of categories such as 'schizophrenic' or 'mentally ill person', which they suggest develop according to a logic which liberates conduct from ethical constraints:

> Definition sets the victimised group apart (all definitions mean splitting the totality into two parts – the marked and the unmarked), as a different category, so that whatever applies to it does not apply to the rest. By the very act of being defined, the group has been targeted for special treatment; what is proper in relation to 'ordinary people' must not necessarily be proper in relation to it. Individual members of the group now become in addition exemplars of a type; something in the nature of the type cannot but seep into their individualised images.
>
> (Bauman quoted in Leudar and Thomas, 2000, p.171)

In the case of tabloid reporting on Broadmoor's criminals/patients, the result is an ironic twist in moral accountability. The 'special treatment' here is permanent public renunciation that their psychiatric condition is bona fide. This becomes all the more appealing in tabloid terms when special treatment can be married with other tabloid pet hates, which recently has included human rights legislation seen as being imposed on Great Britain by meddling European bureaucrats. Thus, in 2008, it was widely reported that Peter Sutcliffe was attempting to gain his freedom via human rights legislation. The bare bones of the story was enough for *The Sun* to heap the following invective on both Sutcliffe and especially his female lawyer, Saimo Chahal, who conveniently for the paper takes a high profile professional interest in the human and legal rights of patients cared for within the forensic psychiatric system:

> EVIL Peter Sutcliffe is making a bid for freedom by claiming his human rights were breached all those years ago when he was found guilty of butchering 13 young women.
> Listen up, you piece of filth – if there was any real justice in this country your human rights would be completely academic by now as you would have done the Saddam shuffle straight to the gallows after your trial.
> You and your lawyer should both shut up.
> I don't care if you're mad or bad but as far as I'm concerned your brief is definitely sad, representing scum like you ...
> I don't know how mother-of-two Saimo Chahal can live with herself as she represents Sutcliffe.
> I guess she's got broad shoulders after being crowned legal rights lawyer of the year and having her award presented by Cherie Blair.
> Saimo, I bet your children are really proud of you.

The Sun also helpfully provided a web forum for readers to express their own antipathy towards Sutcliffe as well as mistrust of his psychiatric status. Contributions to the forum include, 'He should have been hanged in the first place, looney [sic] or sane' and '[S]chizophrenia ... so which Peter Sutcliffe thinks he's now SANE??'

Psychiatric stereotypes provide a convenient template for tabloid reporting on Sutcliffe and other purported mentally ill killers. In 2003 for example, the *News of the World* traded on the popular adage about lunatics taking over the asylum declaring of Broadmoor, 'THEY'VE TAKEN OVER'. The story concerned Broadmoor's lax management and noted that, 'Dangerous lunatics like the Yorkshire Ripper and the Soho Nail Bomber are housed there. But as our report reveals today, there is rampant crime, questionable security and ludicrous luxury. Sex fiends adorn the walls of their "rooms" (note, not "cells") with porn. Inmates carry their own keys' (11 May 2003, p.17). In a rare instance of journalistic self-criticism on tabloid reporting on special hospitals, David Brindle writing in *The Guardian* has noted how it appeals to our prejudice to be told that

> in the words of the cliche, that 'the lunatics have taken over the asylum': that liberalising the old custodial regime has played into the hands of the patients; that killers and rapists, blessed with animal cunning, are running rings round helpless staff; and that therapeutic care is wasted on psychopaths who are beyond treatment and should be banged up for life.
>
> (*The Guardian*, 4 May 1997, p.19)

In an era in which the tabloids are preoccupied by defining psychiatric patients as dangerous predators, the populist notion that we waste therapy on 'killers and rapists, blessed with animal cunning' underlines the symbolic appeal of crazed culpability. Just as we recognise that deference to psychiatric knowledge is contingent on whether it 'fits' with journalistic prejudice, so we need to recognise that tabloid discourses on criminals/patients feeds into culturally embedded journalistic narratives.

Conclusion

My argument in this chapter has been that the tabloid press provide a particular and distinctive frame on the criminally insane that both originates and predominates in this media sector. The logic of tabloid reporting is that it seeks to assert a moral diagnosis on to the sins of psychiatric patients that symbolically displaces and replaces psychiatric notions of criminality as mental sickness. Asserting moral jurisdiction over the wrongdoing of the criminal/patient is the prerogative of the tabloids helped in no small measure by the delineation of the boundaries between sickness, madness and badness that is often far from clear-cut. As Busfield (1994, p.261) notes of these fluid boundaries, 'precisely because these categories are evaluative, boundary disputes cannot be settled simply by resort to the facts; they also involve the realm of judgements, values and ethics'. This is why questions of madness and badness – which is essentially the imperialistic assertion of normative values on mad people, judging them by our rules and our moral values – are a defining fixation of tub-thumping tabloids. There may well be a gravitational effect in other media sectors but I suggest that it is not a defining concern as it is in the populist press.

5
Visualising Madness: Mental Distress and Public Representation

Introduction

The old adage that says, 'madness is as madness looks', suggests a deep-rooted concern with knowing who the mad are. It also indicates a complex relationship between madness and culture that has deep historical roots: 'Ever since Antiquity, the theories of physiognomy, humours and complexions developed by Greek medicine fed the assumption that madness was as madness looked. Melancholics would be passive, listless, withdrawn, broadcasting the "black looks" produced by black bile or the melancholic humour. Maniacs would resemble the brutes to whose bestial condition their inordinate vices had reduced them' (Porter, 1991, p.92). Over the years, as 'madness' has been pressured to give way to modern notions of 'mental illness', psychiatry and psychological medicine has failed to distance itself from traditional notions of possession, violence and creativity.

For instance, I noted in Chapter 1 that the psychiatric label 'schizophrenia' has not been able to lift the popular meaning of the condition out of the realm of lurid tabloid headlines, gothic fantasy and horror. Consequently, for those with a diagnosis of schizophrenia, misconceptions about the condition (that it means a 'split personality', that they are dangerous and criminal, evil or unpredictable, and so on) invoke a double burden. One aspect concerns 'their incorporation within the role of mental patient, within a service-dominated frame of existence in which there are only limited opportunities to practise as an ordinary social agent. The other is incorporation within a set of images and assumptions about schizophrenia and the mentally ill that put the person "off the map", outside the community of ordinary human beings' (Barham and Hayward, 1991, pp.74–5). The notion that schizophrenics belong 'outside the community' jars with the inclusive thrust of community mental health policy in many Western countries.

In Great Britain, for example, the symbolic hold of madness in the popular imagination has become revivified because deinstitutionalisation policies have returned the mentally ill to share our urban space. While the principle of restoring mental patients to mainstream society is seen as laudable, both in terms of alleviating fiscal pressure caused by expensive institutional care and social pressure to end long-term incarceration, the blunt reality of care in the community falls some way short of the rhetorical promises. Despite pronouncements about the social benefits it will bring to mental patients in the community, the suspicion is that cost-cutting priorities have driven asylum closures (Scull, 1989) and that patients are left to fend for themselves.

The inclusive vision of psychiatric care in the community has also to contend with deeply ingrained assumptions that psychiatric patients *per se* pose a dangerous threat. In Britain, media coverage of the reappearance of mental patients as a familiar figure on our streets and in other public spaces, accompanies concern that voice hearers in particular, pose a risk to public safety, which as I noted in Chapter 1 is because of their presumed inability to control their response to whatever the 'voice' is saying to them: 'The hearing of voices ... signify within many media representations as an indication that the person has lost the ability to control his or her own behaviour. The voices signify that the person is a risk, having lost the ability to distinguish self and other, and is consequently viewed as a danger to both him- or herself and the public at large' (Blackman and Walkerdine, 2001, p.126). In short, the cultural image of the community psychiatric mental patient as 'mad, bad and dangerous to know' has simultaneously reinforced their 'otherness' and grounded it in everyday experience.

Madness and its representations

In Chapter 2 I noted some features of the Western artistic tradition of depicting the insane. However, representing visually what is after all an *unobservable* mental phenomenon presented a considerable challenge. The cultural historian Sander Gilman (1988) has persuasively argued that the iconography of illness is an indication of the way in which society deals with and conceptualises disease: 'The portrait of the sufferer, the portrait of the patient is ... the image of the disease anthropormorphized' (p.2). Thus, a standard icon of madness since classical times has been dishevelment; wild, unkempt, hair and tattered clothing have long provided an influential visual stereotype of madness (cf. Kromm, 2002). However, as Gilman points out that stereotypical representations are not necessarily accurate, rather, they enable the intended audience to recognise that it is madness that is being portrayed.

Consider, for a moment, the sort of images that we conventionally associate with madness: wild unkempt hair, tattered clothing, red-veined staring eyes, muttered imprecations, fists shaken at 'things' that are *not there*, outspoken dialogues to the different parts of oneself. These are stereotypical conceptions that make it clear how madness is seen: as *visible differences* of appearance and behaviour, which demarcate a symbolic boundary between 'us' and 'them'. They hark back to earlier regimes of representation in the visual arts – in painting, sculpture and print – where tropes and myths of madness as 'difference' are fast-frozen (Porter, 2002; cf. Rowson, 2001).

Gilman (1982) has also suggested that our *need* to recognise madness as 'difference' is a boundary marking in which our sense that 'we' are not like 'them', nor are we about to become like them, underlines a reassuring psychological message that the devastation of mental illness is not likely to happen to ourselves or people around us; that we can neutralise our fears as to who exactly is 'mad':

> The banality of real mental illness comes in conflict with our need to have the mad identifiable, different from ourselves. Our shock is always that they are really just like us. This moment, when we say, 'they are just like us', is most upsetting. Then we no longer know where lies the line that divides our normal, reliable world, a world that minimizes our fears, from that world in which lurks the fearful, the terrifying, the aggressive. We want – no, we need – the 'mad' to be different, so we create out of the stuff of their reality the myths that make them different.
>
> (p.19)

Gilman argues that by symbolically marking the mentally ill as different, images of madness are internalised by many individuals labelled 'mad'. This internalised mode of representation 'is not merely a mimetic reflection of the daily world of the insane, but is also tied to the long Western tradition of representing psychopathological states' (Gilman, 1982, p.99). Thus, the idea that the mad alone possess true insight into their 'condition' (an idea promoted by the anti-psychiatric movement) and which is rendered visible through their art, is naïve.

In his other work on disease representation, Gilman (1988) notes that in their own endeavours to portray insanity, artists certified as insane have played a role influencing public images of madness. For instance, paintings by Richard Dadd, who in 1843 became violently insane and killed his own father, reveals, a continuity of representation in which Dadd borrows a 'structure of expression' in which icons of madness as difference, have shaped his own artistic perception of insanity's 'difference' (Gilman, 1988, p.99). Thus, in his 1878 painting *Sketch of an Idea for Crazy Jane*, based on the popular stereotype of a lovesick madwoman, he draws on a standard iconography of madness such as ragged clothes and wild hair in conjunction. (Interestingly, Dadd, at this time incarcerated in a male-only ward for the criminally insane in Broadmoor, employed a male patient to model as the female mad icon.)

In the nineteenth century, mass incarceration in European asylums provided an unprecedented opportunity for recording and documenting the physiognomy of madness. As alienism strove to shed connotations of quackery and turn itself into a legitimate science, the notion that clinicians could describe, define and even diagnose the insane according to their *portraiture* became increasingly important (see Chapter 2 for my comments on portraits of monomaniacs painted by Theodore Gericault in the 1820s). Indeed, the ability to catalogue mental pathology from *outward* appearances underpins psychiatry's 'discovery' of madness as a phenomenon amenable to a 'clinical gaze'. The blossoming of psychiatric photography (see Chapter 2) in the second half of the century bears witness to the idea that the mad exhibited differences in appearance, which doctors and scientists could recognise and label (Gilman, 1976).

The notion that mental disorder renders the mad different in appearance and behaviour underpins Denise Jodelet's (1991) account of how social representations of madness operate in French villages, where following closure of an asylum, male ex-patients were housed with local families. Jodelet found social attitudes towards the *bredins* (or 'loonies' in the local dialect) constituted a form of 'otherness', and was 'the product, expression and instrument of a group in its relationship with otherness' (p.8). Thus, Jodelet describes how the villagers mentally divided their lodgers into what she found was recognisable 'types', from the child-like 'innocent' born with a mental disorder, the harmless 'crackpot', to a more recent criminal phenomenon. At the same time, despite careful selection of patients, there was constant discussion among villagers in respect of who was considered dangerous and who was harmless.

Jodelet also examines representations 'in the minds' of individuals as well as 'out there' in the communities in which the *bredins* had been re-housed. On the issue of protecting the community's sense of collective identity from the imagined social contagion or threat posed by integrating a negatively valued and stigmatised group, Jodelet show how symbolic practices were used to keep apart the *bredins* from the community to protect the latter group's identity. This entailed more than the discursive typecasting noted above but included ritualistic practices that were beyond dissent within the community. Thus, lodgers in every home used cutlery and wore clothes that were kept separate from the family's possessions among whom they lodged, and they were also demarcated to their own zone within the household. It is important to note that the mad were not kept apart because of any explicit recognition that they were dangerous. Rather, Jodelet describes a feeling of menace and unease underneath the surface – of lawlessness, and of physical and sexual violence, whether imaginary or real.

Jodelet's study illustrates the power that social representation has in a community to create an identity for a pre-existing social category – 'the mad'. Similarly, Knowles (2000) provides an illuminating ethnographic study of the hardship of city space for mental patients in Montreal. Her title, *Bedlam on the Streets*, vividly captures the notion that the chaos of the asylum, a gothic region populated by shadows and unsettling non-human noise and behaviour, has been transplanted within our urban centres. She uses photographs to depict the *in situ* character of Bedlam on the streets of Montreal to graphically illustrate how madness *is seen* in the context of spaces and places from which it has historically been excluded. Her photographs of disturbed and disturbing mental patients in the city reveal the ambivalent relationship that non–mentally ill society harbours towards the mad: 'they look like everyone else but they are not (Knowles, 2000, p.23).

Knowles' use of black-and-white photographs to depict the forlorn character of madness is another reminder that contemporary images of mental distress must always be placed in the context of conceptualisations and representations from previous times (see Chapter 2). The tabloid image of the dangerous schizophrenic, for example, corresponds closely with the popular image of the criminal lunatic codified in the Criminal Lunatics Act of 1800: 'The picture of the criminal lunatic took on a range of guises but almost certainly the best known and most widely publicised images of insanity in the nineteenth century, as today, surrounded cases of homicide' (Busfield, 1994, p.273). The assumption that violence and madness are intertwined has over time helped form a public register of violently insane people (Wearing, 1993) that prevents media images of the mentally ill from becoming 'too much like us'.

According to Wahl (1995), '[t]he creative professionals of today's media are ... just carrying on traditional depictions of the past. Many of today's images, from children's cartoons through prime time drama to "slasher" movies, are repetitions or residuals of long-standing popular beliefs' (p.114). I have already outlined at length my criticism of any simplistic appeal to historical continuities of mad stereotypes in Chapter 2, so there is no need to repeat my argument here. However, I have sympathy towards the general historical point that Wahl is making. For example, in his discussion of US mass media images of mental illness, he notes how the portrayal of the 'mad murderer' in movies and comics as looking 'different' activates artistic conventions that have evolved over centuries. So, while the single paintings of Gericault and Dadd have evolved into multiple images and mass reproductions of cinema and TV, images of madness as difference remain remarkably constant.

Mental distress and cultural form

In Great Britain, the policy shift from asylum to community-based mental health care has sparked interest in the mediating role of the mass media vis-à-vis promoting 'positive' representations of mental distress. The hope among mental health professionals and campaigners is that 'improved' accuracy in media images and representations of mental distress might eventually lead to a more tolerant social climate in which stigmatisation of the mentally ill is reduced. As I pointed out in Chapter 1, numerous studies of media stereotyping of mental distress conducted in the years immediately following the launch of community-care policies, have noted the saliency of media misrepresentations of psychiatric patients. Indeed, they appear to show how a limited repertoire of mental illness representations is endemic across a wide range of mass media forms. I want to suggest that assumptions of uniformity in media representations of mental distress are misleading, however.

The movement from incarceration to care in the community requires that we view representations of mental illness *historically*. The increasing visibility of representations of mental illness can therefore be seen differently from conventional approaches to (mis)representations of mental illness because it acknowledges the shifting relationship between images of madness and changing contexts of mental health care policy. Recent changes in the social organisation of psychiatry in Great Britain, for example, may have long-term implications for ways in which the mentally distressed are represented in the British media. In order to track past, present and future representations of mental distress, we need an approach that acknowledges different rules of representation governing diverse media output in different national and historical contexts.

While TV and film, for example, share formal aesthetic properties (notably, image and sound combinations), they are distinct cultural forms (see Ellis, 1982). Differences in cultural form however, are not acknowledged in any of the literature on media representations of mental distress (Harper 2005 and 2009 shares my criticism). For example, Philo et al.'s influential book *Media and Mental Distress* (1996) ignores aesthetic differences between film and TV while noting that negative stereotypes of mental distress are dominant across a range of visual media. Indeed, Philo et al. collapse all distinctions between factual and fictional representations and ignore differences between children's cartoons, teenage drama, soap opera and films shown on TV. These elisions conveniently avoid the question of whether similarities in representations of mental illness are more significant than the differences arising from the particular genres and forms being employed. By contrast, this chapter is concerned with the extent and nature of these differences across a range of television current affairs formats, and the ways they mediate visual representations of mental distress.

In their seminal discussion of British television's presentation of discourses around 'terrorism' Schlesinger, Murdock and Elliott (1983) note that 'closed' formats do not constitute the sum of its output, and point to more 'open' programming in which various 'alternative' and 'oppositional' discourses are included. Even in the US, despite the prime-time imperatives that dominate mainstream television's portrayal of mental illness, alternative voices sometimes do manage to obtain airtime and visibility, though the odds are very much against them.

Fred Wiseman's 1967 classic documentary, *Titicut Follies*, is a notable case in point. Taking its title from the annual musical revue performed by inmates and staff of Bridgwater, a Massachusetts prison for the criminally insane, its fly-on-the-wall account of prison life presents a very different portrayal of the mentally ill to the one conventionally portrayed in prime-time drama. The thrust of Wiseman's film is to visualise the prison as a space where the difference between normal and non-normal is policed. However, *Follies'* unstructured narrative collapses any identifiable distinction between normal and non-normal identities within the prison. One consequence of our looking in on the prison, then, is that it opens a significatory space in which *our* 'normalcy' is called into question: 'until we identify what is bad, mad, and dangerous to know, we cannot deny those aspects of ourselves and play others up' (Miller, 1998, p.225).

Wiseman's depiction of madness disturbs our conventional understanding of what madness looks/sounds like. As Miller again puts it, 'What is presented is utterly mad. The maddest of the lot is a leeringly unphlegmatic screw, whose delight in tomfoolery is equaled (sic) only by his craving for attention' (ibid., p.222). Thus a sequence in which the 'mad' screw sings a duet with an inmate he had previously castigated for being black appears to trade on the popular aphorism: 'you don't have to be mad to work here, but it helps!' Wiseman's open-ended style refuses to close down options for identifying the mad within the prison; inmates, guards, psychiatrists *all* appear mad. Indeed, so challenging was Wiseman's depiction of madness *and normality* within the prison that the Commonwealth of Massachusetts upheld the prison authorities' call for it to be banned from public exhibition even though they had previously granted Wiseman permission to film in the prison.

Ironically, one of the legal objections against the broadcasting of Wiseman's film is that it misrepresented prison life, by focusing on its more sensational aspects, for example, naked patient bodies, a prisoner undergoing force-feeding, a dead inmate who turns out to be the inmate previously force-fed. Thus, while sensationalism is the stock-in-trade of drama, it is not supposed to be the motivation behind actuality-based programming. Among other things, then, *Titicut Follies* fell foul of the regulating impact of genre. Its failure to avoid censure reminds us that cultural forms are mechanisms for structuring public discourse (see Golding and Murdock, 1991). It is for this reason that the diversity of documentary television programming, or lack of it, plays such an important role in the orchestration of national public debate.

Documenting mental distress

In Great Britain, for example, TV documentary maintains close affinity to the notion of public service and the viewer-as-citizen (Corner, 1986; Murdock, 1991). It is a cultural form that asserts – in the very process of its representing – an authoritative claim to 'truth' premised on a very specific 'fidelity to the real' (Winston, 1995). Embedded in documentary accounts of the world 'out there' is the pursuit of 'journalism's role in fostering interaction among the audience – in helping audience members to interact as citizens' (Dahlgren, 1995, p.28). Similarly, Corner identifies the 'radical revelatory' consequences of the documentary, where viewers are 'put in touch with one another by revealing infrastructural relations of interdependence' (Corner, 1986, p.x).

Consider Michael Apted's series of *Up* films documenting the lives of two groups of British school friends (beginning with *Seven Up* (first broadcast in1964) and updated at seven-year intervals). The films *28 Up* and *35 Up* document Neil's depression and self-imposed social exile. In *35 Up* Neil also speaks poignantly of his inability to form relationships and his deep regret that he could never meet a woman who might like him enough to consider marriage. Ironically, following the transmission of *35 Up* Neil reportedly received marriage offers from viewers all over the world! Public interest in cementing or affirming Neil's sense of 'belonging' in the community reminds us that television can initiate *relations of recognition* that move beyond an undifferentiated 'we' of spectatorship towards conditions of mutuality.

Apted's interest in documenting Neil's story of depression and social anxiety belies British television's historical indifference towards seeing and hearing about the lives of mental patients. The pioneering 1957 BBC series 'The Hurt Mind' discussed in the previous chapter is an exception here, though in that series no patient is allowed to express their views on the treatment they have received. Thus, while from an early point in its history in Britain, radio, and later television, opened itself to a range of popular voices this did not include the mentally distressed speaking for/as themselves. Mental distress, if it was spoken about at all, was debated by psychiatric experts and addressed by government policies. Mental patients were out of sight, out of mind.

However, the shift from asylums to community care in the 1990s coincided, in Britain, with major changes in the British television system. I will deal more fully with these changes in Chapter 6. Here, I want to point out that the emergence of a new populism in documentary and current affairs programmes has led to a decentring of expertise and an emphasis on common sense and grounded experience (Livingstone and Lunt, 1994). The arrival of populist TV means that marginalised voices have been granted more extensive access opportunities to speak about their experiences than in varieties of paternalism associated with the ethos of public service (Corner, 1994).

The more or less contemporaneous shifts in British TV and mental health systems invite consideration of the terms on which the mentally ill are given a public voice (also addressed in Chapter 6). However, television's production of moving images means that viewers are also able to 'witness' *how things appear* as much as what is said. This is important for subjects who may not have an opportunity to speak directly to others or make known their testimony. In TV programmes, claims to plausibility and authority depend as much on what speakers look like as on what they say. Consequently, televisual images of madness need careful attention if we are to understand the circumstances surrounding mentally ill people's public to representation (Cross, 2002, 2004).

In order to explore televisual images of madness this chapter draws on public representations of mental illness in three contrasting forms of British current affairs television. They are: Whose Mind Is It Anyway? (*Panorama*),[1] A Place of Safety (*Disguises*),[2] and Mad, Bad or Sad? (*Video Diaries*).[3] Each programme deals with issues relating to the release of mental patients into the community following the onset of care in the community legislation in England and Wales in 1993.[4] Despite their contrasting formats, however, a common thematic prompts each programme: understanding the implications of releasing mental patients from asylums. It is significant, therefore, that each of the selected programmes take schizophrenia to be at the core of public concern about mental health care in the community.

Visualising madness

The image of the irrational is never far away. As Gilman notes, 'underlying our understanding of the mentally ill is the continued presence in society of older images of the insane, images that overtly or covertly color our concept and serve to categorize them upon first glance' (Gilman, 1982, p.iii). Following Gilman, we can ask how television programmes depicting schizophrenia represent visually what is after all an unobservable phenomenon *such that viewers can recognise that schizophrenia is what is being portrayed.* For many programme makers, communicating about psychiatric illness is not just a question of accessing personal testimony about the experience of being ill. It is often a matter of *imaging the illness* so that viewers can see what it looks like. This representational challenge links contemporary television producers and other visual artists to painters and sculptors in earlier centuries.

I begin *Panorama*'s examination of Community Supervision Orders (CSOs) to control mental patients who refuse medication. 'Whose Mind Is It Anyway?' opens with the tragic story of a paranoid schizophrenic woman who killed her own two children weeks after her discharge from a mental hospital. Viewers are told that she was not receiving medical support in the community and was therefore left alone to supervise her children. The story of the double murder therefore sets the tone of the programme by constructing violent criminality as an *inevitable* consequence of asylum closures and lack of medical supervision of the mentally distressed.

The popular image of the 'mad' as aggressive and out of control, unable to normalise their actions, finds support in the programme's images of the mentally ill as criminal and potentially dangerous. The programme's makers provide a concrete illustration of potentially dangerous mentally ill people who would be affected by the CSO scheme:

> Presenter: Only those regarded as a threat to themselves or others would have Orders imposed. The charity MIND estimates as many as four thousand sufferers could be affected.

As the presenter's voice-over proceeds, the image track shows one of the apparently 'four thousand sufferers' who represent a possible threat to self/others. We see a man playing pool, followed by a close-up of his face at the moment the narrator says that CSOs would only be imposed on those regarded as a threat to 'others'. His facial expression and dishevelled appearance is key to his identification as a possible threat to others. As I noted earlier, dishevelled hair and tattered clothes is a standard icon of dangerous insanity, which is fully exploited in this shot. The notion that the violent or the dangerous can be identified by their facial appearance has a long history in Western representations of madness, and according to Gilman (1988) derives from 'anxiety tied to a perceived tenuousness of life' (p.11). By picturing those who may harm us we are reassured that we could identify danger before it befalls us. In the context of *Panorama*'s concern about community supervision of the mentally ill, the idea that we can *see* who is dangerous has obvious appeal. The CSO scheme thus finds support in the programme's representation of the pool player as an identifiably dangerous person.

At the heart of *Panorama*'s concern about community care is the apparent absence of a monitoring system to ensure that potentially dangerous mentally ill people take their medication (the corollary of which is that mentally ill people will *not* become dangerous *if* they take their medication). Underpinning the controversy around CSOs, however, is the use of force to implement the scheme. According to *Panorama*, this entails balancing mentally ill people's civil liberty (their right to refuse medication) against public safety. In order to explore this issue, the programme makers mobilise evidence from a CSO scheme operating in the American City of Madison. The US scheme is described by the programme presenter as offering, 'Better care [than in Britain] combined with greater force'. In the process of showing viewers the 'greater force' of the US scheme, the equation of mental illness with danger is embodied in the form of Roger Tollerson. He is represented as the type of schizophrenic whose behaviour necessitates whatever amount of force that it takes to properly protect the public. In Madison, viewers are informed, the use of force to control the mentally ill is the responsibility of specialist police officers.

The sequence in question begins with the *Panorama* presenter inside the car of one of the specialist officers as he takes an emergency call. To-camera, the presenter explains to viewers that a 'mentally disturbed man has been seen brandishing a knife at a local restaurant' and that 'if this man needs medication, as is highly likely, then come what may the police will see him put on treatment tonight whether voluntarily or by force'. We then see a shot of a police car (with siren sounding) moving at speed. In the next shot we see Tollerson in the back of a police car apparently talking to himself. The presenter describes the scene thus:

> A chronic schizophrenic has been arrested. It looks like Roger Tollerson has not been taking his medication.

The myth that schizophrenics are *likely* to be dangerous is amplified by the dramatic image of the speeding police car and the flashing police siren, both of which signify imminent danger. A sense of disaster narrowly avoided is generated in the very next shot where we see a knife on the dashboard of a police car. At this moment Tollerson is transformed into a potentially homicidal schizophrenic whose *unobservable* violent intentions are rendered graphically *observable* in the image of the knife. The presenter's own (patronising) assessment of the situation ('It looks like Roger Tollerson has not been taking his medication') provides a simple cause-and-effect explanation in which Tollerson's dangerous behaviour is the result of a failure to take his medication. The clear implication is that without medication schizophrenics are *compelled* to act in a potentially dangerous and criminal manner.

The connection between schizophrenia and violent criminality is fully realised (indeed, *resolved*) in a final image where we see Tollerson in handcuffs being escorted back to hospital by the police. The use of this image to close the sequence conveys a strong sense of resolution: Tollerson is about to receive appropriate and *deserving punishment* for his menacing public behaviour. While this resolution may provide a certain degree of reassurance, for the programme's viewers the image of Tollerson being led away handcuffed puts in question the wisdom of current British mental health policy in which potentially dangerous mental patients are living among us unsupervised.

In *Disguises'* 'A Place of Safety', the series reporter Adam Holloway, investigates the policy of care in the community by impersonating a homeless, voice-hearing schizophrenic. It will be recalled from my brief comments on this programme in Chapter 4 that the format of the series was to employ hidden cameras as an aid to reporting areas of public controversy, and also to use reportorial disguises as a way of obtaining clandestine footage. This involves Holloway acting out different roles, often over a period of several weeks. It is this in-role performance that forms the 'core' footage of each programme that is then made sense of by Holloway's out-of-role address to the viewer. His reportorial subterfuge combines an extended view of schizophrenic experience 'from the inside' (as it were) while retaining the credentials provided by expert analysis and 'objective' commentary.

The verisimilitude of his in-role behaviour is crucial to the success of his public performance as a 'disturbed schizophrenic'. To authenticate his performance, Holloway first establishes that homeless people *do* behave strangely in public places and that this is a sign they are mentally distressed but do not receive psychiatric help. Using footage obtained by his hidden camera, Holloway presents the spectacle of apparently disturbed (and disturbing) homeless people as icons of the failure of community-care policies. Showing viewers visibly 'strange' behaviour is a crucial part of the programme makers' aim of visualising how community care policies *are* failing the very people that they are intended to serve. However, the care in the community policy is also shown to be failing more than just the mentally ill.

Holloway arrives in London and performs his role as a homeless schizophrenic. Following his apparent failure to find accommodation he explains his decision to move to Hackney and impersonate a disturbed schizophrenic:

> With three hundred per cent more schizophrenics in this borough than the national average, there should be help here [pause].

I impersonate a schizophrenic shouting at his voices in the street
[pause]. Nothing happens. Are people used to this kind of thing
here?

Holloway's in-role plight is signified by the increasingly dramatic
nature of his actions. Throughout the sequence, tension-enhancing
music is used to heighten the sense of drama as the action unfolds.
The visual track shows his attempts to attract public attention by
firstly shouting at his voices in the street, then lying down in the
middle of the road and finally, stripping off his clothes with the aim
of being sectioned (forcibly detained) by the police under the Mental
Health Act. The veracity of his in-role behaviour is guaranteed by
the 'realism' of his strange and potentially dangerous behaviour,
a realism given authenticity by earlier use of footage showing real
homeless people acting strangely (see Chapter 4). Underpinning
Holloway's performance is a presumption that without medical help
schizophrenics will *inevitably* engage in unpredictable, bizarre and
dangerous acts of madness such as lying down in the middle of the
road. This presumption reaches its climax in his impersonation of a
schizophrenic whose behaviour eventually attracts the attention of
the police. Holloway introduces the sequence thus:

To attract attention and get help I begin taking my clothes off
in the street. As a last resort, I try to get the police to section me
using their powers under the Mental Health Act. The police have
powers to take a mentally ill person to a place of safety, either a
police station or a hospital.

Holloway's failure to get help from the police is certainly a dramatic
moment in the programme and perhaps justifies the programme
makers' use of a reporter impersonating a schizophrenic (though
this is arguable). The police's unsympathetic reaction to his in-role
expression of fear about hearing voices (one officer sarcastically tells
him to put his clothes back on and 'go and hear your voices somewhere else', while another waves at him from close quarter and says
'bye-bye' in a childish voice) provides visual and verbal confirmation that care in the community does not work (at least in Hackney)
and that the public cannot rely even on police protection from disturbed schizophrenics. It is here that the failure of community-care

policies is rendered alarmingly visible in the image of a 'disturbed' and potentially dangerous schizophrenic left to roam the streets unsupervised.

The policemen's apparent inaction set up the final sequence of the programme as Holloway to-camera admits that his attempts to find a place of safety have been 'patchy' and that he is now forced to join the ranks of homeless mentally ill people on the streets. However, the social *implications* of the policemen's actions are left to the viewers' own imagination. Deinstitutionalisation thus provides a catalyst for the programme's generation of *anxiety* about the public behaviour of schizophrenics. It is a concern that they will 'turn' their internal madness outwards *onto us* and hurt us, which underpins the programme maker's decision to cast Holloway as an increasingly desperate and (by implication) increasingly 'dangerous schizophrenic'. While the danger posed by Holloway in-role is self-directed, the implication established by the thematic development of the programme is that it is only a matter of time before self-harm becomes transformed into harm to others. Thus, the main finding uncovered by Holloway is not that the mentally ill roam the streets unsupervised, but that they are allowed to do so *despite* their recognisably disturbed and disturbing behaviour.

Disguises' method of combining journalistic reportage with personal testimony based on grounded experience enables Holloway to present a view of the experience of mental illness 'from the inside'. Despite his intermittent first-person testimony, however, we never come close to knowing what it's actually like to be a schizophrenic living in the community. The best we can hope for is perhaps a voyeuristic pleasure in thinking we are seeing something of the experience of the other. Another more radical option is the *Video Diary* approach in which the BBC's Community Programmes Unit provides diaries for those whose voices have traditionally been marginalised by professional broadcasters.

Sharon's video diary, entitled 'Mad, Bad or Sad?', is presented to viewers as a search for her own mother whom she has never met. Sharon theorises that this experience has caused her severe mental distress including her voice hearing experiences (see also Chapter 6 for more discussion on the topic of voice hearing in relation to *Video Diaries*). The implication is that by exploring the circumstances of her adoption, she might slay those 'voices' from her past that torment her present. The notion that Sharon is a traveller/explorer is drawn upon throughout her diary as she takes viewers on a journey to significant places in her life: the white family with whom she was fostered as a child, the asylum where she was institutionalised, the prison she was sent to following an arson attack as a cry for help. By showing these places she provides a visual map that pinpoint the principal locales of her career as a schizophrenic. Thus, the possibility that her diary has been purposefully (i.e. *professionally*) edited as a journey of 'self-discovery' cannot be discounted.

Despite my unease surrounding the editorial circumstances of its story-telling construction, Sharon's diary provides a tangible opportunity to explore Gilman's assertion that stereotyped images of madness are internalised by individuals labelled as 'mad'. It is worth emphasising here that Gilman is not using the term 'internalised' to refer to an ideological fog that descends upon and envelops those labelled mad. Rather, his thesis is that the artistic work of the mentally ill reveals highly symbolic representations of internal states for which a structure of expression has been found in the representation of the idea of madness (Gilman, 1988). In other words, images of madness produced by the mad convey traces of the dominant modes of representing madness as difference. Consider Sharon's opening address to viewers:

> You probably don't think you'll crack up. The chances are you might then you'd be a nutter like me.

Here, Sharon's use of the term 'nutter' reveals her own internalised recognition of her own difference from 'non-nutters', a difference that she conveys throughout her diary. For example, when she introduces her friends from a mental health social club she says: 'A lot of people don't want to know us, so all us nutters stick together.' At the same time, by using 'nutter' she reveals her willingness to identify, though not necessarily *identify with*, the popular terminology that marks her as being somehow 'different'. It deliberately unsettles the fixity of the binary opposition nutter/non-nutter as a distinction between two categorical opposites.

By using it in an address to viewers, Sharon *intentionally* enters into a dialogue about the labelling of her 'difference' from which she (as a 'nutter') is usually excluded. This enables her to publicly affirm her sameness to other non-nutters while acknowledging her difference from them. This apparent contradiction suggests ambivalence towards her internalised sense of difference, which is encapsulated in her choice of 'Mad, Bad Or Sad?' as a subtitle for her diary. That her schizophrenic label is something she *acknowledges and resists* gives the viewer an insight into the difficulties of living with and within this powerful categorisation.

Sharon's sense that she is *visibly* 'different' is articulated at the end of a sequence in which Sharon and friends dance in front of the camera. Their dancing is self-consciously hammed up as the camcorder focuses on each of them in turn. Their behaviour is recognisably 'normal', in the sense that it is a party scene and that people often exaggerate their 'performance' when filmed by a camcorder. At one level the sequence conveys the obvious 'normality' of their fun in playing to an audience (both real and imagined). On another level, however, it reveals something fundamental about Sharon's internalised sense of abnormality. Following her dance, she collapses exhausted into a chair and to-camera says, '[t]he lunatics have taken over Stretford' (i.e. the area of Manchester in which she lives). This comment reflects her self-acknowledgement that their behaviour *can* be seen as something other than strictly 'normal' camcorder-related behaviour. This verbal anchor renders the meaning of what is shown (the dancing) in at least two distinct ways.

Firstly, her statement can be read as a deliberate pun on the widely known aphorism, 'the lunatics have taken over the asylum'.[5] This is something many viewers would immediately recognise as a broadly comical reference to the madcap humour/dancing often generated by the presence of a camcorder at parties, weddings and other social events. At the same time, Sharon's comment 'fixes' the behaviour (not now dancing, but something potentially more sinister) exhibited by Sharon, Mickey and their friend in relation to her own internalised perception of what 'mad' people look and act like. In other words, she articulates her sense of difference at the same time that 'normal' camcorder-related behaviour is being engaged in.

I am reminded here of how the British artist Tracey Emin deployed her own madcap dancing in her video performance-piece, *Why I Never Became a Dancer* (1995). Filmed on similar cheap grainy super 8 medium used by Sharon to record her mad/not mad dance, Emin's film recreates her attempt to win a disco dance competition in her home town of Margate where she was jeered by local lads, some or most of whom she had previously had sex with, hypocritically calling her 'slag'. Who or what is mad here? Is it Tracey Emin for wanting to visualise her personal shame and humiliation in the form of a public performance? Or is it in wanting to create public art out of a highly personal narrative in which one's vulnerability is on public show? For both Emin and Sharon, these questions matter because their dancing is an unsettling performance in terms of seeing/not seeing *some kind of madness*.

In Tracey Emin's film, the recreated scene of public humiliation shifts to another scene in which we see Emin in an empty room dancing to the Sylvester disco song, 'You Make Me Feel (Mighty Real)'. As she dances, she reels off a list of men's names before saying 'this one's for you'. As Sally Hunt (2003) points out, Emin's spewing out of these men's names while she 'spins joyfully out of their orbit, like a Whirling Dervish, liberated and ecstatic', is cathartic for artist and viewer. In this sense, Emin's whirling dervish/dancing is resolved; in Hunt's estimation at least, Emin's mad dancing liberates Emin from the conformity of being only seen as a slag. I would also add that in popular parlance, a Whirling Dervish is seen as a kind of frenetic madness and that Emin's 'whirling dervish' dance in her video represents not only some kind of madness but also that the outcome of her madness is her art.

In Sharon's own case however, the ambiguity about what we are seeing/not seeing in her dance is purposively *not* resolved. This reflects not only the amateur status of the *Video Diary* format, but also Sharon's own preferred *ambivalence* towards her self-identity as schizophrenic/not schizophrenic. The absence of any authoritative interpretation of the madcap dancing sequence ultimately leaves the viewer with a sense of uncertainty about the *status* of the images as representations of 'lunatic' behaviour. How viewers themselves respond to this *uncertainty of meaning* depends of course on the fixity of their own internalised myths about the public (and private) behaviour of those labelled as lunatics/schizophrenics.

Conclusion

My aim in this chapter has been to show that televisual images confirm that schizophrenics in the community are an identifiable public figure, for the most part because of their visibly 'strange' behaviour, which most of us can recognise even though we are not trained psychiatric professionals. My discussion has sought to understand the figure of the schizophrenic as part of a *continuity of representation* that has been enshrined in public images of madness over centuries. Today's TV programme makers (including the amateur Sharon) are, in some ways, reproducing traditional iconographies of madness. As such, televisual representations of mental patients carry a heavy burden for those who are assigned the role of being different.

Herein lies the problem that I identified in Chapter 1, which is that despite (or perhaps because of) no longer separating the mad from the rest of the population, we no longer know exactly who or where the mad are. Not knowing who these people are, it is perhaps no surprise that they have become objects of our concern and fear. It also suggests how, in the absence of institutional boundaries, *symbolic boundaries* help assuage anxiety about those whom we suspect are 'not like us' (See Rose, 1998 for similar arguments relating to television dramatisation of mad folk living in the community).

As the central institution of the public sphere, television is the epicentre of public discourse about what it means to a 'normal' citizen. This means that in TV programmes, claims to normality require participants to *look like they belong* in the world of citizenry. In the context of mentally ill people's struggle for social inclusion, visual images representing them as though they belong elsewhere are manifestly unhelpful. If we want to improve the social prospects of people with mental illness then images suggesting psychiatric symptoms persist, even after the person has left the hospital/asylum, can undermine their claim to citizenship (see Sayce, 2000).

Nevertheless TV programmes depicting mental illness do not inevitably cohere around stereotyped images of 'dangerous looking' or 'abnormal' people. As *Video Diaries* illustrates, instead of reproducing symbolic boundaries between 'us' and 'them', as in the 'closed' genres and formats of prime time television, more 'open' TV formats help initiate 'boundary crossings' into the everyday life-world of the mental distressed similar to the way that mental health care in the community policies erode the physical boundary separating the mad and the non-mad. The challenge that this changed context of care invites for future programme makers is how to mobilise images of mental illness that refuse cultural stereotypes of madness as 'difference'.

This begs the question, though, as to whether 'alternative' forms of public representation change, or simply ameliorate, conventional representations of madness that have built up over the centuries. Sharon's self-representation opportunity in 'Mad, Bad Or Sad' is one way of reconstructing the public image of schizophrenia (as difference/not difference, other/not other). But her ethnographic insights into the voice-hearing world does not in itself provide a corrective balance to the historical and culturally rooted image of madness as difference, including those steadfastly recycled by both the *Panorama* and *Disguises* examples I have discussed. It merely highlights the urgent need for other kinds of 'open' – rather than 'closed' – representational formats that refuse to settle for a highly restricted public image of mental distress. Along with Graham Murdock, I now want to explore the reasons why internet and not television forums are being used by voice hearers to respond to this need.

6
Speaking of Voices: Mediating Talk about Mental Distress

Lost in translation

We encountered London's Bethlem asylum and Bedlam, its mythical other in Chapter 2. For well over a century (from 1728 to 1855), medical care of the inmates was entrusted to successive generations of the Monro family. Like many practitioners of the 'mad-doctoring trade' at that time, they combined their public duties with lucrative private practices ministering to the better-off. In 1766, John Monro kept a notebook of his work with paying patients, detailing how he came to decide whether someone was mentally ill and what treatment to proscribe. Although he was often harsh in his judgements, dismissing patient's speech as 'nonsense' or complaining that they were too 'full of talk' and liable to 'ramble', he did at least listen to what they told him (Stewart, 2003, p.12). In contrast, the speech of those committed to Bedlam, who were mostly either too poor to afford home care or deemed to be a danger to the community, was largely ignored and many were physically restrained with 'leg irons, manacles, straitjackets and other instruments for intimidating patients' (Wing, 1997, p.3). This overt brutality ended in the 1850s following an investigation by the Lunacy Commissioners into the maltreatment of two female patients, but the practice of discounting patients' talk continued.

The conception of orderliness that crystallised in the mid-nineteenth century was built around the practical application of rationality. The emerging role of the citizen, with the right to participate fully in social and cultural life, carried obligations as well as rights. The model citizen was expected to inform themselves on public issues, interrogate the relevant evidence, engage in rational deliberation on competing proposals and register their political choice in the silence of the voting booth. The shouting, incoherent strings of words and 'talking to oneself' associated with madness was citizenship's direct antithesis, the dark other of disorder, and 'Bedlam' passed into common usage as a description of random, disruptive, undisciplined noise and impulsive behaviour (Bailey, 1996, p.54). Having stepped outside the bounds of reason, patients were judged to be 'a danger to themselves and others, and society therefore [had] a right and a duty to control them' (Maitland, 2001, p.77). Confinement to an asylum 'sought to shut them up, literally and metaphorically, in the process invalidating and essentially eliminating their own voices' and 'all too readily' dismissing their speech as 'the raving and importunings of the irrational, epiphenomenal noise of no interest or substantial significance' (Scull, 2006, p.49).

'Visiting an Irish lunatic asylum around 1850, two inspectors were buttonholed by an inmate who complained bitterly that, "they took my language from me"' (Porter, 2002, p.158). This sanctioned theft was central to the institutionalised approach to treatment. Patients' talk about disturbing experiences was treated as data that contributed vital clues to diagnosing their condition and assigning it a label. Once translated from everyday speech to the professional lexicon of medicine, the origins of these experiences and their meaning to the sufferer were of no further interest. Of the various experience patients recounted, claims that they could hear voices came to play a central role in diagnoses, particularly of schizophrenia.

Within the medical model that accompanied psychiatry's increasing domination of the treatment of mental distress, from the mid-nineteenth century onwards, hearing voices has been classified as an 'auditory hallucination' indicating serious mental malfunctioning with little or no intrinsic meaning. Psychiatry's claims to be a branch of medicine rooted in studies of physical disorders separated it sharply from psychoanalysis. In place of a 'talking cure' based on encouraging patients to speak at length about the experiences that most disturbed them, psychiatry worked with drug treatments designed to address imbalances in brain chemistry. The practical corollary is that even though hearing voices is a patient's experience, it is better understood as a psychiatric symptom. As David Ames, a specialist in treating the elderly, recalls, 'When I began training in psychiatry in 1982 I was taught that the form of patients' unusual experiences was usually more important than the content when making a psychiatric diagnosis' (Ames, 2000, p.1537).

A decade earlier, David Rosenhan, an American psychologist with a joint degree in law, set out to show that assuming that voice hearing indicated a serious condition requiring treatment, was likely to generate mistaken diagnoses and treatment that violated patients' human rights. He and eight collaborators, including a psychiatrist and three psychologists, presented themselves at a range of mental institutions saying that friends had told them they were good hospitals and claiming to be hearing a voice saying 'thud' (Rosenhan, 1973), a word chosen deliberately 'because nowhere in the psychiatric literature are there any reports of a person hearing a voice that contains such obvious cartoon angst' (Slater, 2005, p.66). Although they exhibited no other symptoms all were committed to a hospital ward, where, despite reverting to their normal behaviour immediately after admission, they were kept for some time. Rosenhan and seven of his colleagues were diagnosed as 'schizophrenics'. The remaining participant was judged to be suffering from manic depression. Thirty years later, Lauren Slater, repeated Rosenhan's experiment and was diagnosed as having 'psychotic depression'. She was not admitted to any ward but instead was prescribed a course of drugs that she was expected to administer herself (Slater, 2005, Chapter 3).

Her experience points to two important developments. Firstly, despite mounting criticism the medical model remains dominant. Indeed, the 'introduction of new technology for studying the brain and by the development of molecular genetics and the human genome project' (Moncrieff, 1997), coupled with breakthroughs in pharmaceutical research that have produced new drug treatments, has strengthened it. Secondly, the reluctance to admit her to hospital illustrates the decisive shift that has taken place in the location of treatment as the old asylums have been progressively closed and patients either moved into specialist units in general hospitals or discharged into the 'community'.

The original drive to build asylums had been fuelled in large part by the bad reputation gained by the 'trade in lunacy' conducted by private madhouses towards the end of the eighteenth century (Freeman 1997, p.34). Well planned and run public institutions were seen as a thoroughly modern solution to the problem of managing mental distress effectively and humanely prompting the prominent nineteenth-century campaigner, Sir George Paget, to declare that public asylums were 'the most blessed manifestation of true civilisation the world can present' (quoted in Scull, Mackenzie and Hervey, 1996, p.69). Despite these lofty ambitions, asylums never achieved a monopoly of treatment however, and continued to co-exist alongside private forms of care in the community. But as tales of institutionalised abuse accumulated disillusion set in and the original meaning of asylum, as a place of safety, was almost entirely stripped away. As we saw in Chapter 3, Elizabeth Cochrane's savage expose of patient mistreatment in the Blackwell's Island asylum, for Pulitzer's *New York World*, established a vogue for undercover reporting and presented asylum patients as open to exploitation and particularly vulnerable because of their incompetence. This image of victimhood is still very much part of public discourse but it co-exists uneasily with the still resilient image of dangerousness and threat rooted in the assumption that because the mentally distressed lack the restraints of reason they are liable to act impulsively and often violently. In a 2008 survey of the general population almost half (49%) of those asked agreed that a mentally ill person 'cannot be held responsible for their actions' (up from 44% the pervious year) (Department of Health, 2008) and 34% of those polled in a 2009 survey were convinced that 'people with schizophrenia are likely to be violent' (Brimelow, 2009).

The deconstruction of the asylum system began earlier in Britain than on the other side of the Atlantic, prompting a US psychiatrist visiting in the mid-1950s to express unreserved admiration for the growth of a community-oriented psychiatry, which assumed that since 'mentally ill patients are ... competent to control their own behaviour except for brief periods' they can safely be released from institutional care (quoted in Jones, 1993, p.153). This shift towards community-based mental health services did not mean that the hospital had no role to play in the delivery of treatment. The mixed economy of care continued. The central issue was where the balance should be struck between the practice of confinement and the principle of restoring health service users to mainstream society (Barham, 1992).

By the 1980s however, there was growing criticism of the community care strategy, particularly among those who saw the reduction of costly long-term psychiatric beds driven more by the Conservative government's desire to reduce public expenditure and cut taxes than by clinical or social considerations (Busfield, 1986). Concern was intensified by mounting evidence that rather than re-entering the 'mainstream' many discharged patients found themselves confined to the margins. As shopping malls and city centres became subject to more and more intensive surveillance and policing using CCT cameras and private security agencies, anyone acting 'oddly' or 'suspiciously' was increasingly likely to be expelled or moved on. As Caroline Knowles' powerful ethnography of Montreal shows all too clearly, the mentally distressed found themselves steered away from zones of public interaction and confined to a floating world of 'drop-in' centres, church halls, homeless shelters, and bed and break-fast accommodation (Knowles, 2000).

In Britain, the lack of a co-ordinated discharge policy prompted widespread concern that the system was unable to guarantee the supervision or oversight needed to prevent the mentally ill posing a danger to themselves and others. And as we saw in Chapter 1, this fear was vividly dramatised by two widely publicised cases in 1992 involving diagnosed schizophrenics. In December, Jonathan Zito was randomly stabbed to death in the London Underground by Christopher Clunis, who was later incarcerated in Broadmoor high-security hospital. On New Year's Eve, Ben Silcock, who had tried, but failed, to gain admission to his local psychiatric hospital, climbed into the lion enclosure at London Zoo and was badly mauled.

Fuelled by public concern about safety, in 1997 the newly elected Labour Government signalled its view that care in the community was a failed policy and the following year announced plans for changes to the mental health laws. In 2002, it introduced draft legislation revising the existing system, which required the mentally ill to be admitted to hospital before they could be compulsorily treated, and allowing for compulsory treatment in the community. This proposal was met by concerted protest from an alliance of over 50 organisations in the mental health field arguing that it pandered to popular stereotypes of dangerousness, overplayed the risk to the public and eroded patients' rights. The argument for tighter controls over the mentally distressed surfaced again in January 2007, when the House of Lords discussed introducing an element of forced incarceration within a revised system of institutional care.

This movement is of particular concern to voice hearers who have been diagnosed as schizophrenic because of the strong connotations of dangerousness attached to their condition. Popular representations tend to follow closely the medical model in depicting 'The hearing of voices … as an indication that the person is a risk, having lost the ability to distinguish self and other, and is consequently viewed as a danger to both him- or herself and the public at large' (Blackman and Walkerdine, 2001, p.126). This conception has not gone uncontested however.

On the contrary, the status of Voice Hearing as a clear schizoid symptom had come under intense scrutiny in the 1990s, with an increasing number of Voice Hearers, supported by sympathetic professionals, challenging its role as 'a stable and authoritative diagnostic determinant' (Maitland, 2001, p.71). In place of psychiatry's conventional construction of the condition as solely a signifier of 'disease and illness' with no intrinsic meaning or relation to the patient's biography, voice hearers were invited 'to focus on the voices, recount what they are saying, to record them, document them and integrate them into their lives' (Blackman, 2000, p.60). Voice hearers and their families have vigorously promoted this alternative view, but the core ideas were originally formulated by a Dutch psychiatrist, Marius Romme, on the basis of his clinical experience, and developed in collaboration with science journalist, Sandra Escher.

In the mid-1980s, a Dutch woman, Patsy Hage, was hearing intrusive and troubling voices. In her sessions with Romme, then working as Professor of Social Psychiatry at the University of Limberg, she challenged him to accept that voice hearing was a real experience for her and not to dismiss it as an illusion and pigeonhole it as a psychotic symptom. In response, he set up a series of meetings between Hage and other voice hearers and was struck by their inability to manage their experiences. In an effort to contact people who were coping Romme and Hage appeared on a popular Dutch television programme talking about voice hearing and invited people to contact them.

Of the 700 hundred persons who did, 150 claimed to have effective managing strategies. In 1987 this led Romme to organise a conference where voice hearers could exchange experiences and then, together with Sandra Escher, to establish a permanent contact network, *Stichting Weerklank* (Foundation Resonance). This intervention was based on two founding principles: one conceptual, the other practical. Romme insisted that there was no necessary link between voice hearing and schizophrenia, arguing that while 'going to a psychiatrist gives you an 80% chance of getting a diagnosis of schizophrenia', 'only 16% of the whole group of voice hearers can be diagnosed with schizophrenia'. Conceptually, he had come to regard voices as messengers' telling 'us about problems that occurred in the person's life' and that 'instead of not-listening to the message we should look how to help and sustain the person in solving their problems' (Romme, 2000, p.1). This rather baggy conception of 'problems' was later superseded by the more specific argument that 'many people begin to hear voices as a result of extreme stress or trauma' (Hearing Voices Network, 2008). This interpretation validated voice hearers' experiences and invited them to talk them through with sympathetic interlocutors. At a practical level, Romme welcomed contributions made by sympathetic medical professionals and the families and carers of hearers, but saw voice hearers themselves, including those outside the mental health system, playing a central role in the process of finding ways to live with the condition, by sharing experiences and suggesting coping strategies.

In 1988, he came to speak in Manchester. Two years later, following a national conference on voice hearing and a major *Independent on Sunday*, feature on the topic, an English Hearing Voices Network was established to help establish self-help groups where voice hearers could share experiences and discuss strategies for coping. As the organisation's web site made clear, this 'new approach' to the condition was based on the view that, '[p]eople who hear voices and their families can gain great benefits from de-stigmatising the experience, leading to a greater tolerance and understanding' achieved through 'promoting more positive explanations which give people a more positive framework for developing their own ways of coping' (Hearing Voices Network, 2003). The account offered by Sharon, in one of the Network's newsletters catches perfectly the way the organisation's 'alternative view' offered participants a new explanation of their condition and validated them as individuals:

I do have a theory about my voices. I believe that they are memories and recollections that return right back to my early childhood. Being the only black child at school, I think I suffered much racial abuse, blame and abuse. This pattern has remained in my mind, and I am destined to hear constant reminders of terrible emotional trauma .... What is the cure? There is no cure because I do not have a biological illness. I am bruised and hurt by my earlier experiences, and this is part of my roots .... I have made many good friends at the group and at last feel accepted. Not as a mad, crazy nutter; but as a valid human being who has had a lot of *shit* in the past!

> (quoted in Blackman, 2000, p.62) (italics in the original)

We encountered Sharon in the previous chapter discussing her experiences of the day-to-day difficulties living and coping with a diagnosis of schizophrenia for BBC's *Video Diaries* series, and we will return to this account presently.

By the early 1990s then, two diametrically opposed interpretations of voice hearing were competing for visibility and legitimacy. On the one side there was the well-established medical model, underwritten by mainstream psychiatry, which regarded voice hearing as an auditory hallucination indicating a serious mental disorder, in many cases schizophrenia, treatable with drugs but requiring careful supervision since patients who hear 'voices' could not be trusted to act responsibly themselves (see Chapter 1). On the other side stood an alternative perspective that saw voice hearing as a response to distressing or traumatic experiences that needed to be recognised and worked through with the help of sympathetic professionals and other hearers, with the aim of developing coping strategies that did not involve medication.

This dispute about the nature and treatment of the condition was mapped in turn, onto the politics of public policy around the deficiencies of the care in the community strategy and inserted into an arena of popular representations in which images of dangerousness and demands for stricter controls were countered by accusations that those suffering mental distress were being unfairly stigmatised and denied full status as citizens.

In the remainder of this chapter we want to explore how these opposed frameworks of interpretation have been handled in British television documentary and current affairs programmes over the last decade-and-a-half and how the terms of engagement have shifted as a result of changes in the ecology of broadcasting brought about by the twin impact of intensified competition and the rise of the Internet. We begin by looking at the situation in the early 1990s when debate over the failures of community care was beginning to gather momentum and new programme forms were extending the space available for alternative viewpoints.

Experience, analysis, policy

Broadcasting emerged as a major mode of mass communication in the years after World War I. In Britain, its institutionalisation coincided with the arrival of universal political citizenship, as the right to vote was finally extended to every adult. In contrast to the American decision to organise programme provision around market competition, private enterprise and advertising finance, Britain opted to create a monopoly public service corporation, the BBC, funded by a compulsory tax on receiving set ownership. Thus, the US system approached its audiences primarily as consumers of the products promoted in and around the programmes, while the BBC saw its principal role as providing the cultural resources required for the responsible exercise of citizenship (Murdock, 2005). As the pre-eminent sources of the information, analysis and argument, citizens required to make rational choices between competing political positions and policy proposals, news, current affairs and documentary programming were assigned a central role to this project. Within this model of broadcasting as a 'public sphere', independent experts and legitimated political actors were granted a principal speaking role. Drawing on 'scientific' research and professional experience, experts were called on to provide the authoritative information and analysis that allowed contending positions to be rationally evaluated. Politicians were held to account for the failures of present policies and asked to justify proposals for change.

By organising who got to speak about what and how their ideas were valued, the programme forms that broadcasters developed played a pivotal role in orchestrating public knowledge and debate. Interviews, studio discussions and broadcast lectures largely relayed and refereed understandings originating elsewhere. Investigative documentary and current affairs programmes set out to probe behind the official rhetorics. But even these more interventionist projects, more often than not, left the great majority of audience members either listening to other people talk about their situation with few opportunities to speak for themselves, or finding that the accounts they had offered were used as data, illustrations of the issue or problem under discussion. The arrival of a public service variant of commercial television in the mid-1950s introduced a more populist, less exclusive, dynamic to British broadcasting but did little to change the unequal distribution of chances to engage in deliberation on public issues. Experts, politicians and programme makers continued to commandeer the major spaces of expression.

This presented a problem since the definition of citizenship as the right to full social and cultural participation required that the main arenas of public expression be open to the widest possible range of contributors and that everyone should have the opportunity to tell their stories and express their views directly rather than have them ventriloquised by those claiming to 'represent' their best interests.

Demands for greater access to the screen gathered momentum steadily through the 1970s as a variety of minority groups mobilised to lobby for an end to discrimination and greater recognition and respect. Dismantling stereotypes and misperceptions was central to the claims made by the women's movement and by movements within the ethnic, gay and disabled communities. This pressure produced two major responses. Firstly, after a sustained debate, the vacant fourth free-to-air terrestrial channel was awarded to a new public service organisation, Channel 4, with a remit requiring it to pay particular attention to the needs of minorities. Secondly, broadcasters began to experiment with new programme forms that offered extended spaces for the expression of grounded experience and non-expert views. They included video diaries and talk shows on topical issues.

Personifying problems: Experience as data

The relegation of experiential testimony within the best established form of current affairs programming, is well illustrated by the edition of *Panorama* broadcast on 1 March 1993, entitled, 'Whose Mind is It Anyway?'. Launched in 1953 as a magazine programme, *Panorama* assumed its present form two years later and rapidly became the BBC's flagship current affairs programme. Broadcast on the main channel, BBC1, and presented by some of the Corporation's most celebrated and respected journalists and interviewers, including Richard Dimbleby

and Robin Day, it established itself as one of broadcasting's pre-eminent sites of authoritative investigation and comment on public issues.
'Whose Mind is it Anyway?' took up public concern about the community care system's failure to ensure that patients released from hospital continued to take the medication that controlled their condition,
focussing specifically on Community Supervision Orders (CSOs) which
could compel patients living in the community to accept medication.

The programme's working assumption is established at the outset
when the presenter points out that

> Particularly affected would be severe schizophrenics who often
> don't realise when they are ill.

This framing statement that some patients cannot be trusted to
administer their own medication, is followed by an interview shot
in a day-centre with Gordon, one of the attendees, looking dishevelled and unkempt:

Presenter: Do you hear voices?
Interviewee: I've only heard one. It called me a creep, a big
               one like Moses, bigger than the one on the Ten
               Commandments. I'm still trying to find out who
               it was. My psychiatrist said it was my monad, my
               higher self, as in cringe, as in Doctor Monty Python,
               but from the highest level.
Presenter: Are they always different voices?
Interviewee: No, it's the only one I've ever heard. Never heard
               another ... one since that. I just tell it to watch out.
Presenter: Do you feel that you need care? Does anyone super-
               vise you at all? Do you see a doctor?
Interviewee: Oh yes I go to case management that's the new
               psychiatric thing. Kitchen meetings are very popular
               these days with politicians' acts, so they introduce us
               all to kitchen parties and meetings in the afternoon,
               which is very interesting and fulfilling and keeping
               up. You see the idea is to let the undamaged parts of
               the brain come out and let them enjoy themselves
               like any normal person, but the only damaged
               parts are the mental mental mentals and once the
               fingers are gone, we're alive again.

The function of the opening question, 'Do you hear voices?', is to confirm Gordon's status as a 'severe schizophrenic'. The presenter shows no interest in exploring when he first began to hear the voice, whether its arrival was related to particular circumstances in his life, or how he now responds to it. Gordon's comment that he tells his voice 'to watch out' suggests that he has found a way of coping, but asking, 'does anyone supervise you at all?', directly after his description of what he hears ignores this and presents him as unable to function without oversight, an assumption that is at odds with his (ironic?) account of regularly going to 'kitchen meetings' and his voluntary attendance at the day-centre.

Control over the type of drugs administered and the dosage is a major concern for many patients, particularly given the powerful side effects that some anti-psychotics may produce (Barham, 1992, pp.47–9). Under the proposed CSO legislation a patient would not be able to refuse medication, but Gordon is not asked for his views on this element of compulsion or the denial of rights it entails. Policy issues are the protected preserve of medical experts and political actors. Gordon's role is to embody the problem and provide raw data for discussion.

At first sight, political talk shows built around contributions from a studio audience, appear to de-centre expertise and give the floor back to participants' testimony. Extending opportunities to speak does not necessarily bring control over the framing of issues however, as Andra Leurdijk's research on Dutch talk shows dealing with issues around racism and multiculturalism demonstrates. The 21 shows she analysed featured 226 lay speakers (60% from ethnic minorities) as against only 17 academics and other professionals, but these accredited experts were allocated more time and allowed 'to bring forward their expertise and point of view uninterrupted' (Leurdijk, 1997, p.157). This same inequality of treatment also characterised England's major issue-based talk show of the 1990s, *Kilroy*.

Originally titled, *Day by Day*, it was the first British talk programme to adopt the approach pioneered by the early *Oprah Winfrey* shows in the US and set out to give a platform to grounded experiences and to social groups that had been excluded from mainstream network programming. Launched in 1986, two years after the first Winfrey shows, *Day by Day* was hosted by the former Labour Member of Parliament, Robert Kilroy Silk, and went out directly after the breakfast news on the BBC's main channel, BBC1. Soon renamed *Kilroy*, it focused on topical issues taken from the news and confronted politicians and experts with the experiences of people who lived with their categorisations and policies on an everyday basis.

The edition broadcast on 24 January 1993 focussed on the state of community care for schizophrenics and gave extensive space to voice hearers in the studio audience, as in the following exchange:

> Kilroy-Silk: What kind of things are they saying to you?
>
> Participant: Eh, one chap was an old man. I mean I had up to 30 voices, young people, old people.
>
> Kilroy-Silk: Were they voices of people you knew or recognised?
>
> Participant: No. Some of them I recognised as arguing in my favour to keep me alive. They were arguing that I should die of cancer or die of an heart attack. But on one particular occasion I was coming back from Liverpool with my father, to London where I now live, and I was running out of petrol but wouldn't stop at a motorway service station for the simple reason I thought they were alien bases, that they were alien people there. Consequently we ran out of petrol. It was wintertime; my father thought I'd got out the car to ring the AA. In actual fact I'd got out just to walk round I was going to leave him there. I got back in the car and said they'll be here soon. We waited hours and my dad said 'when's the AA [Automobile Association] coming?' I said we're not waiting for the AA, we're waiting for the spaceships to take us home 'cause I thought we were going back to our original planet where we came back from'. [studio audience laughter]

Avoiding evaluative judgements, Kilroy Silk elicits details of *what* the speakers' voices say and *how* he experiences them but he does not ask the speaker for his views on *why* the condition first occurred, what might have prompted it, or for his opinions on the treatment that he has received. Issues of diagnosis and policy evaluation are left to an accredited expert, Dr Tim Crowe, identified as a consultant psychiatrist in an on-screen caption. Having listened to a series of hearer's first-hand accounts, Dr Crowe translates them back into the specialised terms of the dominant medical model:

Kilroy-Silk: Is that typical of what we've heard schizophrenics go through?

Dr Crowe: There are many different features of the disease and I think we've heard some of the spectrum so far .... There are two big categories: hallucinations-disorders of perception: delusions-disorders of belief.

Kilroy-Silk: What causes it?

Dr Crowe: We don't know that anything else is relevant so at the moment we think that probably the genetic part is overwhelming.

At this point a member of the studio audience interrupts and tries to put an alternative perspective on the agenda for discussion by separating voice hearing from the diagnosis of schizophrenia:

Audience member: But ... there are some, some, some, societies erm, you know, the, the, hearing of voices etcetera isn't classified as an illness.

This suggestion, which as we noted earlier, is one of the central arguments in the alternative perspective on voice hearing proposed by Dr Marius Romme and other critical psychiatrists, is immediately discounted and the prevailing medical model reimposed by insisting that voice hearing is always and everywhere, a 'psychotic condition':

Dr Crowe: ... It seems as though similar, erm, psychotic conditions occur and as far as I am aware, all societies would regard the sort of symptom we've, we've, we've heard about as abnormal.

This construction is then underlined by the discussion of treatment that studiously avoids any discussion of alternatives to medication.

Kilroy-Silk: Is there a cure?

Dr Crow: Treatment, the drug treatment we have is quite good. We've had it for thirty years, erm, it improves the acute episodes and er, it er, prevents relapse, which is very important.

The alternative perspective developed by Marius Romme and his associates did receive an extended airing however, eight months after this edition of *Kilroy* went out, in the context of arguably the most radical attempt to enlarge the space available for the articulation of grounded experience, the BBC's *Video Diaries* project.

Video and validation: Listening to the voice hearing experience

The *Video Diaries* experiment ran throughout the 1990s (from 1990 to1999). Housed in the BBC's Community Programmes Unit, it gave selected individuals VHS camcorders to record their lives and their reflections on their situation.

This was not the first time that the daily routines of 'ordinary' lives had been shown in detail, warts and all. In 1974, the English documentary film-maker, Paul Watson, followed the model established two years earlier by the US series, *An American Family*, and filmed the Wilkins family as they negotiated living together in a small flat in Reading. It was very much part of the general push to open up the range of representations shown in prime time. As Watson later noted, he 'wanted to make a film about the kind of people who never got on to television' (Sieder, 2008). The resulting 12-part BBC series, *The Family* established a new style of British television documentary based on filming over an extended time period and shown as a series rather than as a one-off. The emphasis however was still very much on observation and despite the close relationships developed with participants, final editorial control remained firmly in the hands of the programme maker. The *Video Diaries* experiment broke this monopoly by asking participants to film themselves and giving them control over editorial decisions. The production team acted as enablers and advisors with the aim of producing a programme that was as close as possible to the diarist's intentions.

The edition entitled, *Mad, Bad or Sad?*, was shot by Sharon, a young black voice hearer, diagnosed as schizophrenic, who we encountered in Chapter 5 and also earlier in this chapter as an activist in the Hearing Voices Network. The programme is organised around the Network's core assumptions. In line with the movement's approach, Sharon's opening speech to camera rejects her medical label of schizophrenic as reductionist and presents her condition as a response to the discrimination she suffered growing up black in a racist environment:

> A doctor will give you a label that sticks to you for the rest of your life. Mine was schizophrenic. Making this diary was hard, sharing all

my secrets, but I really wanted you to see me, the person I am behind the label. ... I hear voices, echoes of my past. This is the root of my madness. I don't believe I'm schizophrenic. I think a lot of black people get labelled with schizophrenia. ... The main thing is these voices and I hear them about eighty per cent of the day slagging me off.

She returns to the experiential roots of her condition later in the programme, claiming that

My voices are bad memories, personalities from my past who call me 'wog', 'black bastard', 'coon', and 'whore'.

As she demonstrates, with an annotated tour of her medicine cabinet, she is required to take a formidable array of medication prescribed by her psychiatrist, but for her, the 'cure' is worse than the condition.

Every two weeks I get an injection of Depixol ... but it doesn't work for me. I suppose the way they [psychiatrists] see it, I'm so drugged up I can't give them any trouble [pause] but it just leaves me with no energy for life at all, then because I'm bored the voices I hear get worse.

This criticism of conventional treatment, which is spoken over a film of Sharon being injected, is followed by an extended final sequence recorded at a meeting of a Hearing Voices group in Manchester. This gives other members of the group a chance to speak about their experiences and Sharon the opportunity to outline the movement's self-help approach to managing voice hearing:

These groups are starting up all over the county. [pause] Many people who come here are outside the psychiatric system. They're not diagnosed schizophrenic but they hear voices too. [pause] It's a self-help group with no professionals. Because we all hear voices it makes it easier to talk about them.

Shifting ground

By providing an extended space to see and hear the person behind the diagnostic label in ways that she controlled, *Video Diaries* not only validated Sharon's sense of herself and provided a platform

for the expression of a perspective on voice hearing that challenged the medical model, it helped cultivate empathy and understanding among viewers. As we have seen however, authoritative analysis of both the condition and the policy framework surrounding its treatment remained firmly in the hands of designated experts drawn from the medical, academic and political arenas. Each programme was a discrete event. It could be recorded for later or repeat viewing and it might be reviewed in the national press and listing magazines but there was no mechanism for facilitating more open discussion of its contents or for linking one programme to another. The rise of the Internet has the potential to overcome both these limitations and to transform programming from an event to a gateway, in which what appears on screen is linked to a whole series of web-based resources. This 'digital dividend' has the capacity to transform popular access to understanding and debate around mental distress, but realising its potential depends, firstly, on the range and diversity of the programmes that provide the initial platform for viewers' navigations of the Net and secondly on the forms developed for online presentation.

Although the *Video Diaries* series ended in 1999, programmes built around self-made videos continued. In 1993 the BBC's Community Programmes Unit had launched *Video Nation*, with the aim of producing a comprehensive video archive of everyday life in Britain. People were given Hi-8 cameras for a year and asked to record their lives and thoughts. During its first decade, 10,000 tapes were submitted which were sifted and edited to produce around 1300 short films that were broadcast, initially individually and then in themed programmes. The project is still running and still generating the occasional broadcast but the archive is now housed on the BBC's web site. At the time of writing there were two contributions from voice hearers, Mike Matthews' *Life Changed*, and Hardip Singh Leader's *Out of Nowhere*. Both can be viewed by anyone accessing the site and both offer first-hand accounts, but they are much briefer than Sharon's programme-length contribution to *Video Diaries*. This compression is characteristic of video file sites, which tend to follow the lead set by *YouTube* by encouraging submissions of five minutes or less. The result is a tension between greater openness to a diversity of voices and experiences but less space for the development of arguments and nuanced representations.

Increasingly, commentators familiar with the situation in the 1980s and early 1990s when broadcasting was experimenting with new, more inclusive, ways of addressing public issues, see developments since then as abandoning this project. A number would follow Alastair Campbell, Tony Blair's former Press Secretary in arguing that

> The media has more space than ever but, it seems to me, less ability to handle really complex subjects. The combination of intense competition, negativity, trivialisation, obsession with celebrity ... programmes now only interested in making a splash, rather than genuinely illuminating an issue – it all means there are few places where complexity is dealt with.
>
> (Campbell, 2006, p.7)

The last 15 years have seen a major shift in the ecology of British broadcasting as the rise of multi-channel systems has intensified competition for viewers, and continuing political debate about the future funding of the BBC has put the Corporation under mounting pressure. Broadcasters have responded by increasingly addressing viewers as consumers, making personal choices in the marketplace, rather than as citizens participating in debates around public issues and the quality of public life. In the field of actuality programming, this general reorientation has been marked by two shifts; firstly, the increasing tendency to personalise public issues, reproducing the 'make-overs' at the centre of consumerist programming dealing with home decoration and personal appearance, and secondly, the reassertion of control over the terms of representation by programme makers.

Personalising public issues

In 1996, the topics dealt with in *Kilroy* were still firmly rooted in the policy agenda with topics such as 'Emergency bed shortage' (17 January). Two years later the rota included many more of the personal dilemmas, such as 'My Husband Wants to Become a Woman' (31 March), that had long been the stock-in-trade of the leading US talk show, *The Oprah Winfrey Show* (Murdock, 2000, p.210). This model found its fullest expression in 1998 when Trisha

Goddard, a young black woman, was offered the slot left vacant by the departure of the former host of Anglia Television's day-time talk show.

Goddard had a particular interest in issues around mental distress having herself been referred to a psychiatric unit following a breakdown. After her discharge from hospital she started work for the mental health services in Australia where she met and married the head of the Australian branch of MIND, the major mental health charity.

Her decline and recovery is recounted in detail on her personal web site and serves as a template for her approach to the guests on her show, who are encouraged to think positively about ways they can change their lives. The structural conditions that may have caused or exacerbated the situations they find themselves in remain invisible and unexamined. The proposed solutions revolve around therapy rather than political debate and action. As her web site is at pains to emphasise: 'As a programme maker, she has ensured the ongoing involvement of mental health counsellors ... with programme guests' (Trisha TV Ltd, 2009). By shifting the emphasis from deliberation to entertainment, the drama of witnessing people struggle with adversity fits snugly with the demands of intensified competition. As Oprah Winfrey candidly admitted, commercial television 'pays you based on the numbers watching ... although my attitude was, "Let's get something out of this" ... Entertainment was the real goal' (Duncan, 1999, p.16). A similar shift towards personal decisions and dramatised situations took place in documentary production with the rise of docu-soaps and 'reality TV'.

Docu-soaps borrowed heavily from soap opera form, following a stable group of characters as they encountered and dealt with incidents and crisis in their working environments. These locations needed to generate a variety of immediately recognisable situations that were amusing, touching or dramatic, with characters that audiences could easily empathise with. This ruled out mental hospitals and community care centres. St James' Hospital in Leeds, Europe's largest teaching hospital, on the other hand, met these requirements perfectly, with the added advantage that the long tradition of hospital dramas, had already primed viewers to respond to many of the situations portrayed. *Jimmy's*, which ran from 1987 to 1994, was a pioneer of the docu-soap form, along with other programmes set in locales that viewers were likely to be familiar with, such as airports (*Airport* 1996–2005) and driving schools (*Driving School* 1997). As with soap operas, the focus was on the central characters and the everyday dramas they had to negotiate, a characteristic typified by one of the most successful examples of the genre, *Vets in Practice* (1997–2002). As one reviewer noted, 'while some attempts were made to raise public awareness of issues relating to animal welfare and veterinary practice ... more commonly the spotlight fell on the more tragic, humorous or sentimental aspects of the animal-centred stories' (Boschi, 2008). Symptomatically, the programme's arrival in prime time coincided with Granada's decision to cancel its long-running, and highly respected, investigative current affairs series, *World In Action*, which had included the mental health system in its excavations of abuses of power, most notably in its broadcast of 20 May 1968, *Ward F13*, which had documented the plight of geriatric patients (for discussion of *Ward F13* see Chapter 3).

This deletion of social and political context was replicated, and reinforced, in the other major innovation in actuality programming, 'Reality TV'. As Stephen Lambert, director of programmes at RDF media, one of the main originators of the form, has pointed out, he and his colleagues worked on the assumption that, 'These days people are less interested in politics and more concerned about all those life choices they feel under pressure to make. That's what this whole spate of reality programming is about' (Hoggard, 2003, p.9). To ensure that 'pressure' is paced and applied to maximum effect, the programme makers manufacture it. As Daisy Goodwin, another major force in developing the genre, admits: 'The shows I make tend to be real people in real situations, although constructed by us' adding that, '[a] pure reality show is a planned fiction' (op cit. p.9).

All programmes that give the producer the final cut involve a degree of manipulation. As Paul Watson told an interviewer: 'We all know what manipulation is, it's called editing. I used to be a painter and you put a colour next to a colour and they interact with each other. It's the same with films but you have to move things around with honesty to the subjects otherwise you might as well write a drama' (Ogle, 2002, p.2). For Watson, and other programme makers of his generation, the manipulation involved in 'reality TV's' studied construction of situations and scenarios marks a decisive move from observation to exploitation. As he told an interviewer who asked him how he felt about being described as the 'godfather' of reality television, 'Who'd want to be a godfather to such bastards' (Armstrong, 2006, p.2).

All film-making runs the risk that participants will play to the camera but 'Reality TV' expressly invites them to perform. This demand for carefully crafted self-presentation militated against the participation of anyone suffering from serious mental distress. The boundaries of acceptably bizarre behaviour were however tested in 1996 in the most successful 'Reality TV' show, Channel 4's, *Big Brother*. In this format, viewers watch a group of people confined together in a specially built house, performing set tasks and interacting with each other, and then vote for the participant they think should be expelled until only one participant is left and declared the winner. The 1996 series was won by Pete Bennett, a sufferer from Tourette Syndrome, a neurological disorder characterised by involuntary movements and vocalisations (known as tics), including swearing. The Tourette Syndrome (UK) Association credited Bennett's momentary celebrity with increasing public sympathy and interest in the syndrome, but the publicity he attracted was embedded in a wider programming context where once again attempts to understand how sufferers coped has been displaced by entertainment.

In 1989 the BBC broadcast a documentary entitled, *John's not Mad*, in its *QED* science series. It followed 15-year-old John Davidson, from Galashiels in Scotland, as he encountered a range of reactions and explored how he and his family coped. It brought what was then a relatively unknown condition into the public domain and deconstructed the popular assumption that it was a form of madness. Sixteen years later, the BBC screened a follow up, *The Boy Can't Help It*, exploring John's adult life and the impact that the original programme had had on him. Both programmes employed sympathetic observation to illuminate the realities of living with an incurable condition on a day-to-day basis. In 2006, Davidson was featured in another documentary, in his capacity as a full-time worker for Tourette's Scotland, a support group that organises holidays for teenage sufferers. The programme, *Tourette de France*, broadcast on Channel 4, featured the actor/comedian, Keith Allen, accompanying Davidson and one of his groups on a countrywide bus tour, taking in the Parisian asylum where in 1885, Gilles de la Tourette, first described the condition that bears his name. The promotional material claimed that the programme:

By turns, funny and touching, gives the viewer a rare insight into a group of normal, likeable, and occasionally mischievous teenagers who are managing to live fulfilling and rewarding lives, despite the bizarre hand that fate has dealt them.

Some critics saw it differently. As one pointed out, the fact that 'Allen reacts with laughter to every tic and the producers flash up "nigger" and "cunt" on screen in case you misunderstood what the kids were shouting' suggests that 'this documentary is more about entertainment than educating the public' (McCalmont, 2007, pp.1–2). This re-orientation offers little or no space to explore either the distress the condition causes many sufferers or the debates around the most effective form of treatment and support.

The choice of a well-known television actor and comedian as the programme's presenter, points to another important trend, the celebrification of suffering and treatment, exemplified by a 2006 BBC2 programme, *The Secret Life of a Manic Depressive*, in which the comedian, Stephen Fry, who had been diagnosed with bi-polar disorder, explored the roots of the condition and talked to other celebrity sufferers. As he told an interviewer, 'I always heard voices in my head saying what a useless bastard I am', but he came to recognise that 'the voice is my own. It's my own voice, telling me what a worthless lump of shit I am' (Owen, 2006, p.1). Left undiagnosed, his condition worsened. He attempted suicide and had a very public breakdown. He saw making the programme as a chance 'to speak out, to fight the public stigma and to give a clearer picture of a mental illness most people know little about' (op cit.) comparing the struggle for the rights of the mentally distressed as a continuation of the Civil Rights movement and the campaigns for gay rights. Two years later, in October 2008, BBC2 broadcast another major celebrity-based programme, *Cracking Up*, in which Alastair Campbell, famous for his tough, even brutal, approach to media management and 'spin', recounted his experience of severe depression, his hospitalisation and subsequent recovery.

This celebrity orientation is not confined to accounts of suffering it extends to the presentation of treatment. The section of the BBC's on-line Headroom site which tackles a range of mental health issues with people with first-hand experience of them (BBC, 2009a) for example, is hosted by the comedienne, Ruby Wax. Titled *Ruby's*

Room, it promises a 'cosy place to air feelings about those things we all tend to brush under the carpet' (BBC, 2009b). Although Wax read psychology at university and is currently training as a psychotherapist, her familiarity with mental distress and her diagnostic expertise is inevitably more limited than a practitioner with years of experience. The filmed interviews on the site do provide spaces for the articulation of first-hand accounts, but again, some of these are pre-empted by celebrity contributors. The interview on 'breakdown' for example is with Alastair Campbell.

The arrival of the celebrity-turned-doctor, represented by Ruby Wax, is mirrored by the emergence of doctor-turned-celebrity.

In 2006, BBC3, the Corporation's digital channel particularly aimed at younger audiences, broadcast *I Love Being Mad*, featuring four people who had overcome mental health problems and were highly critical of the mainstream approach to treatment. One section recorded the 'Great Escape Bed Push' showing the participants symbolically escaping from a secure psychiatric hospital pursued by a giant syringe as they push a psychiatric bed from Bradford to Manchester in their pyjamas. The programme was nominated for a Mental Health Media Award, a prize introduced that year to acknowledge 'the best portrayal and most sensitive reporting [of mental health issues] in the broadcast media' (Mental Health Media Awards 2009). One of the participants was Rufus May, who had been diagnosed as schizophrenic and confined to a psychiatric hospital at the age of 18. As he later explained, 'I had gone through the strange process of being talked to as if I was not there, of professionals trying to suppress my odd and disturbing behaviour with drugs without trying to understand why I was acting as I was. No one seemed willing to walk in my shoes' (Intervoice, 2007, p.1). Discharged from hospital, he abandoned his medication (against psychiatric advice) and eventually trained as a psychologist committed to alternative treatment. His approach provided the basis for *The Doctor who Hears Voices*, a Channel 4 dramatised documentary based on his treatment of a female hospital doctor who hears a male voice telling her to kill herself. She was suspended when she admitted to feeling suicidal but was convinced that if she spoke about her voice hearing she would never work again. Played by an actress, to protect her anonymity, she is treated by May who is described in the publicity for the programme as 'a maverick psychologist [who] believes there is no such thing as schizophrenia, that medication can destroy lives and that there is nothing wrong with hearing voices' (Channel 4 2009). The programme was nominated for a Mental Health Media Award. This instance illustrates the contradictory impact of anchoring programmes around celebrities. On the one hand, Rufus May's own dramatic life history and the national exposure he received as a result of *I Love being Mad*, gave him a highly visible platform on which to demonstrate the alternative approach to voice hearing dramatised in *The Doctor Who Hears Voices*. On the other hand, by focusing so centrally on him, as a charismatic personality, and the case of one of his own patients, the programme raises questions about how well the approach might work in more mundane circumstances and less imaginative hands.

Programmes based around the psychiatric histories of television celebrities raise this same question of representativeness. While there is no doubt that by 'coming out' and recounting their experiences of mental distress, Stephen Fry, Alastair Campbell and other prominent personalities, such as the comedian Paul Merton, have raised the public profile of mental health issues, their interventions have also limited debate in important ways. Firstly, their prior status as celebrities, and the further coverage Fry and Campbell attracted when their programmes both won Mental Health Media awards, ensured that the conditions they suffered from, depression and bi-polar disorder, moved to the top of the agenda for discussion. Conditions without celebrity sufferers do not enjoy the same advantaged access to publicity. Secondly, by presenting their conditions as something that 'could happen to anyone' and their recoveries and coping strategies as within everyone's reach, the attention given to their cases has sidestepped the role of social conditions in structuring both experience and access to treatment. Where are the voices of sufferers who are poor and socially excluded?

The answer, as the extract from Sharon's posting on the Voice Hearing Network web site quoted earlier suggests, is increasingly, on the Web.

Networks and navigations

There is abundant evidence to show that the computer's historic monopoly over access to the Internet has generated enduring 'digital divides' which have excluded substantial numbers of the elderly and poor. As access migrates towards mobile phones and web-enabled digital television sets, basic inequalities in access are likely to lessen widening the potential for both use and participation. The problem is that the Internet, and particularly the most widely used section of it, the World Wide Web, offers access to wide range of materials which pull in different directions.

Take the popular micro-blogging site, Twitter, for example. Anyone can join and contribute diary entries, jokes and comments on topical issues, but postings are limited to 180 characters. Anyone logging on the morning of 13 August 2009, and searching for entries related to schizophrenia would have found links to recent academic research alongside links to commercial drug development sites. They would also have found a number of postings relaying the tired joke, 'Schizophrenia beats being alone', and supposedly humorous observations such as, 'Things are so tough in Detroit ... my neighbour went to his shrink for his schizophrenia and asked for a group rate'.

When asked in a recent British survey to choose from a list of descriptions of people who are mentally ill, almost two-thirds (63%) of respondents selected 'someone who is suffering from schizophrenia' and 59% opted for 'someone who has a split personality' (Department of Health, 2008). By continually reproducing these stereotypes, Twitter helps perpetuate popular understandings that do nothing to dismantle discrimination. In this context, the ways information, imagery and argument around mental distress is organised on the Internet assumes a critical role.

Social organisations of all kinds have been quick to use the web's connective and interactive capacities to develop and extend their visibility and reach. These capacities can be employed in one of two ways. They can help organisations improve their visibility and reach by strengthening and diversifying vertical channels of distribution. Or, they can be used to develop, horizontal, peer-to-peer, exchange networks. The web site of the major mental health charities, MIND, is a good example of the first while the site of *National Perceptions Forum* (formerly the National Voices Forum) illustrates the second. In addition to its main site, MIND employs a variety of additional channels, from the Chief Executive's blog to the organisation's page on the social networking site, Facebook, to provide users with access to a wide range of information, analysis and debate on mental health issues and links to other relevant sources. The section on user empowerment for example, profiles the work of the Hearing Voices Network while the current edition of MIND's bi-monthly magazine *Open Mind*, available electronically at the time of writing, has a feature on the Living with Voices group for deaf voice listeners. There is, however, no extended opportunity for users of the mental health services or their carers, to recount their experiences outside of these mediated spaces. In contrast, the site developed by the *National Perceptions Forum* is constructed almost entirely around first-hand accounts and user contributions. Describing itself on its home page as a 'a forum which gives an active voice to people who hear voices in the head', it takes the model of the voice hearing self-help groups and extends it beyond the time and space constraints of face-to-face meetings. It provides sections giving first-hand accounts of experiences, information on self management, discussions of proposed changes to mental health legislation, and links to participants' home page recounting their biographies, offering tips on coping on a day-to-day basis, and critical commentary on conventional treatment.

At the same time, broadcasting organisations have been developing their own web presence with the BBC's site currently the most extensive and widely used. In addition to sections organised around particular programmes, it currently hosts three general domains devoted to health that deal with issues around mental distress; the main health site (www.bbc.co.uk/health), *Ouch!* 'reflecting the lives and experiences of disabled people', and *Headroom*, which aims 'to help you cope with the everyday stresses and strains of life and provide a safe place to start finding answers to more complex problems'. Users looking across these three sites would encounter a range of views. The description of schizophrenia given on the main health site, for example, follows the medical model in categorising voice hearing as a hallucination and a major symptom of the condition and privileging 'treatment with medication in the form of tablets or long-acting injections'. Although the page offers no links to the web sites of voice hearing activists, anyone following the link to the section of the NHS Direct site on schizophrenia would find an article by Stevie White-McQuillan entitled 'I hear voices' reprinted from the newsletter of the office where he works, outing himself as a voice hearer. In it he recounts finding out that he had been diagnosed with paranoid schizophrenia after being admitted to hospital and thinking 'I'm hearing voices, so I must have schizophrenia' but insists that he now considers himself 'just an ordinary bloke who happens to hear voices' (NHS Choices, 2009).

Although the BBC is not responsible for the content on the external web sites it provides links to, it does arguably, have an obligation to offer users guidance on navigating their way through the thicket of available web sources, by annotating and contextualising the positions they advance. It also has an unrivalled opportunity to become the principal node in an emerging network of public and civil initiatives that, taken together, offer the basis for a public digital commons providing a comprehensive alternative to the commercially driven and advertising funded initiatives that are presently pushing to commandeer the Internet (Murdock, 2005). By bringing first-hand testimony, expert analysis and critical debate together in one place for the first time, this intervention would overcome the separations between grounded experience and general analysis, professional production and amateur contributions that have characterised broadcasting up until now and lay the basis for a more dialogic and inclusive way of working. This will require greater integration of the various sections on the Corporation's own web site, a continuing extension of the on-line spaces available for users to post material and engage in debate, and the development of a new public search system linking users to the widest possible range of non-commercial sources.

As commercial pressures on programming continue to increase, with the consequences for programming that we have detailed here, re-making the practice of public service for the digital age is an absolute precondition for the survival and expansion of the information, analysis, understanding, empathy and argumentation, on which active citizenship depends. Mental distress, where sufferers are still subjected to widespread misunderstanding, hostility and discrimination, is arguably, the area where these resources are needed most.

7
Concluding Remarks

What has this book been about? Unfortunately, there is no short-cut summary here. To get a sense of the book's main themes the reader will have to undertake a journey, reading the chapters to understand how mediations of madness emerge, disappear and interleave, only to re-emerge at unexpected moments. When writing about the interplay between historical and contemporary images and representations of madness, I found that there is no neat procession of discrete elements (I wish there was!). However, I had hoped, as I came towards writing this conclusion, that I could pursue a straightforward option of summarising the chapters and synthesising some grand overarching argument. I found instead that I wanted to discuss the implications of my critique.

In my introduction, I noted how this book was a contribution to a growing body of work critical of media representations of mental distress. However, it may strike some readers as odd that the arguments and ideas contained in and across the chapters of *Mediating Madness* do not 'fit' with the existing literature. That summation would be correct. For example, I have not included anywhere in the book the now-standard appeal that newspaper editors, journalists and other media workers desist from misrepresenting the 'facts' of mental illnesses such as schizophrenia by providing what psychiatrists tell us is more accurate, less sensationalized, information about psychiatric illness. What would these facts consist of when we consider that 'schizophrenia' is now a discredited label even among psychiatrists and psychologists? Should journalists ignore, for example, arguments by the Campaign for Abolition of the Schizophrenia Label in preference to more mainstream psychiatric 'facts'?

I certainly understand why mental health professionals want to hold tabloid reporting on mental health to account for its scary headlines and one-dimensional treatment of psychiatric-related topics. Morris (2006) is a typical example of those who want to alert readers about the overwhelmingly negative image of psychiatry and mental illness in the media and to contrast this with promotional messages about the caring and sensitive nature of contemporary psychiatric treatment. Psychiatrists and psychiatric nurses are required to deal with the day-to-day difficulties of caring for the mentally distressed often under difficult and stressful conditions. As a former psychiatric nurse, I have enough insight and experience to know that the poor self-image of the mentally distressed is compounded by their predominantly devalued public image.

Equally, as a 'media studies' academic I also understand why tabloid newspaper editors and journalists would disregard appeals for more accurate or balanced information about mental illness not least given the old journalistic truism that says, 'never let the facts get in the way of a good story'. Nor am I minded to try to identify some kind of middle ground on which anti-stigma campaigners and tabloid journalists can find a happy median where interests pertaining to both sides can somehow be accommodated. What would this accommodation look or read like exactly? Indeed, my argument in this book has purposefully strayed away from special pleading for balanced treatment of the imbalanced (as it were). This is not meant to be facetious but to highlight how in the context of media reporting on mental distress, notions of 'balance' and 'imbalance' are negotiable concerns.

So where *does* this book fit? I have two responses. My first response is to acknowledge that the chapters of this book read like an edited collection of chapters each broadly concerned with the cultural politics of representing madness. This individualization of chapters has been a deliberate strategy on my part so as to illustrate some of the many complexities involved in thinking and writing about historical and contemporary mediated images madness. My second response to where this book fits is that it should be seen as a counterpoint what I consider to be a politically 'cold', indeed analytically frozen approach to media images of madness and mental distress emanating from within the media studies literature.

I want to illustrate this point by returning to *Media and Mental Distress*, the analysis of British media images of mental distress by Greg Philo and his colleagues in the Glasgow Media Group. Published in 1996, and now cited as *the* seminal British study of how the media shape public beliefs about mental distress, this book has become a kind of 'year zero' for recognition as to how poorly represented in the media is psychiatry and psychiatric patients. I, too, am respectful of Philo et al.'s work on this topic because it put the relationship between media and stigmatizing images of mental distress onto the media and cultural studies map. Prior to the publication of their book there was a dearth of British writing on the topic of media and mental distress.

And yet it has always left me questioning that there is so much more that could be said on the topic of madness and representation not least by borrowing valuable insights from social historians such as Roy Porter who have taken madness seriously both as a shifting historical and cultural concept. Taking into account a historical perspective on this topic has allowed me to use the term 'madness' productively (I hope), and is not at all evidence of a media-generated trap into which me and others who use the term culturally and politically, have fallen.

I have already made some critical comments on Philo et al.'s methodology in Chapter 5 so there is no need to repeat these points. What I do want to note here, however, is that the empirical template used by the Glasgow Media Group to analyse all manner of social ills (the template they use can just as easily address 'bad news' about the Israel–Palestine conflict as it can negative media reporting of mental distress), in the case of mental distress fails to recognise how schizophrenia (a condition that they pay close attention to in their writing for its link to violence in news reporting) is not just a 'condition' but also a construction. This is important because the tabloid image of schizophrenia as dangerous, split personality, chronically debilitating and so on, is a cultural *not* a tabloid construction.

In pointing out that schizophrenia is a cultural construction, I want to be clear that I am not aligning myself to an anti-psychiatric narrative. As a former psychiatric nurse who has witnessed the misery of those tormented with a florid psychosis, I find it hard to reconcile with R. D. Laing's cosy narrative of schizophrenia as a heroic journey through madness. At the same time however,

Laing's image of schizophrenia is as much a construction as Eugene Bleuler's inventive account of 'schizophrenia' as a disease entity a century ago (see Gilman, 1988, Chapter 12). When we get into these kinds of debates, what we find is that the media and mental illness relationship takes unexpected twists and turns, which I think are difficult to reconcile analytically and creatively from within the limited purview of the Glasgow Media Group template.

In making these critical observations about the limitations of the Glasgow Media Group's work on media and mental distress I am aware that my own preferred cross-discipline approach that I have aimed for in this book goes against the flow of current thinking about stigmatizing images of mental illness. I simply do not hold out any prospect of ending the media's reliance on stigmatizing words and images associated with 'madness' (the best we can hope for is an extension of liberal-sounding terms like 'mental distress'). Derogatory words such as 'mad', 'loony', 'nutter' and so on are so much a part of our linguistic and cultural repertoire that the idea of banishing them strikes me as realistic as mad folk setting sail on a ship of fools. Nor do I want to see the demise of 'mad' terminology because to banish these terms would be to dismiss past ways of thinking about cultures of madness that I have shown also continue to shape in unexpected ways contemporary cultures of madness.

To understand the complexity of past and current cultures of madness, I suggest that we need to better understand their terms and our definitions. This is what I have attempted to do in the various illustrations and case studies used in this book. However, this also includes interrogating the continuing use of the rhetorical device of 'their' and 'our' to signify those who (erroneously) perceive madness as a set of behaviour(s) that are readily identifiable as different from 'normality'. The language that really matters, it seems to me, is that which acts as an exclusionary device demarcating 'them' from 'us'. On the contrary, the notion that there is a 'we' (who identify as sane) and 'them' (who are identified as mad) divide is undermined by the salutary fact that mental distress currently affects about one in four people in Britain (and some 450 million people worldwide). Clearly, 'we' are also 'them'.

What I suggest to anti-stigma campaigners is that we acknowledge instead that madness is not a good place to be but it's a place that many people inhabit in varying degrees. For example, writing this book *felt* at times like I was going mad. This may seem pithy; insensitive to those who experience real madness (whatever that is like), the more so when the subject matter happens to be madness. But I want to acknowledge that this is sometimes how those sleepless nights felt worrying about how to develop the next idea. In the midst of writer's block and its accompanying anxieties, I often found myself describing the process of writing this book as 'madness', and those friends and colleagues to whom I said this shared the humour. In Chapter 1 I noted that the late social historian Roy Porter advocated using the term 'madness' in his own writings popularising the history of mad culture because it applies not only to the clinically certifiable but also includes all manner of thought and emotion. I have spent so much time at my computer accompanied by Porter's writings that it seems apt to use the term to define my experience writing this book.

Notes

1 Madness and the Popular Imagination

1. Despite the change of headline, the paper's editor Rebbekah Wade was unprepared for the backlash from mental health and psychiatric user groups. Using press releases and Internet chat forums, the editor encountered a storm of national and international protest about its stigmatizing of Bruno. So much so in fact, that the next day Bruno received the paper's good wishes for his recovery (though no public apology) and a commitment to financial help. So apparently contrite was the *Sun* that it was reported that Marjorie Wallace of SANE would educate Wade in mental health issues (although ironically Wallace/SANE have been criticised by service users for their own stigmatizing media promotional practices – see Crossley, 2006, pp.192–9).

5 Visualising Madness: Mental Distress and Public Representation

1. *Panorama*: 'Whose Mind Is It Anyway' (broadcast BBC1, 1 March 1993). *Panorama* is the longest-running public affairs TV programme in the world. Broadcasting since 1965, it currently gets around five million viewers and is still considered the BBC's 'flagship' current affairs programme.
2. *Disguises*: 'A Place of Safety' (broadcast ITV, 25 February and 4 March 1993). Made by Granada TV, *Disguises* was launched in 1993 as the series that can 'get to parts of a story others can't reach' (Granada publicity material for *Disguises*, March 1993). However, the format provoked strong reaction from critics concerned that its 'voyeuristic' appeal based on journalist subterfuge and 'spying' with a hidden camera outweighed its public service merit (see Corner, 1995, pp.100–1).
3. *Video Diaries*: 'Mad, Bad or Sad?' (broadcast BBC2, 14 September 1994). Made under the auspices of the BBC's Community Programmes Unit (CPU), *Video Diaries'* camcorder-based format was a major advance in broadcasting the testimony of people under-represented, misrepresented or ignored by mainstream television (Dovey, 1991). Towards the end of its run in 1999, the CPU was accused of ignoring its remit of accessing marginal voices and selecting diarists with more avowedly 'sensational' interests.
4. Scotland has a separate legislative process within the political context of Great Britain. However, Scotland also introduced mental health care in the community in 1993.

5. The expression 'the lunatics have taken over Stretford' can also be taken as a satirical comment on the ambiguous impact of the care in the community policy. Similar to the satire on Thatcherite and Reaganite economic policies by the eighties British pop group Fun Boy Three, in their song 'The Lunatics Have Taken Over the Asylum', the expression signifies a topsy-turvy world of policymaking gone mad, and that that which one first imagined to be of benefit to the economic health of the nation (the savings to the public purse generated by asylum closures) may have unintended consequences for those communities who must now live with the (human) consequences of asylum closures.

Bibliography

Allderidge, P. H. (1985) Bedlam: Fact or fantasy?, in W. F. Bynum, R. Porter and M. Sheperd (eds) *The Anatomy of Madness*, Vol. 2, London: Tavistock, pp. 17–33.

Altheide, D. and Snow, R. (1979) *Media Logic*, London: Sage.

Ames, D. (2000) Review of Ivan Leudar and Philip Thomas *Voices of Reason, Voices of Insanity*, *British Medical Journal*, Vol. 321, p. 1537.

Anderson, M. (2003) One flew over the psychiatric unit: Mental illness and the media. *Journal of Psychiatric and Mental Health Nursing*, Vol. 10, pp. 297–306.

Andrews, J., Briggs, A., Porter, R., Tucker, P., Waddington, K. (1997) *The History of Bethlem*, London: Routledge.

Appleby, L., Shaw, J., Kapur, N., et al. (2006) *Avoidable Deaths, Five Year Report of the National Confidential Inquiry into Suicide and Homicide by People with Mental Illness*, London: National Confidential Inquiry Into Suicide and Homicide by People with Mental Illness. Full executive report available at www.nmhdu.org.uk/silo/files/avoidable-deaths-five-year-report-.pdf.

Armstrong, S. (2006) Candid cameraman: An interview with Paul Watson, http://www.guardia.co.uk/media/2006/nov/20/mondatmediasection (accessed 9 August 2009).

Arnold, C. (2008) *Bedlam: London and Its Mad*, London: Simon and Schuster.

Bailey, P. (1996) Breaking the Sound Barrier: A Historian Listens to Noise. *Body and Society*, Vol. 2(2), pp. 49–66.

Barham, P. (1992) *Closing The Asylum*, London: Penguin Books (second edition).

Barham, P. and Hayward, R. (1991) *From The Mental Patient To The Person*, London: Tavistock/Routledge.

Bartlett, P. and Wright, D. (1999) *Outside the Walls of the Asylum: The history of care in the community, 1750–2000*, London: Athlone Press.

BBC (2009a) www.bbc.co.uk/headroom/wellbeing/ (accessed 16 December 2009).

—— (2009b) www.bbc.co.uk/headroom/rubys/ (accessed 16 December 2009).

Bean, P. (2008) *Madness and Crime*, Cullompton: Willan Publishing.

Benbow, A. (2007) Mental Illness, Stigma, and the Media, *Journal of Clinical Psychiatry*, Vol. 68 (supplement 2), pp. 31–5.

Benson, T. and Anderson, C. (2002) *Reality Fictions: The Films of Frederick Wiseman*, Carbondale: Southern Illinois University Press.

Beresford, P. (2001) Service users, social policy and the future of welfare. *Critical Social Policy*, Vol. 21(4), pp. 494–512.

Bilton, M. (2003) *Wicked Beyond Belief. The Hunt for the Yorkshire Ripper*, London: HarperCollins Publishers.

Blackman, L. (2000) Ethics, Embodiment and the Voice-hearing Experience, *Theory, Culture and Society*, Vol. 17(5), pp. 55–74.

Blackman, L. and Walkerdine, V. (2001) *Mass Hysteria: Critical Psychology and Media Studies*. London: Palgrave Macmillan.

Blackman, L. (2007) Psychiatric Culture and Bodies of Resistance, *Body and Society*, Vol. 13(2), pp. 1–23.

Blumler, J. and Gurevtich, M. (1999) *The Crisis of Public Communication*, London: Routledge.

Bly, N. [Elizabeth Jane Cochrane Seaman] (1887) *Ten Days in a Mad-House*, New York: Ian L Munro Publisher. Available at http://digital.library.upenn. edu/women/bly/madhouse/madhouse.html (Accessed 12 December 2007).

Boschi, A. (2008) Vets in Practice (1997–2002), BFI Screenonline, http:www. screenonline.org.uk/tv/id/1178610/ (Accessed 8 August 2009).

Brady, I. (2001) *The Gates of Janus: Serial Killing and its Analysis*, Port Townsend, WA: Feral House.

Brimelow, A. (2009) 'Schizophrenia: The Horror Movie', http://news.bbc. co.uk/i/hi/health/8190036.stm (Accessed 15 August 2009).

Brindle, D. (2006) 'Why was tabloid tosh met with silence?', *The Guardian Society*, Vol. 21(June), p. 4.

Browne, J. (1985) Darwin and the face of madness, in W.F. Bynum, R. Porter and M. Sheperd (eds) *The Anatomy of Madness*, Vol. 1, London: Tavistock, pp. 151–65.

Busfield, J. (1986) *Managing Madness: Changing Ideas and Practice*, London: Hutchinson.

—— (1996) *Men, Women and Madness*, London: Routledge.

—— (1994) The Female Malady? Men, Women And Madness In Nineteenth Century Britain, *Sociology*, Vol. 28(1), pp. 259–77.

—— (2002) 'Psychiatric disorder and individual violence: Imagined death, risk and mental health policy', in A. Buchanan (ed.) *Care of the Mentally Disordered Offender in the Community*, Oxford: Oxford University Press, pp. 65–86.

Byrne, P. (1999) Stigma of mental illness: Changing minds, changing behaviour. *British Journal of Psychiatry*, Vol. 174, pp. 1–3.

Cameron, D. and Frazer, E. (1987) *The Lust to Kill: A feminist investigation of sexual murder*, Cambridge: Polity Press.

Campbell, A. (2006) 'I tell this paper about my depression and guess what happens', *The Independent*, Vol. 15(October), p. 7.

Carroll, W. C. (2002) Songs of Madness: The Lyric Afterlife of Shakespeare's Poor Tom, in P. Holland (ed.) *Shakespeare Survey: An Annual Survey of Shakespeare Studies and Production*, Vol. 55, pp. 82–95.

Castel, R. (1991) From dangerousness to risk, in G. Burchill, C. Gordon, and P. Miller (eds) *The Foucault Effect: Studies in Governmentality*, London: Harvester Wheatsheaf.

Clare, A. (1980) *Psychiatry in Dissent: Controversial Issues In Thought And Practice*, London: Tavistock Publications (second edition).

Coleman, R. (1999) Hearing voices and the politics of oppression, in C. Newnes, C. Dunn, G. Holmes (eds) *This is Madness: A Critical Look at Psychiatry and the future of the Mental Health Services*, Ross-on-Wye: PCCS Books.

Conolly, J. (1976) Case Studies From the Physiognomy of Insanity (The Medical Times and Gazette), in S. Gilman (ed.) *The Face of Madness: Hugh W.*

Diamond and the Origin of Psychiatric Photography, New York: Brunner/Mazel, pp. 25–78.

Cooper, D. (1978) *The Language of Madness*, London: Penguin.

Corner, J. (1986) (ed.) *Documentary and the Mass Media*, London: Routledge.

—— (1994) Mediating the Ordinary: The 'Access Idea and Television Form', in M. Aldrich and N. Hewitt (eds) *Controlling Broadcasting. Access Policy and Practice in North America and Europe*. Manchester: Manchester University Press, pp. 20–33.

—— (1995) *Television Form and Public Address*, London: Edward Arnold.

Cottle, S. (2003) News, Public Relations and Power: Mapping the Field, in S. Cottle (ed.) *News, Public Relations and Power*, London: Sage, pp. 3–24.

—— (2008) Reporting demonstrations: the changing media politics of dissent, *Media, Culture and Society*, Vol. 30(6), pp. 853–72.

Crepaz-Keay, D. (2005) Who benefits from the new act?, *British Medical Journal*, Vol. 331, pp. 1470–1.

—— (2008) About the National Survivor User Network, *Openmind*, No. 149, pp. 8–9.

Crisp, A. H. (2000) Changing minds: every family in the land: An update on the College's campaign, *Psychiatric Bulletin*, Vol. 24, pp. 267–8.

—— (2004) (ed.) *Every Family in the Land: Understanding Prejudice and Discrimination Against People with Mental Illness* (Revised Edition), London: Royal College of Psychiatrists.

Cross, S. (2002) Hearing Voices: Mental Illness and Cultural Recognition. *Inter/Sections: Journal of Global Media and Culture*, Vol. 2(3/4), pp. 69–78.

—— (2004) Visualising Madness: Mental Illness and Public Representation, *Television and New Media*, 5(1), pp. 197–216.

Crossley, N. (2006) *Contesting Psychiatry: Social Movements in Mental Health*, London: Routledge.

Curran, J. and Seaton, J. (1997) *Power Without Responsibility: The Press and Broadcasting in Britain*, London: Routledge (fifth edition).

Curran, J. (2002) *Media and Power*, London: Routledge.

Curtis, T., Dellar, R., Leslie, E., Watson, B. (2000) (eds) *Mad Pride: A celebration of mad culture*, London: Spare Change Books.

Dahlgren, P. (1995) *Television and the Public Sphere*. London: Sage.

Dalrymple, T. (2001) Inside the mind of a monster, *Sunday Telegraph*, 2 December, p. 1.

Darnton, R. (1984) *The Great Cat Massacre and Other Episodes in French Cultural History*, London: Harmondsworth.

Davies, K. (2001) 'Silent and Censured Travellers'? Patients' Narratives and Patients' Voices: Perspectives on the History of mental Illness since 1948. *Social History of Medicine*, Vol. 14(2), pp. 267–92.

Department of Health (2008) *Attitudes to Mental Health 2008 Research Report*, London: Department of Health.

Deutsch, A. (1937/1967) *The Mentally Ill in America*, London: Columbia University Press.

—— (1948) *The Shame of the States*, New York: Harcourt, Brace and Company.

Diamond, H. W. (1976) On the Application of Photography to the Physiognomic and Mental Phenomena of Insanity, in S. Gilman (ed.) *The Face of Madness: Hugh W. Diamond and the Origin of Psychiatric Photography*, New York, NY: Brunner/Mazel, pp. 18–24.

Di Bello, P. (2005) Vision and Touch: Photography and Women's Popular Culture in the Nineteenth Century, in V. Toulmin and S. Popple (eds) *Visual Delights Two: Exhibition and Reception*, Eastleigh, UK: John Libbey, pp. 3–16.

Dickens, C. (1842/2001) *American Notes for General Circulation*, London: Viking Penguin.

—— (1852/1968) A Curious Dance Round a Curious Tree in H. Stone (ed.) *Uncollected Writings from 'Household Words', 1850–1859*, Bloomington: Indiana University Press, pp. 3–14.

Dickinson, R. (2005) The Air Loom: An Influencing Machine, in S. Rushton, A. Bangma and F. Wurst (2005) (eds), *Experience, Memory, Re-enactment*, Rotterdam: Piet Zwart Institute, pp. 81–7.

Didi-Huberman, G. (2003) *Invention of Hysteria: Charcot and the Photographic Iconography of the Salpêtrière*, Cambridge: The MIT Press.

Disher, M. W. (1955) *Victorian Song: From Dive to Drawing Room*, London: Phoenix House.

Dovey, J. (1991) Old Dogs And New Tricks: Access Television in the UK, in T. Dowmunt (ed.) *Channels of Resistance*, London: BFI.

Duncan, A. (1999) 'Interview with Oprah Winfrey', *Radio Times*, 27 February– 5 March, pp. 16–19.

Dunn, S. (1999) *Creating Accepting Communities: Report of the Mind Enquiry into Social Exclusion and Mental Health problems*, London: Mind.

Ellis, J. (1982) *Visible Fictions*. London: Routledge.

Foster, J. (2006) Media presentation of the mental health bill and representations of mental health problems, *Journal of Community & Applied Social Psychology*, Vol. 16(4), pp. 285–300.

Foucault, M. (1977) *Discipline and Punish: The Birth of the Prison*, London: Tavistock.

—— (1980) *Power/Knowledge*, Brighton: Harvester.

—— (1982) 'The subject and power' in P. Rabinow and H. Dreyfus (eds) *Michel Foucault: Beyond structuralism and hermeneutics*, Hemel Hempstead: Harvester Wheatsheaf, pp. 208–28.

—— (2001) *Madness and Civilization. A History of Insanity in the Age of Reason*, London: Routledge.

—— (2003) *Abnormal. Lectures at the College de France 1974–1975*, London: Verso.

Fraser, N. (2000) Rethinking Recognition. *New Left Review*, Vol. 3 (May–June), pp. 107–20.

Freedland, J. (1996) Hearing is believing. *The Guardian Review*, 22 April, pp. 34–8.

—— (1998) Out of the bin and Glad to be Mad. *The Guardian*, p. 17.

Freeman, H. (1997) 'Mad-docs and Englishmen', *The Times Higher*, 17 October, p. 34.

Fuller Torrey, E. and Miller, J. (2001) *The invisible plague: The rise of mental illness from 1750 to the present*, Piscataway, NJ: Rutgers University Press.

Giddens, A. (1990) *The Consequences of Modernity*, Cambridge: Polity Press.

Gilman, S. (1976) *The Face of Madness: Hugh Diamond and the Origins of Psychiatric Photography*. New York: Palatine.

—— (1982) *Seeing the Insane*. New York: Wiley.

—— (1988) *Disease and Representation: Images of Illness from Madness to AIDS*. Ithaca: Cornell University Press.

Glass, J. (1989) *Private Terror/Public Life: Psychosis and the Politics of Community*. Ithaca, NY: Cornell University Press.

Goffman, E. (1961/1984) *Asylums: Essays on the social situation of mental patients and other inmates*, Harmondsworth: Penguin Books.

Gramsci, A. (1971) *Selections from the prison notebooks of Antonio Gramsci*, London: Lawrence and Wishart.

Green, V. (2003) *The Madness of Kings*. Thrupp: Sutton Publishing.

Grob, G. N. (1991) *From Asylum to Community: Mental Health Policy in Modern America*, Princeton, NJ: Princeton University Press.

Golding, P. and Murdock, G. (1991) Culture, Communications, and Political Economy, in J. Curran and M. Gurevitch (eds), *Mass Media and Society*. London: Edward Arnold, pp. 15–32.

Hall, S., Critcher, C., Jefferson, T., Clarke, J. and Roberts, B. (1978) (eds) *Policing the Crisis: Mugging, the State and Law and Order*, London: Macmillan.

Hall, S. (1997) The Spectacle of the 'Other', in S. Hall (ed.) *Representation: Cultural Representations and Signifying Practices*, London: Sage, pp. 223–90.

Hallam, A. (2002) Media influences on mental health policy: Long-term effects of the Clunis and Silcock cases, *International Review of Psychiatry*, Vol. 14(1), pp. 26–33.

Hargreaves, I. (2003) *Journalism: Truth or Dare?*, Oxford: Oxford University Press.

Harper, S. (2005) Media, Madness and Misrepresentation: Critical Reflections on Anti-Stigma Discourse. *European Journal of Communication*, Vol. 20(4), pp. 460–83.

—— (2009) *Madness, Power and the Media: Class, Gender and Race in Popular Representations of Mental Distress*, London: Palgrave Macmillan.

Hart, D. and Phillipson, J. (1999) *Changing media minds: a practical guide*. Psychiatric Bulletin, Vol. 23, pp. 428–9.

Haslam, J. (1989) *Illustrations of Madness*. London: Routledge (Facsimile of 1810 edition edited by Roy Porter).

Hattori, N. (1995) The pleasure of your Bedlam: The theatre of madness in the Renaissance, *History of Psychiatry*, Vol. 6(23), pp. 283–308.

Hearing Voices Network (2003) Assisting people who hear voices: A new approach, http://www.hearing-voices.org.uk/about.htm (Accessed 6 August 2003).

—— (2008) Welcome to the Hearing Voices Network, http://www.hearing-voices.org/ (Accessed 3 August 2009).

Henderson, L. (2007) *Social Issues in Television Fiction*, Edinburgh: Edinburgh University Press.

Hoggard, L. (2003) 'Thinking Outside the Box', *The Observer Review*, 29 June, p. 9.

Holloway, W. (1981) 'I just wanted to kill a woman' Why? The Ripper and Male Sexuality, *Feminist Review*, No. 9, October, pp. 33–41.

Hunter, R. and Macalpine, I. (1963) *Three Hundred Years of Psychiatry: 1535–1860*, London: Oxford University Press.

Huxley, P. and Thornicroft, G. (2003) Social inclusion, social quality and mental illness, *British Journal of Psychiatry*, Vol. 182(4), pp. 289–90.

Ingram, A. (2005) *Cultural Constructions of Madness in Eighteenth-Century Writing: Representing the Insane*, Houndmills: Palgrave Macmillan.

Intervoice (2007) The Mad Doctor: The extraordinary story of DR Rufus May, the former psychiatric patient, http://www.intervoiceonline.org/2007/3/19/the-mad-doctor (Accessed 2 August 2009).

Jay, M. (2003) *The Air Loom Gang. The Strange and True Story of the James Tilly Matthews and his Visionary Madness*, London: Bantam Press.

Jodelet, D. (1991) *Madness and Social Representations*. Hemel Hempstead: Harvester Wheatsheaf.

Jones, K. (1993) *Asylums and After: A Revised History of the Mental Health Services: From the Early 18th Century to the 1990s*, London: The Athlone Press.

Klein, N. (2007) *The Shock Doctrine*, London: Penguin.

Knowles, C. (2000) *Bedlam on the Streets*, London: Routledge.

Kromm, J. (2002) *The Art of Frenzy: Public Madness in the Visual Culture of Europe, 1500–1850*, London: Continuum.

Kuhn, T. (1970) *The Structure of Scientific Revolutions*, Chicago: Chicago University Press (second edition).

Kullman, C. H. (1985) Exquisite Madness: The Madhouse Motif in Popular Humorous Satire. *Studies in Contemporary Satire*, Vol. 12, pp. 1–5.

Laing, R. D. (1965) *The Divided Self*, London: Pelican.

Large, M., Smith, G., Swinson, N. Shaw, J. and Nielssen, O. (2008) Homicide due to mental disorder in England and Wales over 50 years. *The British Journal of Psychiatry*, Vol. 193, pp. 130–3.

Lawton-Smith, S. (2005) A Question of Numbers: The potential of community-based treatment orders in England and Wales, Kings Fund Working Paper. Available at www.image.guardian.co.uk/sys-files/Society/documents/2005/09/20/Kings_Fund.pdf (Accessed 24 September 2008).

Lavis, A. (2005) 'La Muse Malade', 'The Fool's Perceptions' & 'Il Furore dell'Arte': An Examination of the Socio-cultural Construction of Genius through Madness, *Anthropology and Medicine*, Vol. 12(2), pp. 151–63.

Leff, J. (2001) Why is care in the community perceived as a failure?. *British Journal of Psychiatry*, Vol. 179, pp. 381–3.

Leudar, I. and Thomas, P. (2000) *Voices of Reason, Voices of Insanity*, London: Routledge.

Leurdijk, A. (1997) Common sense versus political discourse: Debating racism and multicultural society in Dutch Talk shows. *European Journal of Communication*, Vol. 12(2), pp. 147–68.

Livingstone, S. and Lunt, P. (1994) *Talk On Television: Audience Participation and Public Debate*, London: Routledge.

MacDonald, M. (1981) *Mystical Bedlam: Anxiety and Healing in Seventeenth-Century England*, Cambridge: Cambridge University Press.

MacGregor, J. M. (1989) *The Discovery of the Art of the Insane*, Princeton, NJ: Princeton University Press.

MacKinnon, D., (2001) 'Poor senseless Bess clothed in her rags and folly': Early Modern Women, Madness, and Song in Seventeenth-Century England, *Parergon*, Vol. 18(3), pp. 119–51.

—— (2003) 'The Trustworthy Agency of the Eyes': Reading Images of Music and Madness in Historical Context. *Health and History*, Vol. 5(2), pp. 123–49.

Maisel, A. (1946) 'Bedlam 1946', *Life Magazine*, 5 June 1946. Available at www.mnddc.org/parallels2/prologue/6a-bedlam/bedlam-life1946.pdf (Accessed 15 February 2008).

Maitland, S. (2001) The Changing Shape of Madness. *Index on Censorship*, Vol. 30(4), pp. 69–80.

Martin, J. (1984) *Hospitals in Trouble*, Oxford: Blackwell.

Mazzoleni, G. and Schulz, W. (1999) 'Mediatization' of Politics: A Challenge for Democracy. *Political Communication*, Vol. 16, pp. 247–61.

McCalmont, J. (2007) 'Tourette De France', *Video Vista Monthly VHS and DVD Review*. http:www.videovista.net/reviews/july07/tourette.html (Accessed 10 August 2009).

Micale, M. and Porter, R. (eds) *Discovering the History of Psychiatry*, Oxford: Oxford University Press.

Midelfort, H. C. E. (1980) Madness and civilization in early modern Europe, in B. C. Malament (ed.) *After the Reformation: Essays in Honor of J. H. Hexter*, Philadelphia, PA: University of Pennsylvania Press, pp. 247–65.

Miller, T. (1998) *Technologies of Truth: Cultural Citizenship and the Popular Media*, Minneapolis: University of Minnesota Press.

Milmo, C. (2000) Psychologists in trouble for 'Big Brother', *The Independent*, 1 August, p. 18.

Moir, D. and Jessel, A. (1995) *A Mind to Crime*, London: Signet.

Monahan, J. and Steadman, H. J. (1994) (eds) *Violence and Mental Disorder: Developments in Risk Assessment*, London: University of Chicago Press.

Moncrieff, J. (1997) Psychiatric Imperialism: The Medicalisation of Modern Living, http://www.critpsynet.freeuk.com/sound.htm (Accessed 2 August 2009).

Morris, G. (2006) *Mental Health Issues and the Media: An Introduction for Mental Health Professionals*, London: Routledge.

Murdock, G. (1991) Communications, Modernity and the Human Sciences, in H. Ronning and K. Lundby (eds), *Media and Communication: Readings in methodology, history and culture*, Oslo: Norwegian University Press, pp. 32–54.

—— (2000) Talk shows: Democratic Debates and Tabloid Tales, in J. Weiten, G. Murdock and P. Dahlgren (eds) *Television Across Europe: A Comparative Perspective*, London: Sage, pp. 198–220.

—— (2005) Public Broadcasting and Democratic Culture: Consumers, Citizens, and Communards, in J. Wasko (ed.) *A Companion to Television*, Oxford: Blackwell, pp. 174–98.

NHS Choices (2009) 'I Hear Voices', http://www.nhs.uk/Livewell. mentalhealth/Pages/schizophreniareal stories (Accessed 3 August 2009).

O'Farrell, M. (2006) The Vanished. *The Guardian G2 Women*, 2 October, p. 18.

Ogle, T. (2002) 'Lord of the fly-on-the walls', http:www.guardian.co.uk. theobserver/2002/jan/features.review27 (Accessed 14 August 2009).

Olstead, R. (2002) Contesting the text: Canadian media depictions of the conflation of mental illness and criminality. *Sociology of Health & Illness*, Vol. 24(5), pp. 621–43.

Owen, J. (2006) Stephen Fry: My Battle with mental illness, *The Independent on Sunday*, 17 September, p. 22.

Parr, H. (2000) Interpreting the 'hidden social geographies' of mental health: ethnographies of inclusion and exclusion in semi-institutional places. *Health and Place*, Vol. 6, pp. 225–37.

Peterson, D. (1982) (ed.) *A Mad People's History of Madness*, Pittsburgh: University of Pittsburgh Press.

Perry, D. W., Cormack, I. D., Campbell, C. and Reed A. (1998) Weapon carrying: An important part of risk assessment, *Psychiatric Bulletin*, Vol. 22, pp. 92–3.

Phillips, Anne (1999) *Which Equalities Matter?*, Cambridge: Polity Press.

Phillips, Adam (2001) Round and about madness. *Index on Censorship*, Vol. 4(01), pp. 42–50.

Philo, G., Henderson, L. and McLaughlin, G. (1993) *Mass Media Representations of Mental Health/Illness: Report for Health Education Board for Scotland*, Glasgow: Glasgow University Media Group.

Philo G. (1996) (ed.) *Media and Mental Distress*, Harlow: Addison Wesley Longman.

Philo, G., McLaughlin, G. and Henderson, L. (1996) Media Content, in G. Philo (ed.) *Media and Mental Distress*, Harlow: Addison Wesley Longman, pp. 45–81.

Pickering, M. (2001) *Stereotyping: The Politics of Representation*, London: Palgrave.

—— (2009) Engaging with History, in M. Pickering (ed.) *Research Methods for Cultural Studies*, Edinburgh: Edinburgh University Press, pp. 193–213.

Pilgrim, D. and Rogers A. (1999) *A Sociology of Mental Health and Illness*, Buckingham: Open University Press (second edition).

Porter, R. (1987a) *Mind-Forg'd Manacles, A History of Madness in England from the Restoration to the Regency*, London: Weidenfeld and Nicholson.

—— (1987b) *A Social History of Madness*, London: Weidenfeld and Nicholson.

—— (1991) (ed.) *The Faber Book of Madness*, London: Faber and Faber.

—— (1997) Bethlem/Bedlam Methods of Madness?. *History Today*, Vol. 47(10), pp. 41–6.

—— (2002) *Madness. A Brief History*, Oxford: Oxford University Press.

—— (2004) Is mental illness inevitably stigmatising?, in A. Crisp (ed.) *Every family in the land: understanding prejudice and discrimination against people with mental illness*, London: Royal Society of Medicine Press.

Prins, H. (2005) Mental disorder and violent crime: A Problematic relationship. *The Journal of Community and Criminal Justice*, Vol. 52(4), pp. 333–57.

Read, J. and Baker, S. (1996) *Not Just Sticks and Stones: A Survey of the Stigma, Taboos and Discrimination Experienced by People with Mental Health Problems*, London: Mind.

Repper, J., Sayce, L., Strong, S., Willmot, J., Haines, M. (1997) *Tall Stories from the Back Yard. A survey of 'Nimby' Opposition to Community Mental Health Facilities Experienced by Key Service Providers in England and Wales*, London: Mind.

Rogers, A and Pilgrim, D. (2001) *Mental Health Policy in Britain: A Critical Introduction*, London: Palgrave.

Rogers, A., Pilgrim, D. and Lacey, R. (1993) *Experiencing Psychiatry: Users' Views of Services*, London: Macmillan/MIND publications.

Romme, M. (2000) Redefining hearing voices, http://www.psycminded.co.uk/critical/marius.htm (Accessed 5 August 2009).

Rose, D. (1998) Television, Madness and Community Care. *Journal of Community and Applied Social Psychology*, Vol. 8, pp. 213–28.

Rose, N. (2002) At risk of madness, in T. Baker and J. Simon (eds) *Embracing risk*, Chicago, IL: University of Chicago Press, pp. 209–37.

—— (2005) In Search of Certainty: Risk Management in a Biological Age. *Journal of Public Mental Health*, Vol. 4(3), pp. 14–21.

Rosenhan, D. L. (1973) On being sane in insane places. *Science*, Vol. 179, pp. 250–8.

Roth, M. and Kroll, J. (1986) *The Reality of Mental Illness*, Cambridge: Cambridge University Press.

Rowson, M. (2001) Fools, knaves and lunatics, *Index on Censorship*, Vol. 4(01), pp. 55–63.

Salmon, R. (2000) Intimacy and Abstraction in the Rhetoric of the New Journalism, in L. Brake, B. Bell and D. Finkestein (eds) *Nineteenth-Century Media and the Construction of Identities*, London: Palgrave Macmillan.

Sass, L. (1994) *Madness and Modernism: Insanity in the Light of Modern Art, Literature and Thought*, Cambridge, MA: Harvard University Press.

Sartorius, N. and Schulze, N. (2005) *Reducing the Stigma of Mental Illness. A Report from a Global Programme of the World Psychiatric Association*, Cambridge: Cambridge University Press.

Sayce, L. (1995) Responses to Violence: A Framework for Fair Treatment, in J. Crichton (ed.), *Psychiatric Patient Violence*, London: Duckworth, pp. 127–50.

—— (1998) Stigma, discrimination and social exclusion: What's in a word?. *Journal of Mental Health*, Vol. 7(4), pp. 331–43.

—— (2000) *From Psychiatric Patient to Citizen: Overcoming Discrimination and Social Exclusion*, London: Routledge.

Scheff, T. (1999) *Being Mentally Ill: A Sociological Theory*, New York: Aldine de Gruyter (third edition).

Schlesinger, P., Murdock, G. and Elliott, P. (1983) *Televising Terrorism: Political Violence in Popular Culture*. London: Comedia.

Schlesinger, P. and Tumber, H. (1994) *Reporting Crime: The Media Politics of Crime and Criminal Justice*, Oxford: Oxford University Press.

Scull, A. (1979) *Museums of Madness: The Social Organisation of Insanity in Nineteenth Century England*, London: Allen Lane/Penguin Books.

—— (1989) *Social Order/Mental Disorder: Anglo American Psychiatry in Historical Context*, London: Routledge.

—— (2006) *The Insanity of Place/The Place of Insanity: Essays on the history of psychiatry*, London: Routledge.

—— (2007) *Madhouse: A Tragic Tale of Megalomania and Modern Medicine*, London: Yale University Press.

Scull, A., Mackenzie, C. and Hervey, N. (1996) *Masters of Bedlam. The Transformation Of The Mad-Doctoring Trade*, Chichester: Princeton University Press.

Shorter, E. (1997) *A History of Psychiatry: From the Era of the Asylum to the Age of Prozac*, New York: John Wiley.

Showalter, E. (1985) Representing Ophelia: Women, madness and the responsibilities of feminist criticism, in P. Parker and G. Hartman (eds) *Shakespeare and the Question of Theory*, London: Routledge, pp. 77–94.

—— (1987) *The Female Malady: Women, Madness and English Culture, 1830–1980*. London: Virago.

Sieder, Joe (2008) *Family, The* (1974) http://www.screenonline.org.uk/tv/id/444743/ (Accessed 9 August 2009).

Slater, L. (2005) *Opening Skinner's Box: Great Psychological Experiments of the Twentieth Century*, London: Bloomsbury.

Small, H. (1998) *Love's Madness: Medicine, the novel and female insanity, 1800–1865*, Oxford: Oxford University Press.

Smith, R. (1981) *Trial by Medicine: Insanity and Responsibility in Victorian Trials*, Edinburgh: Edinburgh University Press.

Stevenson, C. (2000) *Medicine and Magnificence: British Hospital and Asylum Architecture, 1660–1815*. London: Yale University Press.

Stewart, H. (2003) Sheer Bedlam, *The Guardian*, 3 May, p. 12.

Stigma Shout Survey (2008) *Service user and carer experiences of stigma and discrimination*. Available at www.mentalhealthshop.org/products/rethink_publications/stigma_shout_survey.html (Accessed 5 July 2009).

Swift, J. (1966) *A tale of a tub: And other satires*, London: Dent.

Szasz, T. (1974) *The Myth of Mental Illness*, New York: Harper and Row.

—— (2007) The Titicut Follies: The forgotten story of a case of psychiatric censorship, *History of Psychiatry*, Vol. 18, pp. 123–5.

Tagg, J. (1988) *The Burden of Representation*, London: Macmillan.

Taylor, P. and Gunn, J. (1999) Homicides by people with mental illness: Myth and reality, *British Journal of Psychiatry*, Vol. 174, pp. 9–14.

Thornicroft, G. (2006) *Shunned: Discrimination against people with mental illness*, New York: Oxford University Press.

TNS (2007) *Attitudes to mental illness in England 2007*, Shift/CSIP. Available at: www.dh.gov.uk/en/Publicationsandstatistics/Publications/PublicationsStatistics/DH_076516 (Accessed 4 July 2009).

Trisha TV (2009) Trisha Goddard Official Website-Biography-Mental Health, http://www.trishatv.com/biography-mental-health (Accessed 9 August 2009).

Tully, J. C. H. (1997) *Prisoner 1167: The Madman Who Was Jack the Ripper*, New York, NY: Carrol and Graf Publishing.

Wahl, O. (1995) *Media Madness: Public Images of Mental Illness*, New Brunswick: Rutgers University Press.

Wahl, O. F. (2004). Stop the presses: Journalistic treatment of mental illness, in L. Friedman (ed.) *Cultural sutures: Medicine, morals, and media*, Durham, NC: Duke University Press, pp. 55–69.

Walkowitz, J. (1992) *City of Dreadful Delight: Narratives of Sexual Danger in Late-Victorian London*, London: Virago.

Wallace, M. (1992) A Journalist's View, in K. Jones and H. Freeman (eds) *Community Care and Schizophrenia: The Need for Social Research*, London: SANE pamphlet, pp. 27–30.

Warner, R. (2004) Recovery from Schizophrenia: Psychiatry and Political Economy, London: Routledge (third edition).

Wearing, M. (1993) Professional discourse and sensational journalism: Media constructions of violent insanity. *Australian Journal of Communication*, Vol. 20(1), pp. 84–96.

Williams, K. (1997) *Get Me a Murder a Day! The History of Mass Communications in Britain*, London: Hodder Arnold.

Wilson, B. (2005) *The Laughter of Triumph: William Hone and the Fight for the Free Press*, London: Faber and Faber.

Wilson, C., Nairn, R., Coverdale, J., Panapa, A. (1999) Constructing mental illness as dangerous: A pilot study. *Australian and New Zealand Journal of Psychiatry*, Vol. 33, pp. 240–7.

Wiltenburg, J. (1988) Madness and Society in the Street Ballads of Early Modern England. *Journal of Popular Culture*, Vol. 21(4), pp. 101–27.

Winchester, S. (1998) *The Surgeon of Crowthorne: a tale of murder, madness and the Oxford English Dictionary*, London: Penguin.

Wing, J. K. (1997) A place of refuge. *Times Literary Supplement*, 12 December, pp. 3–4.

Winston, B. (1995) *Claiming The Real: the documentary film revisited*. London: BFI.

—— (2005) *Messages: Free Expression, Media and the West From Gutenberg to Google*, London: Routledge.

Wolff, G. (1997) Attitudes of the media and the public, in J. Leff (ed.) *Care In The Community: Illusion or Reality*, Chichester: Wiley.

Index